Understanding Pointers In C & C++

Fifth Edition

Yashavant Kanetkar

FIFTH REVISED AND UPDATED VERSION 2019

Copyright © BPB Publications, INDIA
ISBN :978-93-8817-637-8

LIMITS OF LIABILITY AND DISCLAIMER OF WARRANTY

Distributors:

BPB PUBLICATIONS
20, Ansari Road, Darya Ganj
New Delhi-110002
Ph: 23254990/23254991

BPB BOOK CENTRE 376
Old Lajpat Rai Market,
Delhi-110006
Ph: 23861747

MICRO MEDIA
Shop No. 5, Mahendra Chambers, 150
DN Rd. Next to Capital Cinema, V.T.
(C.S.T.) Station, MUMBAI-400 001 Ph:
22078296/22078297

DECCAN AGENCIES
4-3-329, Bank Street,
Hyderabad-500195
Ph: 24756967/24756400

Published by Manish Jain for BPB Publications, 20, Ansari Road, Darya Ganj, New Delhi-110002 and Printed him at Repro India Ltd, Mumbai

About the Author

Through his books and Quest Video Courseware DVDs on C, C++, Data Structures, VC++, .NET, Embedded Systems, etc. Yashavant Kanetkar has created, moulded and groomed lacs of IT careers in the last two and half decades. Yashavant's books and Quest DVDs have made a significant contribution in creating top-notch IT manpower in India and abroad.

Yashavant's books are globally recognized and millions of students / professionals have benefitted from them. Yashavant's books have been translated into Hindi, Gujarati, Japanese, Korean and Chinese languages. Many of his books are published in India, USA, Japan, Singapore, Korea and China.

Yashavant is a much sought after speaker in the IT field and has conducted seminars/workshops at TedEx, IITs, RECs and global software companies.

Yashavant has been honored with the prestigious "Distinguished Alumnus Award" by IIT Kanpur for his entrepreneurial, professional and academic excellence. This award was given to top 50 alumni of IIT Kanpur who have made significant contribution towards their profession and betterment of society in the last 50 years.

In recognition of his immense contribution to IT education in India, he has been awarded the "Best .NET Technical Contributor" and "Most Valuable Professional" awards by Microsoft for 5 successive years.

Yashavant holds a BE from VJTI Mumbai and M.Tech. from IIT Kanpur.

Acknowledgments

During the entire project, of writing this book I have received endless help from Niranjan Bakre and Pravin Bagde, right from deciding topics, finalizing the method of presentation, framing the exercises, developing the cover idea and what not...

While working with pointers my computers crashed several times. And at all such times I always found Niranjan smiling. He more often than not knew why it crashed and could explain it logically in his inimitable style. Life for him is C and pointers!

Having done the compilation of my earlier book, Pravin Bagde was ready to take this one head on. He knows only one way of working—clean and efficient. He set a really hot pace for this book and I confess that he almost always won hands down.

The best way to have a good idea is to have a lot of ideas. And Manish Jain of BPB has them in plenty. More importantly he implements most of them. The book that you are holding in your, hands is the result of one such idea.

Thanks also to Shakil Ali who wrote and tested most of the programs on Data Structures. The speed at which he is absorbing things I am sure he would go far in life.

N. Kamleshwar Rao was instrumental in designing and executing most of the programs that have been added in this edition. I am confident that the computer world would hear more about him in time to come.

Monali Mohadikar did most of the rework on programs to make them ANSI C compliant. Many thanks to her for her hard work and devotion.

Preface to Fifth Edition

I must take this opportunity to thank the readers profusely. They sent quite a few mails suggesting what I need to do make this book still better. I have accepted their comments gladly. What you are holding in your hands is the result of my action on these suggestions.

One dominant suggestion was to make sure that the programs in this book should also run on modern compilers like Visual Studio and gcc, apart from the good old Turbo C/Turbo C++. I have now modified all the programs to make them work with Visual Studio. I have also indicated in Appendix A how to obtain this compiler and how to install it. I believe that this would help the readers a lot. I derive this conclusion from the fact that over the last three years many readers of my books have benefitted a lot from my Quest video courses on C, C++ and other languages and technologies. As usual, do let me know your comments on this book at sales@bpbonline.com

I have also added a brand new chapter titled Pointers in C++ which explains the new additions that have been done in C++ to the world of pointers. I hope readers would find this addition useful.

Yashavant Kanetkar

Contents

viii

## CHAPTER 01

Understanding
Pointers in
C & C++

Introduction
To Pointers

*Well begun is half done! So concentrate on
the basics of pointers, so that you are
comfortable grasping the advanced features
of pointers in chapters to follow...*

Which feature of C do beginners find most difficult to understand? The answer is easy—pointers. Other languages have pointers but few use them so freely, with such abandon, as C does. And why not? It is C's clever use of pointers that makes it the excellent language it is.

The difficulty beginners have with pointers has much to do with C's pointer terminology than the actual concept. For instance, when a C programmer says that a certain variable is a "pointer", what does that mean? It is hard to see how a variable can point to something, or in a certain direction.

It is difficult to get a grip on pointers just by listening to programmer's jargon. In our discussion of C pointers, we would try to avoid this difficulty by explaining them in terms of simple programming concepts. The first thing we want to do is understand the rationale of C's pointer notation.

The & and * Operators

Consider the declaration,

int i = 3 ;

This declaration tells the C compiler to

(a)   Reserve space in memory to hold the integer value.
(b)   Associate the name **i** with this memory location.
(c)   Store the value 3 at this location.

We may represent **i**'s location in memory by the following memory map:

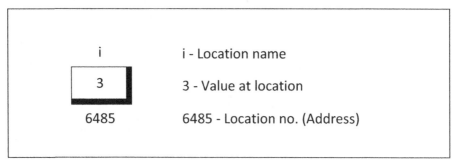

Figure 1.1

From Figure 1.1 we can see that location 6485 has been selected in memory as the place to store the value 3. This location number 6485 is not a number to be relied upon, because some other time the compiler may choose a different location for storing the value 3. The important point is, **i**'s address in memory is a number. We can print this address through the following program:

```
/* Program 1 */
#include <stdio.h>
int main( )
{
    int i = 3 ;
    printf ( "Address of i = %u\n", &i ) ;
    printf ( "Value of i = %u\n", i ) ;
    return 0 ;
}
```

The output of Program 1 compiled with any suitable C compiler would be:

Address of i = 6485
Value of i = 3

Look at the first **printf( )** statement carefully. The '&' operator used in this statement is C's 'address of' operator. The expression **&i** returns the address of the variable **i**, which in this case happens to be 6485. Note that when you execute the program you may get an address different than 6485, depending upon where the variable **i** has been stored in memory when you executed the program.

The other pointer operator available in C is '*', called 'value at address' operator. It returns the value stored at a particular address. The 'value at address' operator is also called an 'indirection' operator.

Compilation and Execution

Once you have written the program, you need to type it and instruct the machine to execute it. Two other programs are needed to do this— Editor and Compiler. Editor lets us type our program, whereas Compiler converts our program into machine language program. This conversion is necessary, since machine understand only machine language.

Apart from these two, there are other programs which you may need to improve your programming efficiency—Preprocessor, Linker and Debugger. Working with each one of them individually is a tedious job. Hence, often all these are bundled together with a layer of GUI on top of them. This GUI makes using these programs easier for you. This bundle is often called Integrated Development Environment (IDE).

There are many IDEs available. Each is targeted towards different operating systems and microprocessors. Details of which IDE to use, from where to download it, how to install and use it are given in Appendix A. Please go through this appendix and install the right IDE on your machine before you try any program in this book.

Observe carefully the output of the following program:

```c
/* Program 2 */
#include <stdio.h>
int main( )
{
    int i = 3 ;
    printf ( "Address of i = %u\n", &i ) ;
    printf ( "Value of i = %d\n", i ) ;
    printf ( "Value of i = %d\n", *( &i ) ) ;
    return 0 ;
}
```

The output of the above program would be:

Address of i = 6485
Value of i = 3
Value of i = 3

Note that printing the value of ***(&i)** is same as printing the value of **i**.

Pointer Expressions

Let us now see what are pointers and how they can be used in various expressions. We have seen in the previous section that the expression **&i** returns the address of **i**. If we so desire, this address can be collected in a variable through the statement,

j = &i ;

Remember that **j** is a special variable. It contains the address of another variable (**i** in this case). Since **j** is a variable the compiler must provide it space in memory. Once again, the memory map shown in Figure 1.2 would illustrate the contents of **i** and **j**.

Figure 1.2

As you can see, **i**'s value is 3 and **j**'s value is **i**'s address.

But wait, we can't use **j** in a program without declaring it. And since **j** is a variable, which contains the address of **i**, it is declared as,

int *j ;

This declaration tells the compiler that **j** would be used to store the address of an integer value—in other words, **j** points to an integer. How do we justify the usage of * in the declaration? Let us go by the meaning of *. It stands for 'value at address'. Thus, **int *j** would mean, the value at the address stored in **j** is an **int**.

Here is a program that demonstrates the relationships we have been discussing.

```
/* Program 3 */
#include <stdio.h>
int main( )
{
    int i = 3 ;
    int *j ;
    j = &i ;
    printf ( "Address of i = %u\n", &i ) ;
    printf ( "Address of i = %u\n", j ) ;
    printf ( "Address of j = %u\n", &j ) ;
    printf ( "Value of j = %d\n", j ) ;
    printf ( "Value of i = %d\n", i ) ;
    printf ( "Value of i = %d\n", *( &i ) ) ;
    printf ( "Value of i = %d\n", *j ) ;
    return 0 ;
}
```

The output of the above program would be:

Address of i = 6485
Address of i = 6485
Address of j = 3276
Value of j = 6485
Value of i = 3
Value of i = 3
Value of i = 3

Work through the above program carefully, taking help of the memory locations of **i** and **j** shown in Figure 1.2. This program summarizes everything that we have discussed so far. If you don't understand the program's output, or the meaning of expressions **&i, &j, *j** and ***(&i)**, re-read the last few pages. Everything we say about pointers from here onwards would depend on your understanding of these expressions thoroughly.

Look at the following declarations,

int *alpha ;
char *ch ;
float *s ;

Here, **alpha, ch** and **s** are declared as pointer variables, i.e. variables capable of holding addresses. Remember that, addresses (location nos.) are always going to be whole numbers; therefore pointers always contain whole numbers.

The declaration **float *s** means that **s** is going to contain the address of a floating-point value. Or in other words, the value at address stored in **s** is going to be a **float**. Similarly, **char *ch** means that **ch** is going to contain the address of a **char** value.

The concept of pointer can be further extended. Pointer, we know, is a variable that contains address of another variable. Now this variable itself could be another pointer. Thus, we now have a pointer that contains another pointer's address. The following example should make this point clear.

```
/* Program 4 */
#include <stdio.h>
int main( )
{
```

```
    int i = 3 ;
    int *j ;
    int **k ;
    j = &i ;
    k = &j ;
    printf ( "Address of i = %u\n", &i ) ;
    printf ( "Address of i = %u\n", j ) ;
    printf ( "Address of i = %u\n", *k ) ;
    printf ( "Address of j = %u\n", &j ) ;
    printf ( "Address of j = %u\n", k ) ;
    printf ( "Address of k = %u\n\n", &k ) ;
    printf ( "Value of j = %u\n", j ) ;
    printf ( "Value of k = %u\n", k ) ;
    printf ( "Value of i = %d\n", i ) ;
    printf ( "Value of i = %d\n", *( &i ) ) ;
    printf ( "Value of i = %d\n", *j ) ;
    printf ( "Value of i = %d\n", **k ) ;
    return 0 ;
}
```

The output of the above program would be:

Address of i = 6485
Address of i = 6485
Address of i = 6485
Address of j = 3276
Address of j = 3276
Address of k = 7234

Value of j = 6485
Value of k = 3276
Value of i = 3
Value of i = 3
Value of i = 3
Value of i = 3

The memory map shown in Figure 1.3 would help you in tracing out how the program prints the above output.

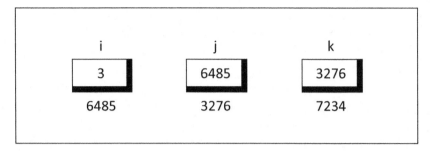

Figure 1.3

Observe how the variables **i**, **j** and **k** have been declared,

int i ;
int *j ;
int **k ;

Here, **i** is an **int**, **j** is a pointer to an **int**, whereas **k** is a pointer to a pointer an **int**. In principle, there could be a pointer to a pointer to a pointer, or a pointer to a pointer to a pointer to a pointer. There is no limit on how far can we go on extending this definition. Possibly, till the point we can comprehend it. And that point of comprehension is usually a pointer to a pointer. Beyond this, one rarely requires to extend the definition of a pointer. But just in case...

The Jargon of Pointers

Consider the following program segment:

int a = 35 ;
int *b ;
b = &a ;

Now can you guess which of the following statements are correct:

(a) **b** contains address of an **int**.
(b) Value at address contained in **b** is an **int**.
(c) **b** is an **int** pointer.
(d) **b** points to an **int**.
(e) **b** is a pointer which points in the direction of an **int**.

Well, all these statements are correct. That's pointer jargon for you. All the statements are trying to establish the same fact—that since **b** contains address of an **int**, it's an **int** pointer. Likewise, had **b** contained an address of a **float** it would have become a **float** pointer. With the same argument if we have three pointer variables first containing address of an array, second containing address of a structure and third containing address of a function then it would be appropriate to call these as an array pointer, a structure pointer and a function pointer respectively.

char, *int* and *float* Pointers

Consider the following program:

```
/* Program 5 */
#include <stdio.h>
int main( )
{
    char c, *cc ;
    int i, *ii ;
    float a, *aa ;

    c = 'A' ; /* ascii value of A gets stored in c */
    i = 54 ;
    a = 3.14 ;
    cc = &c ;
    ii = &i ;
    aa = &a ;
    printf ( "Address contained in cc = %u\n", cc ) ;
    printf ( "Address contained in ii = %u\n", ii ) ;
    printf ( "Address contained in aa = %u\n", aa ) ;
    printf ( "Value of c = %c\n", *cc ) ;
    printf ( "Value of i = %d\n", *ii ) ;
    printf ( "Value of a = %f\n", *aa ) ;
    return 0 ;
}
```

And here is the output...

```
Address contained in cc = 1004     ;
Address contained in ii = 2008
Address contained in aa = 7006
Value of c = A
Value of i = 54
Value of a = 3.140000
```

Note that in **printf( )**s addresses of **char, int** and **float** all have been printed using the format specifier **%u**. Also observe that though the integer variable **i** occupies four bytes in memory the statement **ii = &i** stores only the address of the first byte, 2008 in **ii** (refer Figure 1.4). Similarly, **aa = &a** stores only the address of the first byte (7006) out of four bytes occupied by the **float** variable **a**.

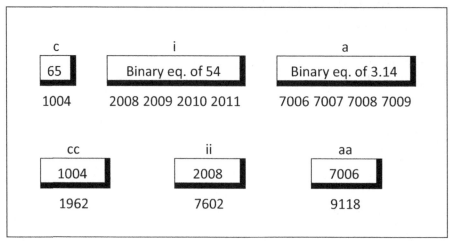

Figure 1.6

The address of first byte is often known as the base address. Though **ii** and **aa** contain only the base addresses, the expressions ***ii** and ***aa** allow access to all the bytes occupied by the integer **i** and **a** respectively. This is because **ii** and **aa** have been declared as **int** and **float** pointers respectively. Since **ii** is an **int** pointer, ***ii** must fetch an **int**. Similarly, since **aa** is a **float** pointer ***aa** must fetch a **float**.

Do you think the following program would work? And if it does what would be its output?

```
/* Program 6 */
#include <stdio.h>
int main( )
{
    int i = 54 ;
    float a = 3.14 ;
    char *ii, *aa  ;

    ii = ( char * ) &i ;
    aa = ( char * ) &a ;
    printf ( "Address contained in ii = %u\n", ii ) ;
```

```
        printf ( "Address contained in aa = %u\n", aa ) ;
        printf ( "Value at the address contained in ii = %d\n", *ii ) ;
        printf ( "Value at the address contained in aa = %d\n", *aa ) ;
        return 0 ;
}
```

Note that here **ii** and **aa** have been declared as **char** pointers. Still the statements **ii = &i** and **aa = &a** work. Once again the addresses 2008 and 7006 (refer Figure 1.5) get stored in **ii** and **aa** which are printed through the first two **printf( )**'s. However, the program falters at the next two **printf( )**'s. This is so since **ii** is a character pointer *ii gives value at address 2008 and not the one present at 2008, 2009, 2010 and 2011. Similarly, *aa gives the value at 7006 and not the one contained in 7006, 7007, 7008 and 7009.

Moral is, if you wish to access an integer value stored in a variable using its address, it's necessary that the address be stored in an integer pointer. Likewise, if you wish to access a float value stored in a variable using its address, it's necessary to store the address in a float pointer.

Passing Addresses to Functions

Arguments are generally passed to functions in one of the two ways:

(a)   sending the value of the arguments
(b)   sending the address of the arguments

In the first method the 'value' of each *actual* argument in the calling function is copied into corresponding *formal* argument of the called function. With this method, changes made to the formal arguments in the called function have no effect on the values of the actual arguments in the calling function.

The following program illustrates the 'Call by Value'.

```
/* Program 7 */
#include <stdio.h>
void swapv ( int, int ) ;
int main( )
{
    int a = 10 ;
    int b = 20 ;
    swapv ( a, b ) ;
    printf ( "a = %d\n", a ) ;
```

```
        printf ( "b = %d\n", b ) ;
        return 0 ;
}
void swapv ( int x, int y )
{
        int t ;
        t = x ;
        x = y ;
        y = t ;
        printf ( "x = %d\n", x ) ;
        printf ( "y = %d\n", y ) ;
}
```

The output of the above program would be

```
x = 20
y = 10
a = 10
b = 20
```

Note that values of **a** and **b** remain unchanged even after exchanging the values of **x** and **y**.

In the second method (call by reference) the addresses of actual arguments in the calling function are copied into formal arguments of the called function. This means that using the formal arguments in the called function we can make changes in the actual arguments of the calling function. The following program illustrates this fact.

```
/* Program 8 */
#include <stdio.h>
void swapr ( int *, int * ) ;
int main( )
{
        int a = 10 ;
        int b = 20 ;
        swapr ( &a, &b ) ;
        printf ( "a = %d\n", a ) ;
        printf ( "b = %d\n", b ) ;
        return 0 ;
}
void swapr ( int *x, int *y )
{
```

```
    int t ;
    t = *x ;
    *x = *y ;
    *y = t ;
}
```

The output of the above program would be:

a = 20
b = 10

Using 'call by reference' intelligently we can make a function indirectly return more than one value at a time, which is not possible ordinarily. This is shown in the program given below.

```
/* Program 9 */
#include <stdio.h>
void areaperi ( int, float *, float * ) ;
int main( )
{
    int radius ;
    float area, perimeter ;
    printf ( "Enter radius of a circle\n" ) ;
    scanf ( "%d", &radius ) ;
    areaperi ( radius, &area, &perimeter ) ;
    printf ( "Area = %f\n", area ) ;
    printf ( "Perimeter = %f\n", perimeter ) ;
    return 0 ;
}
void areaperi ( int r, float *a, float *p )
{
    *a = 3.14 * r * r ;
    *p = 2 * 3.14 * r ;
}
```

And here is the output...

Enter radius of a circle
5
Area = 78.500000
Perimeter = 31 .400000

Here, we are making a mixed call, i.e. we are passing the value of **radius** but, addresses of **area** and **perimeter**. And since we are passing the addresses, any change that we make in values stored at addresses contained in variables **a** and **p**, would make the change effective in **main( )**. That's why when control returns from **areaperi( )**, we are able to output the values of **area** and **perimeter**.

Thus, we have been able to return two values from a called function. This helps us to overcome the limitation of the **return** statement, which can return only one value from a function at a time.

Functions Returning Pointers

The way functions return an **int**, a **float**, a **double** or any other data type, it can even return a pointer. However, to make a function return a pointer it has to be explicitly mentioned in the function's prototype declaration as well as in function definition. The following program illustrates this:

```
/* Program 10 */
#include <stdio.h>
int *fun( ) ;
int main( )
{
    int *p ;
    p = fun( ) ;
    printf ( "%u\n", p ) ;
    printf ( "%d\n", *p ) ;
    return 0 ;
}
int *fun( ) /* function definition */
{
    int i = 20 ;
    return ( &i ) ;
}
```

This program shows how a pointer can be returned from a function. Note that the prototype declaration tells the compiler that **fun( )** is a function which receives nothing but returns an integer pointer. The first **printf( )** would output the address contained in **p** (address of **i**). Can you guess what the second **printf( )** would output? No, it won't print 20. This is because, when the control comes back from **fun( )**, **i** dies. So even if we have its address in **p** we can't access **i** since it is already dead. If you want **i** to survive and ***p** to give 20 then make sure that you declare **i** as **static** as shown below:

static int i = 20 ;

Differences Across Compilers

There are some minor differences across different C compilers like TC/TC++, Visual Studio and gcc. These are mentioned below:

(a) Size of an integer is 2 bytes in a 16-bit compiler like TC/TC++, whereas it is 4 bytes under a 32-bit compiler like Visual Studio and gcc.

(b) Size of a pointer is 2 bytes in TC/TC++, whereas it is 4 bytes under Visual Studio and gcc.

(c) To clear the contents of the screen you should use the library function **clrscr( )** in TC/TC++ and **system( )** function in Visual Studio.

clrscr( ) ; /* in TC/TC++ */
system ("cls") ; /* in Visual Studio */

To use **system( )** function you must include the file **windows.h** at the top of the program above **main( )**.

It would be tedious to mention these differences at each and every place in this book. Hence I am mentioning them in the first chapter itself. All programs in this book have been compiled using Visual Studio Express Edition. So if you are using a different compiler like TC/TC++, you would have to make the relevant changes mentioned above.

Solved Problems

[A] What would be the output of the following programs:

(1)
```c
#include <stdio.h>
void fun ( int, int * ) ;
int main( )
{
    int i = -5, j = -2 ;
    fun ( i, &j ) ;
    printf ( "i = %d j = %d\n", i, j ) ;
    return 0 ;
}
void fun ( int i, int *j )
{
    i = i * i ;
    *j = *j * *j ;
}
```

Output

i = -5 j = 4

Explanation

One doubt immediately comes to the mind—can we use same variable names in different functions? Yes, by all means, without absolutely any conflict. Thus, the two sets of **i** and **j** are two totally different sets of variables. While calling the function **fun( )** the value of **i** and the address of **j** are passed to it. Naturally, in **fun( ) i** is declared as an **int**, whereas, **j** is declared as a pointer to an **int.**

Even though the value of **i** is changed to 25 in **fun( )**, this change would not be reflected back in **main( )**. As against this, since **j**'s address is being passed to **fun( )**, any change in **fun( )** gets reflected back in **main( )**. Hence result of *j * *j, which evaluates to 4 is reflected back in **main( )**.

(2)
```c
#include <stdio.h>
int main( )
{
    int a, b = 5 ;
    a = b + NULL ;
```

```
        printf ( "%d\n", a ) ;
        return 0 ;
}
```

Output

5

Explanation

NULL has been defined in "stdio.h" as follows:

#define NULL 0

Hence, during preprocessing NULL would be replaced by 0, resulting into 5 getting stored in **a**.

(3)
```
#include <stdio.h>
int main( )
{
    printf ( "%d %d\n", sizeof ( NULL ), sizeof ( "" ) ) ;
    return 0 ;
}
```

Output

4 1

Explanation

While finding out size of **NULL**, we are truly speaking finding out size of 0. This is an integer, hence its size is reported as 4 bytes.

Even though the string "" is empty it still contains the   character, '\0'. Hence its size turns out to be 1 byte.

(4)
```
#include <stdio.h>
int main( )
{
    float a = 7.999999 ;
    float *b,*c ;
    b = &a ;
    c = b ;
    printf ( "%u %u %u\n", &a, b, c ) ;
```

```
        printf ( "%d %d %d %d\n", a, *( &a ), *b, *c ) ;
        return 0 ;
}
```

Output

```
4200 4200 4200
-1073741824 1075838975 -1073741824 1075838975
```

Explanation

b contains the address of variable **a**. Since **a** is a **float**, **b** must be a **float** pointer. The same address is then assigned to **c**. Therefore **c** has also been declared as a **float** pointer. The first **printf( )** prints the address of **a** in three different ways. No problem there. What is surprising is the output of the second **printf( )**. Through this **printf( )** we are attempting to print 7.999999 by applying pointer operators on **a**, **b** and **c**. **a**, ***(&a)**, ***b**, ***c** all yield 7.999999 but when they are printed using **%d**, **printf( )** blows it up as the output above would justify.

So always remember to use **%f** to print floating point values. Don't rely on **printf( )** to truncate a **float** value to an integer during printing by using a **%d**. Vice versa is also true. The following statements would not print 7.000000. Don't be surprised if you get some odd value.

```
int i = 7 ;
printf ( "%f", i ) ;
```

(5) ```
     #include <stdio.h>
     int main( )
     {
         int *c ;
         c = check (10, 20) ;
         printf ("c = %u\n", c) ;
         return 0 ;
     }
     int check (int i, int j)
     {
         int *p, *q ;
         p = &i ;
         q = &j ;
     ```
     ```

```
        if ( i >= 45 )
            return ( p ) ;
        else
            return ( q ) ;
    }
```

Output

Error message: Cannot convert from int * to int
                    Return value type doesn't match the function type

Explanation

The integers being passed to **check( )** are collected in **i** and **j**, and then their addresses are assigned to **p** and **q**. Then in the next statement the value of **i** is tested against 45, and either the address stored in **p** or the address stored in **q** is returned. It appears that this address would be collected in **c** in **main( )**, and then would be printed out. And there lies the error. The function **check( )** is not capable of returning an integer pointer. All that it can return is an ordinary integer. Thus just declaring **c** as an integer pointer is not sufficient. We must make the following modifications in the program to make it work properly.

```
#include <stdio.h>
int *check ( int, int ) ;
int main( )
{
    int *c ;
    c = check ( 10, 20 ) ;
    printf ( "c = %u\n", c ) ;
    return 0 ;
}
int *check ( int i, int j )
{
    ....
    ....
}
```

(6)
```
#include <stdio.h>
float *fun ( float* ) ;
int main( )
{
```

```
        float p = 23.5, *q ;
        q = &p ;
        printf ( "q before call = %u\n", q ) ;
        q = fun ( &p ) ;
        printf ( "q after call = %u\n", q ) ;
        return 0 ;
}
float *fun( float *r )
{
        r = r + 1 ;
        return ( r ) ;
}
```

Output

```
q before call = 5498
q after call = 5502
```

Explanation

In **main( )**, **q** has been declared as a **float** pointer. It means **q** is capable of holding address of a **float**. Through **q = &p** the address of **p**, a **float**, is stored in **q** and then printed out through **printf( )**. This is the value of **q** before **fun( )** is called. When **fun( )** is called address of **p** is sent to it and is collected in **r**. At this juncture **r** contains 5498 (when I executed the program it was 5498; when you execute it, this may turn out to be some other address). When **r** is incremented it would become 5502. Why a step of 4? Because **r** is a **float** pointer and on incrementing it by 1 it would point to the next **float** which would be present 4 bytes hence, since every **float** is 4 bytes long. The **return** statement then returns this address 5502 back to **main( )**.

Since a **float** pointer is being returned, a declaration **float *fun (float *)** is necessary above **main( )**, which would tell the compiler that down the line there exists a function called **fun( )** that would receive a **float** pointer and would return a **float** pointer.

[B] Answer the following:

(1) Can you write another expression which does the same job as **++*ptr?**

Explanation

(*ptr)++

(2) In the following program add a statement to function **fun( )** such that address of **a** gets stored in **j**.

```
#include <stdio.h>
void fun ( int ** ) ;
int main( )
{
    int *j ;
    fun ( &j ) ;
    return 0 ;
}
void fun ( int **k )
{
    int a =10 ;
    /* add statement here */
}
```

Explanation

*k = &a ;

(3) Are the expressions ***ptr++** and **++*ptr** same?

Explanation

No. ***ptr++** increments the pointer and not the value pointed by it, whereas, **++*ptr** increments the value being pointed to by **ptr**.

(4) Where can pointers be used?

Explanation

At lot of places, some of which are:
− Accessing array or string elements
− Dynamic memory allocation
− Call by reference
− Implementing linked lists, trees, graphs and many other data structures

(5) Would the following program give a compilation error or warning? [Yes/No]

```
#include <stdio.h>
int main( )
{
     float i = 10, *j ;
     void *k ;
     k = &i ;
     j = k ;
     printf ( "%f\n", *j ) ;
     return 0 ;
}
```

Explanation

No. No typecasting is required while assigning the value to and from **k** because in C conversions are applied automatically when other types are assigned to and from void *.

However, when the same program is compiled using a C++ compiler it reports an error 'Cannot convert from **void** * to **float** *'. This is because in C++ conversions from any pointer type to **void** * are implicit, but **void** * to anything else requires a typecast.

(6) Would the following program compile?

```
#include <stdio.h>
int main( )
{
     int a = 10, *j ;
     void *k ;
     j = k = &a ;
     j++ ;
     k++ ;
     printf ( "%u %u\n", j, k ) ;
     return 0 ;
}
```

Explanation

No. An error would be reported in the statement **k++** since arithmetic on **void** pointers is not permitted unless the **void** pointer is appropriately typecasted.

(7) Would the following program give any error on compilation?

```
#include <stdio.h>
int main( )
{
    int *p1, i = 25 ;
    void *p2 ;
    p1 = &i ;
    p2 = &i ;
    p1 = p2 ;
    p2 = p1 ;
    return 0 ;
}
```

Explanation

No, if compiled using C compiler. If compiled using a C++ compiler you would get an error 'cannot convert from **void** * to **int** *'.

(8)   Would the following program report error on compilation?

```
#include <stdio.h>
int main( )
{
    float *p1, i = 25.50 ;
    char *p2 ;
    p1 = &i ;
    p2 = &i ;
    return 0 ;
}
```

Explanation

When compiled using a C compiler you would get a warning 'assignment from incompatible pointer type p2 = &i'. With a C++ compiler an error is reported 'cannot convert from **float** * to **char** *'.

(9)   What is a null pointer?

Explanation

For each pointer type (like say a **char** pointer) C defines a special pointer value that is guaranteed not to point to any object or function of that type. Usually, the null pointer constant used for representing a null pointer is the integer 0.

(10) What's the difference between a null pointer, a NULL macro, the ASCII NUL character and null string?

Explanation

A null pointer is a pointer, which doesn't point anywhere.

A NULL macro is used to represent the null pointer in source code. It has a value 0 associated with it.

The ASCII NUL character has all its bits as 0 but doesn't have any relationship with the null pointer.

The null string is just another name for an empty string "".

(11) In which header file is the NULL macro defined?

Explanation

In files <stdio.h> and <stddef.h>.

(12) Is the NULL pointer same as an uninitialised pointer? [Yes/No]

Explanation

No

[C] What do the following declarations stand for?

```
int ***i ;
float **j ;
char ****k ;
void f ( int *, char * ) ;
float *g ( float*, float** ) ;
int **h ( float*, char** ) ;
```

Explanation

i is a pointer to a pointer to a pointer to an **int**.

j is a pointer to a pointer to a **float**.

k is a pointer to a pointer to a pointer to a pointer to a **char**.

f is a function which receives an **int** pointer and a **char** pointer and returns nothing.

g is a function which receives a **float** pointer and a pointer to a **float** pointer and in turn returns a **float** pointer.

h is a function which receives a **float** pointer and a pointer to a **char** pointer and returns a pointer to an **int** pointer.

Exercise

[A] What would be the output of the following programs?

(1) #include <stdio.h>
```
int main( )
{
    int a, *b, **c, ***d, ****e ;
    a = 10 ;
    b = &a ;
    c = &b ;
    d = &c ;
    e = &d ;
    printf ( "a = %d b = %u c = %u d = %u e = %u\n", a, b, c, d, e )   ;
    printf ( "%d %d %d\n", a, a + *b, **c + ***d + , ****e ) ;
    return 0 ;
}
```

(2) #include <stdio.h>
```
int main( )
{
    char c, *cc ;
    int i ;  long l;  float f ;
    c = 'Z' ;
    i = 15 ;
    l = 77777 ;
    f = 3.14 ;
    cc = &c ;
    printf ( "c = %c cc = %u\n", *cc, cc ) ;
    cc = &i ;
    printf ( "i = %d cc = %u\n", *cc, cc ) ;
    cc = &l ;
    printf ( "l = %ld cc = %u\n", *cc, cc ) ;
    cc = &f ;
    printf ( "f = %f cc = %u\n", *cc, cc ) ;
    return 0 ;
}
```

(3) #include <stdio.h>
```
void swap ( int, int ) ;
void change ( int, int ) ;
int main( )
```

```
        {
            int c = 10, d = 20 ;
            printf ( "We are in main( )....\n" ) ;
            printf ( "Address of c = %u Address of d = %u\n", &c, &d ) ;
            printf ( "Before swap( ), c = %d d = %d\n", c, d ) ;
            swap ( c, d ) ;
            printf ( "Back to main( )....\n" ) ;
            printf ( "After swap( ), c = %d d = %d\n", c, d ) ;
            return 0 ;
        }
        void swap ( int c, int d )
        {
            printf ( "We are in swap( )....\n" ) ;
            printf ( "Address of c = %u Address of d = %u\n", &c, &d ) ;
            printf ( "Before change( ), c = %d d = %d\n", c, d ) ;
            change ( c, d ) ;
            printf ( "Back to swap( )....\n" ) ;
            printf ( "After change( ), c = %d d = %d\n", c, d ) ;
        }
        void change ( int c, int d )
        {
            int t ;
            printf ( "We are in change( )....\n" ) ;
            printf ( "Address of c = %u Address of d = %u\n", &c, &d ) ;
            printf ( "Before interchanging, c = %d d = %d\n", c, d ) ;
            t = c ;
            c = d ;
            d = t ;
            printf ( "After interchanging, c = %d d = %d\n", c, d ) ;
        }
(4)  #include <stdio.h>
     void swap ( int *, int * ) ;
     void exchange ( int **, int * ) ;
     int main( )
     {
            int c = 10, d = 20 ;
            printf ( "Before swap, c = %d d = %d\n", c, d ) ;
            swap ( &c, &d ) ;
            printf ( "After swap, c = %d d = %d\n", c, d ) ;
            return 0 ;
     }
```

```
void swap ( int *cc, int *dd )
{
    exchange ( &cc, dd ) ;
}
void exchange ( int **cc, int *dd )
{
    int t ;
    t = **cc ;
    **cc = *dd ;
    *dd = t ;
}
```

(5)
```
#include <stdio.h>
int power ( int ** ) ;
int main( )
{
    int a = 5, *aa ;
    aa = &a ;
    a = power ( &aa ) ;
    printf ( "a = %d aa = %u\n", a, aa ) ;
    return 0 ;
}
int power ( int **ptr )
{
    int b ;
    b = **ptr ***ptr ;
    return ( b ) ;
}
```

(6)
```
#include <stdio.h>
float * multiply ( int, float ) ;
int main( )
{
    int i = 3 ;
    float f = 3.50, *prod ;
    prod = multiply ( i, f ) ;
    printf ( "prod = %u value at address = %f\n", prod, *prod ) ;
    return 0 ;
}
float * multiply ( int ii, float ff )
{
    float product ;
```

```
        product = ii * ff ;
        printf ( "product = %f  address of product = %u\n", product,
                &product ) ;
        return ( &product ) ;
    }
```

(7)
```
#include <stdio.h>
int main( )
{
        char *c = 4000 ; /* use char *c = ( char * ) 4000 for C++ */
        int *i = 4000 ;
        long *l = 4000 ;
        float *f = 4000 ;
        double *d = 4000 ;
        printf ( "c = %u, c + 1 = %u\n", c, c + 1 ) ;
        printf ( "i = %u, i + 1 = %u\n", i, i + 1 ) ;
        printf ( "l = %u, l + 1 = %u\n", l, l + 1 ) ;
        printf ( "f = %u, f + 1 = %u\n", f, f + 1 ) ;
        printf ( "d = %u, d + 1 = %u\n", d, d + 1 ) ;
        return 0 ;
}
```

(8)
```
#include <stdio.h>
int main( )
{
        int i = 10, j = 20, diff ;
        diff = &j - &i ;
        printf ( "address of i = %u address of j = %u\n", &i, &j ) ;
        printf ( "difference of addresses of i and j is %d\n", diff ) ;
        return 0 ;
}
```

(9)
```
#include <stdio.h>
int main( )
{
        int *i, *j ;
        j = i * 2 ;
        printf ( "j = %u\n", j ) ;
        return 0 ;
}
```

(10)
```
#include <stdio.h>
int main( )
```

```
    {
        int i = 10 ;
        printf ( "value of i = %d address of i = %u\n", i, &i ) ;
        &i = 7200 ;
        printf ( "new value of i = %d new address of i = %u\n", i, &i ) ;
        return 0 ;
    }
```

(11)
```
#include <stdio.h>
float a = 3.14 ;
float **z ; float **y ; float ***x ;
float ****v ; float ****w ;
float ** fun1 ( float* ) ;
float **** fun2 ( float*** ) ;
int main( )
{
    z = fun1 ( &a ) ;
    printf ( "%u %f \n", z, **z ) ;
    return 0 ;
}
float ** fun1 ( float *z )
{
    y = &z ;
    v = fun2 ( &y ) ;
    return ( **v ) ;
}
float **** fun2 ( float ***x )
{
    w = &x ;
    return ( w ) ;
}
```

[B] State True or False:

(1) Multiplication of a pointer and an **unsigned** integer is allowed.

(2) Address of a **float** can be assigned to a **char** pointer.

(3) A **float** pointer always contains a whole number.

(4) A pointer **p** contains address of a pointer to a pointer to an integer pointer. To reach the integer value we should use the expression ******p**.

Understanding
**Pointers in
C & C++**

Pointers and Arrays

Arrays and pointers are inseparably tied. When you are using one, you are using the other. This chapter explains how...

C language provides a capability that enables the user to design a set of similar data types, called array. Pointers and arrays are very closely related. This relationship is discussed in this chapter.

What are Arrays?

Suppose we wish to arrange the percentage marks obtained by 100 students in ascending order. For this we can either construct 100 variables, each variable containing one student's marks; or construct one variable capable of storing or holding all the hundred values. Obviously, the second alternative is better as it would be much easier to handle one variable than handling 100 different variables. Such a variable is called an array or a subscripted variable.

Now a formal definition of an array—An array is a collection of similar elements. These similar elements could be percentage marks of 100 students, or salaries of 300 employees, or ages of 50 employees. What is important is that the elements must be 'similar'. We cannot have an array of 10 numbers, of which 5 are **int**s and 5 are **float**s. Usually, the array of characters is called a 'string', whereas an array of **int**s or **float**s is called simply an array.

Like other variables an array needs to be declared, so that the compiler knows what kind of an array and how large an array we want. For example,

int marks[30] ;

Here, **int** specifies the type of the variable, just as it does with ordinary variables and the word **marks** is the name of the variable. The number 30 tells how many elements of the type **int** will be in our array. This number is often known as 'dimension' of the array. The bracket ([ ]) tells the compiler that we are dealing with an array.

To fix our ideas, let us note down a few facts about arrays:

(a) An array is a collection of similar elements. It is also known as a subscripted variable.

(b) Before using an array its type and size must be declared. For example,

    int arr[30] ;
    float a[60] ;
    char ch[25] ;

(c) The first element in the array is numbered 0, so the last element is 1 less than the size of the array.

(d) However big an array may be, its elements are always stored in contiguous memory locations. This is a very important point that we would discuss in more detail later on.

(e) If we so desire an array can be initialized at the same place where it is declared. For example,

int num[6] = { 2, 4, 12, 5, 45, 5 } ;
int n[ ] = { 2, 4, 12, 5, 45, 5 } ;
float press[ ] = { 12.3, 34.2, -23.4, -11.3 } ;

If the array is initialized where it is defined, mentioning the dimension of array is optional as in second example above.

(f) If the array elements are not given any specific values, they are supposed to contain garbage values.

(g) In C there is no check to see if the subscript used for an array exceeds the size of the array. Data entered with a subscript exceeding the array size will simply be placed in memory outside the array; probably on top of other data or on the program itself. This will lead to unpredictable results, to say the least, and there will be no error message to warn you that you are going beyond the array size. In some cases the computer may just hang. Thus, the following program may turn out to be suicidal:

```
/* Program 11 */
#include <stdio.h>
int main( )
{
    int num[40], i ;
    for ( i = 0 ; i <= 100 ; i++ )
        num[i] = i ;
    return 0 ;
}
```

So do remember that, ensuring that we do not reach beyond the array size is entirely the programmer's botheration and not the compiler's.

Passing Array Elements to a Function

Array elements can be passed to a function by value, or by reference. These two calls are illustrated below.

```
/* Program 12 */
/* Demonstration of call by value & call by reference */
# include <stdio.h>
void display1 ( int ) ;
void display2 ( int * ) ;
int main( )
{
    int i ;
    int  marks[ ] = { 55, 65, 75, 56, 78, 78, 90 } ;
    for ( i = 0 ; i <= 6 ; i++ )
        display1 ( marks[i] ) ;
    for ( i = 0 ; i <= 6 ; i++ )
        display2 ( &marks[i] ) ;
    return 0 ;
}
void display1 ( int  m )
{
    printf ( "%d ", m ) ;
}
void display2 ( int  *n )
{
    printf ( "%d ", *n ) ;
}
```

And here's the output...

```
55 65 75 56 78 78 90
55 65 75 56 78 78 90
```

Here, to **display1( )** we are passing value of an array element, whereas to **display2( )** we are passing address of an array element. Since at a time only one element or its address is being passed, this element or its address is collected in an integer variable **m**, or an integer pointer **n**. Since **n** contains the address of array element, to print out the array element, we are using the 'value at address' operator **(*)**.

Pointers and Arrays

To be able to see what pointers have got to do with arrays, let us first learn some pointer arithmetic. Consider the following example:

```
/* Program 13 */
# include <stdio.h>
int main( )
{
    int  i = 3, *x ;
    float  j = 1.5, *y ;
    char  k = 'c', *z ;
    printf ( "Value of i = %d\n", i ) ;
    printf ( "Value of j = %f\n", j ) ;
    printf ( "Value of k = %c\n", k ) ;
    x = &i ;  y = &j ;  z = &k ;
    printf ( "Original address in x = %u\n", x ) ;
    printf ( "Original address in y = %u\n", y ) ;
    printf ( "Original address in z = %u\n", z ) ;
    x++ ;  y++ ; z++ ;
    printf ( "New address in x = %u\n", x ) ;
    printf ( "New address in y = %u\n", y ) ;
    printf ( "New address in z = %u\n", z ) ;
    return 0 ;
}
```

Here is the output of the program.

```
Value of i = 3
Value of j = 1.500000
Value of k = c
Original address in x = 65524
Original address in y = 65520
Original address in z = 65519
New address in x = 65528
New address in y = 65524
New address in z = 65520
```

Observe the last three lines of the output. 65528 is original value in **x** plus 4, 65524 is original value in **y** plus 4, and 65520 is original value in **z** plus 1. This so happens because every time a pointer is incremented, it points to the immediately next location of its type. So, when an integer pointer **x** is incremented, it points to an address four locations after the current location, since an **int** is always 4 bytes long (under TC/TC++, since **int** is 2 bytes long, new value of **x** would be 65526). Similarly, **y** points to an address 4 locations after the current location and **z** points 1 location after the current location. This is a very important result and can be effectively used while passing the entire array to a function.

The way a pointer can be incremented, it can be decremented as well, to point to earlier locations. Thus, the following operations can be performed on a pointer:

(a)   Addition of a number to a pointer.
(b)   Subtraction of a number from a pointer.
(c)   Subtraction of one pointer from another.
(d)   Comparison of two pointer variables.

The program given below illustrates these operations.

```
/* Program 14 */
# include <stdio.h>
int main( )
{
    int  arr[ ] = { 10, 20, 30, 45, 67, 56, 74 } ;
    int  i = 4, *j, *k, *x, *y ;
    j = &i ;
    j = j + 9 ;  /* pointer plus number */
    k = &i ;
    k = k - 3 ;  /* pointer minus number */
    x = &arr[1] ;
    y = &arr[5] ;
    printf ( "%d\n", y - x ) ;
    j = &arr [4] ;
    k = ( arr + 4 ) ;
    if ( j == k )
        printf ( "The two pointers point to the same location\n" ) ;
    else
        printf ( "The two pointers point to different locations\n" ) ;
    return 0 ;
}
```

We are already familiar with the operation of addition/subtraction of a number to/from a pointer. That brings us to the third operation— subtraction of pointers.

x and **y** have been declared as integer pointers and are holding addresses of first and fifth element of the array, respectively. Suppose the array begins at location 65502, then **arr[1]** and **arr[5]** would be present at locations 65506 and 65522 respectively, since each integer in the array occupies 4 bytes in memory. The expression **y - x** would print a value 4, as **y** and **x** are pointing to locations that are 4 integers apart.

Pointer variables can be compared provided both variables point to objects of the same data type. Such comparisons can be useful when both pointer variables point to elements of the same array. The comparison can test for either equality or inequality. Moreover, a pointer variable can be compared with zero (usually expressed as NULL).

Do not attempt the any other operations on pointers, other than the 4 operations mentioned above... they would never work out.

Accessing Array Elements using Pointers

We have learnt these two facts above:

(a) Array elements are always stored in contiguous memory locations.
(b) A pointer when incremented always points to the next location of its type.

Let us now correlate these two facts and access array elements using pointers.

```
/* Program 15 */
# include <stdio.h>
int main( )
{
    int  num[ ] = { 23, 34, 12, 44, 56, 17 } ;
    int i, *j ;
    j = &num[0] ;  /* assign address of zeroth element */
    for ( i = 0 ; i <= 5 ; i++ )
    {
        printf ( "address = %u element = %d\n", j, *j ) ;
        j++ ;  /* increment pointer to point to next location */
    }
    return 0 ;
}
```

The output of this program would be:

address = 65512 element = 23
address = 65516 element = 34
address = 65520 element = 12
address = 65524 element = 44
address = 65528 element = 56
address = 65532 element = 17

To understand this output, let us first see how the array elements are arranged in memory. This is shown in Figure 2.1.

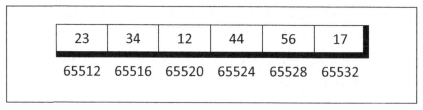

Figure 2.1

In the program, to begin with, we have collected the base address of the array (address of the 0th element) in the variable **j** using the statement,

j = &num[0] ; /* assigns address 65512 to j */

When we are inside the loop for the first time, **j** contains the address 65512, and the value at this address is 24. These are printed using the statement,

printf ("address = %u element = %d\n", j, *j) ;

On incrementing **j**, it points to the next memory location of its type (that is location no. 65516). But location no. 65516 contains the second element of the array, therefore when the **printf( )** is executed for the second time, it prints out the second element of the array and its address (i.e., 34 and 65516)... and so on till the last element of the array has been printed.

So now we know how to access array elements using subscript and using pointer. Obviously, a question arises as to which of the two methods should be used when? Accessing array elements by pointers is **always** faster than accessing them by subscripts. However, from the point of view of convenience in programming, we should observe the following:

Array elements should be accessed using pointers, if the elements are to be accessed in a fixed order, say from beginning to end, or from end to beginning, or every alternate element or any such definite logic.

Instead, it would be easier to access the elements using a subscript if there is no fixed logic in accessing the elements.

Passing an Array to a Function

We already know how to pass individual elements of an array or addresses of individual elements of an array to a function. Let us now see how to pass an entire array to a function. Consider the following program:

```c
/* Program 16 */
/* Demonstration of passing an array to a function */
# include <stdio.h>
void display1 ( int  *, int ) ;
void display2 ( int  [ ], int ) ;
int main( )
{
    int  num[ ] = { 24, 34, 12, 44, 56, 17 } ;
    display1 ( &num[0], 6 ) ;
    display2 ( &num[0], 6 ) ;
    return 0 ;
}
void display1 ( int  *j, int  n )
{
    int  i ;
    for ( i = 0 ; i <= n - 1 ; i++ )
    {
        printf ( "element = %d\n", *j ) ;
        j++ ;  /* increment pointer to point to next element */
    }
}
void display2 ( int  j[ ], int  n )
{
    int  i ;
    for ( i = 0 ; i <= n - 1 ; i++ )
        printf ( "element = %d\n", j[i] ) ;
}
```

Here, the address of the zeroth element and the number of elements in the array are being passed to the **display1( )** function. The **for** loop accesses the array elements using pointers. Note that it is necessary to pass the total number of elements in the array, otherwise the function would not know when to terminate the **for** loop.

Same parameters are also being passed to **display2( )**. But they are received in a different form

void display2 (int j[ ], int n)

Here, though **j** is still an integer pointer, the array notation gives the convenience of accessing the array elements using the expression **j[i]**, without being required to perform any pointer arithmetic on **j**.

Note that the address of the zeroth element (often called the base address) can also be passed by just passing the name of the array. Thus, the following two function calls are same:

display1 (&num[0], 6) ;
display1 (num, 6) ;

The Real Thing

If you have grasped the concept of storage of array elements in memory and the arithmetic of pointers, here is some real food for thought. Once again consider the following array:

int num[ ] = { 24, 34, 12, 44, 56, 17 } ;

We know, that on mentioning the name of the array, we get its base address. Thus, by saying ***num**, we would be able to refer to the zeroth element of the array, that is, 24. One can easily see that ***num** and ***(num + 0)** both refer to 24.

Similarly, by saying ***(num + 1)**, we can refer the first element of the array, that is, 34. In fact, this is what the C compiler does internally. When we say, **num[i]**, the C compiler internally converts it to ***(num + i)**. This means that all the following notations are same:

num[i]
*(num + i)
*(i + num)
i[num]

And here is a program to prove my point.

```
/* Program 17 */
/* Accessing array elements in different ways */
# include <stdio.h>
int main( )
{
    int  num[ ] = { 24, 34, 12, 44, 56, 17 } ;
    int  i ;
    for ( i = 0 ; i <= 5 ; i++ )
    {
        printf ( "address = %u ", &num[i] ) ;
        printf ( "element = %d %d ", num[i], *( num + i ) ) ;
        printf ( "%d %d\n", *( i + num ), i[num] ) ;
    }
    return 0 ;
}
```

The output of this program would be:

```
address = 65512 element = 24 24 24 24
address = 65516 element = 34 34 34 34
address = 65520 element = 12 12 12 12
address = 65524 element = 44 44 44 44
address = 65528 element = 56 56 56 56
address = 65532 element = 17 17 17 17
```

Dynamic Memory Allocation

Consider the array declaration,

int marks[100] ;

Such a declaration would typically be used if 100 student's marks were to be stored in memory. The moment we make this declaration, 400 bytes are reserved in memory for storing 100 integers in it. However, it may so happen that when we actually run the program, we might be interested in storing only 60 student's marks. Even in this case 400 bytes would get reserved in memory, which would result in wastage of memory.

Other way round there always exists a possibility that when you run the program you need to store more than 100 student's marks. In this case the array would fall short in size. Moreover, there is no way to increase or decrease the array size during execution of the program. In other words, when we use arrays static memory allocation takes place. What if we want to allocate memory only at the time of execution? This is done using standard library functions **malloc( )** and **calloc( )**. Since these functions allocate memory on the fly (during execution) they are often known as 'Dynamic memory allocation functions'. Let us now see a program, which uses the concept of dynamic memory allocation.

```
/* Program 18 */
#include <stdlib.h>
#include <stdio.h>
int main( )
{
    int n, avg, i, *p, sum = 0 ;
    printf ( "Enter the number of students\n" ) ;
    scanf ( "%d", &n ) ;
    p = ( int * ) malloc ( n * 4 ) ;
    if ( p == NULL )
    {
        printf ( "Memory allocation unsuccessful\n" ) ;
        exit ( 0 ) ;
    }
    printf ( "Enter marks\n" ) ;
    for ( i = 0 ; i < n ; i++ )
        scanf ( "%d", ( p + i ) ) ;
    for ( i = 0 ; i < n ; i++ )
        sum = sum + *( p + i ) ;
    avg = sum / n ;
    printf ( "Average marks = %d\n", avg ) ;
    return 0 ;
}
```

Here, we have first asked for the number of students whose marks are to be entered and then allocated only as much memory as is really required to store these marks. Not a byte more, not a byte less. The allocation job is done using the standard library function **malloc( )**. **malloc( )** returns a NULL if memory allocation is unsuccessful. If successful it returns the address of the memory chunk that is allocated. We have collected this address in an integer pointer **p**. Since **malloc( )** returns a **void** pointer we have typecasted it into an integer pointer. In the first **for** loop using simple pointer arithmetic we have stored the marks entered from keyboard into the memory that has been allocated. In the second **for** loop we have accessed the same values to find the average marks.

The **calloc( )** functions works exactly similar to **malloc( )** except for the fact that it needs two arguments. For example,

```
int *p ;
p = ( int * ) calloc ( 10, 4 ) ;
```

Here 4 indicates that we wish to allocate memory for storing integers, (since an integer is a 4-byte entity) and 10 indicates that we want to reserve space for storing 10 integers. Another minor difference between **malloc( )** and **calloc( )** is that, by default, the memory allocated by **malloc( )** contains garbage values, whereas that allocated by **calloc( )** contains all zeros. While using these functions it is necessary to include the file "stdlib.h" at the beginning of the program.

More Than One Dimension

So far we have looked at arrays with only one dimension. It is also possible for arrays to have two or more dimensions. The two-dimensional array is also called a matrix. Here is a sample program that initializes a 2-D array and prints out its elements.

```
/* Program 19 */
#include <stdio.h>
int main( )
{
    int s[4][2] = {
                    { 1234, 56 },
                    { 1212, 33 },
                    { 1434, 80 },
                    { 1312, 78 }
                };
    int i, j ;
    for ( i = 0 ; i <= 3 ; i++ )
    {
        printf ( "\n" ) ;
        for ( j = 0 ; j <= 1 ; j++ )
            printf ( "%d ", s[i][j] ) ;
    }
    return 0 ;
```

}

Look at the **printf( )** statement...

printf ("%d ", s[i][j]) ;

In **s[i][j]** the first subscript is row number. The second subscript tells which of the two columns are we talking about—the zeroth column or the first column. Remember that counting of rows and columns begins with zero. The complete array arrangement is shown in Figure 2.2.

s[0][0]	s[0][1]	s[1][0]	s[1][1]	s[2][0]	s[2][1]	s[3][0]	s[3][1]
1234	56	1212	33	1434	80	1312	78
4001	4005	4009	4013	4017	4021	4025	4029

Figure 2.2

Thus, 1234 is stored in **s[0][0]**, 56 is stored in **s[0][1]** and so on. The above arrangement highlights the fact that a two-dimensional array is nothing but a collection of a number of one-dimensional arrays placed one after another.

Remember that the arrangement of a 2-D array into row and columns is only conceptually true. This is because in memory there are no rows and columns. In memory whether it's a 1-D or a 2-D array the elements are stored in one continuous chain.

Pointers and Two Dimensional Arrays

Can we not refer elements of a 2-D array using pointer notation, the way we did in one-dimensional array? Answer is yes, only the procedure is slightly difficult to understand. So, read on...

C language embodies an unusual but powerful capability—it can treat parts of arrays as arrays. More specifically, each row of a 2-D array can be thought of as a 1-D array.

Thus, the declaration,

int s[5][2] ;

can be thought of as setting up an array of 5 elements, each of which is a 1-D array containing 2 integers. We refer to an element of a 1-D array using one subscript. Similarly, if we can imagine **s** to be a 1-D array, then we can refer to its zeroth element as **s[0]**, the next element as **s[1]** and so on. More specifically, **s[0]** gives the address of the zeroth 1-D array, **s[1]** gives the address of the first 1-D array and so on. This fact can be demonstrated by the following program:

```
/* Program 20 */
/* 2-D array is an array of arrays */
# include <stdio.h>
int main( )
{
    int  s[4][2] = {
                        { 1234, 56 },
                        { 1212, 33 },
                        { 1434, 80 },
                        { 1312, 78 }
                   };
    int  i ;
    for ( i = 0 ; i <= 3 ; i++ )
        printf ( "Address of %d th 1-D array = %u\n", i, s[i] ) ;
    return 0 ;
}
```

And here is the output...

```
Address of 0 th 1-D array = 65508
Address of 1 th 1-D array = 65516
Address of 2 th 1-D array = 65524
Address of 3 th 1-D array = 65532
```

This output is consistent with the addresses shown in Figure 2.2. Each 1-D array starts 8 bytes further along than the last one. Thus the expressions **s[0]** and **s[1]** would yield addresses 65508 and 65516.

Suppose we want to refer to the element **s[2][1]** using pointers. We know that **s[2]** would give the address 65524, the address of the second 1-D array. So (**s[2] + 1**) or (65524 + 1) would give the address 65528. The value at this address can be obtained through ***(s[2] + 1)**. We have already studied while learning 1-D arrays that **num[i]** is same as ***(num + i)**. Similarly, ***(s[2] + 1)** is same as, ***(*(s + 2) + 1)**. Thus, all the following expressions refer to the same element:

s[2][1]
* (s[2] + 1)
* (* (s + 2) + 1)

Using these concepts, the following program prints out each element of a 2-D array using pointer notation:

```
/* Program 21 */
/* Pointer notation to access 2-D array elements */
# include <stdio.h>
int main( )
{
    int  s[4][2] = {
                        { 1234, 56 },
                        { 1212, 33 },
                        { 1434, 80 },
                        { 1312, 78 }
                    };
    int  i, j ;
    for ( i = 0 ; i <= 3 ; i++ )
    {
        for ( j = 0 ; j <= 1 ; j++ )
            printf ( "%d ", *( *( s + i ) + j ) );
        printf ( "\n" ) ;
    }
    return 0 ;
}
```

And here is the output...

```
1234  56
1212  33
1434  80
1312  78
```

Pointer to an Array

If we can have a pointer to an integer, a pointer to a float, a pointer to a char, then can we not have a pointer to an array? We certainly can. The following program shows how to build and use it:

```
/* Program 22 */
/* Usage of pointer to an array */
# include <stdio.h>
int main( )
{
    int  s[4][2] = {
                        { 1234, 56 },
                        { 1212, 33 },
                        { 1434, 80 },
                        { 1312, 78 }
                    } ;
    int  ( *p )[2] ;
    int  i, j, *pint ;
    for ( i = 0 ; i <= 3 ; i++ )
    {
        p = &s[i] ;
        pint = ( int * ) p ;
        printf ( "\n" ) ;
        for ( j = 0 ; j <= 1 ; j++ )
            printf ( "%d ", *( pint + j ) ) ;
    }
    return 0 ;
}
```

And here is the output...

```
1234 56
1212 33
1434 80
1312 78
```

Here **p** is a pointer to an array of two integers. Note that the parentheses in the declaration of **p** are necessary. Absence of them would make **p** an array of 2 integer pointers. Array of pointers is covered in a later section in this chapter.

In the outer **for** loop, each time we store the address of a new 1-D array. Thus, first time through this loop, **p** would contain the address of the zeroth 1-D array. This address is then assigned to an integer pointer **pint**. Lastly, in the inner **for** loop using the pointer **pint**, we have printed the individual elements of the 1-D array to which **p** is pointing.

But why should we use a pointer to an array to print elements of a 2-D array. Is there any situation where we can appreciate its usage better? The entity pointer to an array is immensely useful when we need to pass a 2-D array to a function. This is discussed in the next section.

Passing 2-D Array to a Function

The following program shows how we can pass a 2-D array to a function.

```
/* Program 23 */
/* Passing 2-D array to a function */
# include <stdio.h>
void display ( int  q[ ][4], int , int ) ;
int main( )
{
    int  a[3][4] = {
                        1, 2, 3, 4,
                        5, 6, 7, 8,
                        9, 0, 1, 6
                    } ;
    display ( a, 3, 4 ) ;
    return 0 ;
}
void display ( int  q[ ][4], int  row, int  col )
{
    int  i, j ;
    for ( i = 0 ; i < row ; i++ )
    {
        for ( j = 0 ; j < col ; j++ )
            printf ( "%d ", q[i][j] ) ;
        printf ( "\n" ) ;
    }
    printf ( "\n" ) ;
}
```

And here is the output...

```
1 2 3 4
5 6 7 8
9 0 1 6
```

In the **display( )** function, we have collected the base address of the 2-D array being passed to it in **q**, where **q** is pointer to an array of 4 integers. The declaration of **q** looks like this

int q[ ][4] ;

This is same as saying **int (*q)[4]**. The only advantage in using the form **q[ ][4]** is that, we can now use the more familiar expression **q[i][j]** to access array elements.

Array of Pointers

The way there can be an array of **int**s or an array of **float**s, similarly, there can be an array of pointers. An array of pointers would be a collection of addresses. The addresses present in it can be addresses of isolated variables or addresses of array elements or any other addresses. All rules that apply to an ordinary array apply to the array of pointers as well. I think a program would clarify the concept.

```
/* Program 24 */
# include <stdio.h>
int main( )
{
    int *arr[4] ; /* array of integer pointers */
    int i = 31, j = 5, k = 19, l = 71, m ;
    arr[0] = &i ;
    arr[1] = &j ;
    arr[2] = &k ;
    arr[3] = &l ;
    for ( m = 0 ; m <= 3 ; m++ )
        printf ( "%d\n", * ( arr[m] ) ) ;
    return 0 ;
}
```

Figure 2.3 shows the contents and the arrangement of the array of pointers in memory. As you can observe, **arr** contains addresses of isolated **int** variables **i, j, k** and **l**. The **for** loop in the program picks up the addresses present in **arr** and prints the values present at these addresses.

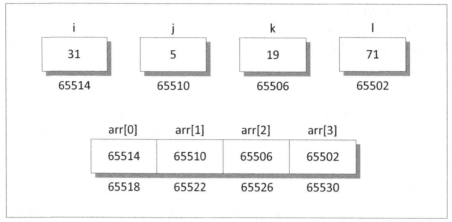

Figure 2.3

An array of pointers can even contain the addresses of other arrays' elements. The following program would justify this:

```
/* Program 25 */
# include <stdio.h>
int main( )
{
    static int a[ ] = { 0, 1, 2, 3, 4 };
    int *p[ ] = { a, a + 1, a + 2, a + 3, a + 4 };
    printf ( "%u %u %d\n", p, *p, * ( *p ) );
    return 0 ;
}
```

I would leave it for you to figure out the output of this program.

3-D Array

I am not going to show a programming example that uses a 3-D array. However, an example of initializing a 3-D array will consolidate your understanding of arrays.

```
int arr[3][4][2] = {
                    {
                        { 2, 4 },
                        { 7, 8 },
                        { 3, 4 },
                        { 5, 6 }
                    },
                    {
```

```
        { 7, 6 },
        { 3, 4 },
        { 5, 3 },
        { 2, 3 }
    },
    {
        { 8, 9 },
        { 7, 2 },
        { 3, 4 },
        { 5, 1 },
    }
};
```

A 3-D array can be thought of as an array of arrays of arrays. The outer array has three elements, each of which is a 2-D array of four 1-D arrays, each of which contains two integers. Figure 2.4 would possibly help you in visualizing the situation better.

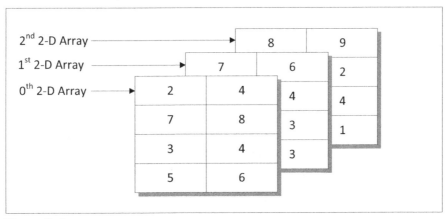

Figure 2.4

Again remember that the arrangement shown in Figure 2.4 is only conceptually true. In memory, the array elements are stored linearly as shown in Figure 2.5.

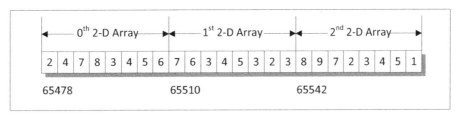

Figure 2.5

How would you refer to the array element 1 in the above array? The first subscript should be [2], since the element is in third 2-D array; the second subscript should be [3] since the element is in fourth row of the 2-D array; and the third subscript should be [1] since the element is in second position in the 1-D array. So element 1 can be referred as **arr[2][3][1]**.

It may be noted here that the counting of array elements even for a 3-D array begins with zero. Can we not refer to this element using pointer notation? Of course, yes. For example, the following two expressions refer to the same element in the 3-D array:

arr[2][3][1]
*(*(*(arr + 2) + 3) + 1)

Returning Array from a Function

Now that we know how to pass a 2-D or a 3-D array to a function, let us find out how to return an array from a function. There are again three methods to achieve this. Suppose we wish to return a 2-D array of integers from a function we can return the base address of the array as:

-   A pointer to an integer
-   A pointer to the zeroth 1-D array
-   A pointer to the 2-D array

This is shown in the following program. The function **fun1( )** returns the base address as pointer to integer, the function **fun2( )** returns it as pointer to zeroth 1-D array, whereas **fun3( )** returns it as pointer to 2-D array of integers. Note the prototype declarations of the functions carefully.

```
/* Program 26 */
/* Three ways of returning a 2-D array from a function */
#include <stdio.h>
#define ROW 3
#define COL 4
int main( )
{
    int i, j ;
    int *a ;
    int *fun1( ) ;
    int ( *b )[COL] ;
    int ( *fun2( ) )[COL] ;
```

```
    int *p ;
    int ( *c )[ROW][COL] ;
    int ( *fun3( ) )[ROW][COL] ;
    a = fun1( ) ;
    printf ( "Array a[ ][ ] in main( ):\n" ) ;
    for ( i = 0 ; i < ROW ; i++ )
    {
        for ( j = 0 ; j < COL ; j++ )
            printf ( "%d ", * ( a + i * COL+ j ) ) ;
        printf ( "\n" ) ;
    }
    b = fun2( ) ;
    printf ( "Array b[ ][ ] in main( ):\n" ) ;
    for ( i = 0 ; i < ROW ; i++ )
    {
        p = ( int * ) ( b + i ) ;
        for ( j = 0 ; j < COL ; j++ )
        {
            printf ( "%d ", *p ) ;
            p++ ;
        }
        printf ( "\n" ) ;
    }
    c = fun3( ) ;
    printf ( "Array c[ ][ ] in main( ):\n" ) ;
    for ( i = 0 ; i < ROW ; i++ )
    {
        for ( j = 0 ; j < COL ; j++ )
            printf ( "%d ", ( *c )[i][j] ) ;
        printf ( "\n" ) ;
    }
    return 0 ;
}
int *fun1( )
{
    static int a[ROW][COL] = {
                                1, 2, 3, 4,
                                5, 6, 7, 8,
                                9, 0, 1, 6
                        } ;
    int i, j ;
```

```
        printf ( "Array a[ ][ ] in fun1( ):\n" ) ;
        for ( i = 0 ; i < ROW ; i++ )
        {
            for ( j = 0 ; j < COL ; j++ )
                printf ( "%d ", a[i][j]  ) ;
            printf ( "\n" ) ;
        }
        return ( int * ) a ;
}
int ( *fun2( ) )[COL]
{
        static int b[ROW][COL] = {
                                    9, 4, 6, 4,
                                    1, 3, 2, 1,
                                    7, 5, 1, 6
                                 } ;
        int i, j ;
        printf ( "Array b[ ][ ] in fun2( ):\n" ) ;
        for ( i = 0 ; i < ROW ; i++ )
        {
         for ( j = 0 ; j < COL ; j++ )
             printf ( "%d ", b[i][j] ) ;
         printf ( "\n" ) ;
        }
        return b ;
}
int ( *fun3( ) )[ROW][COL]
{
        static int c[ROW][COL] = {
                                    6, 3, 9, 1,
                                    2, 1, 5, 7,
                                    4, 1, 1, 6
                                 } ;
        int i, j ;
        printf ( "Array c[ ][ ] in fun3( ):\n" ) ;
        for ( i = 0 ; i < ROW ; i++ )
        {
         for ( j = 0 ; j < COL ; j++ )
             printf ( "%d ", c[i][j] ) ;
         printf ( "\n" ) ;
        }
```

```
        return ( int ( * )[ROW][COL] ) c ;
}
```

And here is the output...

Array a[ ][ ] in fun1( ):
1 2 3 4
5 6 7 8
9 0 1 6

Array a[ ][ ] in main( ):
1 2 3 4
5 6 7 8
9 0 1 6

Array b[ ][ ] in fun2( ):
9 4 6 4
1 3 2 1
7 5 1 6

Array b[ ][ ] in main( ):
9 4 6 4
1 3 2 1
7 5 1 6

Array c[ ][ ] in fun3( ):
6 3 9 1
2 1 5 7
4 1 1 6

Array c[ ][ ] in main( ):
6 3 9 1
2 1 5 7
4 1 1 6

Solved Problems

[A] What will be the output of the following programs:

(1)
```
#include <stdio.h>
int main( )
{
    int a[ ] = { 10, 20, 30, 40, 50 } ;
    int j ;
    for ( j = 0 ; j < 5 ; j++ )
    {
        printf ( "%d\n", *a ) ;
        a++ ;
    }
    return 0 ;
}
```

Output

Error message: Lvalue required in function main

Explanation

Whenever we mention the name of the array, we get its base address. Therefore, first time through the loop, the **printf( )** should print the value at this base address. There is no problem up to this. The problem lies in the next statement, **a++**. Since C doesn't perform bounds checking on an array, the only thing that it remembers about an array is its base address. And **a++** attempts to change this base address, which C won't allow because if it does so, it would be equivalent to shifting the array in memory. Anything, which can change is called lvalue in compiler's language. Since value of **a** cannot be changed through **a++**, it flashes an error saying 'Lvalue required' so that ++ operator can change it.

(2)
```
#include <stdio.h>
int main( )
{
    float a[ ] = { 13.24, 1.5, 1.5, 5.4, 3.5 } ;
    float *j, *k ;
    j = a ;
    k = a + 4 ;
```

```
        j = j * 2 ;
        k = k / 2 ;
        printf ( "%f %f\n", *j, *k ) ;
        return 0 ;
    }
```

Output

Error message: Illegal use of pointer in function main

Explanation

j and **k** have been declared as pointer variables, which would contain addresses of **float**s. In other words, **j** and **k** are **float** pointers. To begin with, the base address of the array **a[ ]** is stored in **j**. The next statement is perfectly acceptable; the address of the 4th **float** from the base address is stored in **k**. The next two statements are erroneous. This is because the only operations that can be performed on pointers are addition and subtraction. Multiplication or division of a pointer is not allowed. Hence the error message.

(3) ```
     #include <stdio.h>
     int main( )
     {
         int n[25] ;
         n[0] = 100 ;
         n[24] = 200 ;
         printf ("%d %d\n", *n, *(n + 24) + *(n + 0)) ;
         return 0 ;
     }
     ```

*Output*

100 300

*Explanation*

**n[ ]** has been declared as an array capable of holding 25 elements numbered from 0 to 24. Then 100 and 200 are assigned to **n[0]** and **n[24]** respectively. Then comes the most important part—the **printf( )** statement. Whenever we mention the name of the array,
     ```

we get its base address (i.e. address of the zeroth element of the array). Thus, ***n** would give the value at this base address, which in this case is 100. This is then printed out. Look at the next expression,

*(n + 24) + *(n + 0)

n gives the address of the zeroth element, **n + 1** gives the address of the next element of the array, and so on. Thus, **n + 24** would give the address of the last element of the array. Therefore ***(n + 24)** would give the value at this address, which is 200 in our case. Similarly, ***(n + 0)** would give 100 and the addition of the two would result into 300, which is then printed out.

(4)
```c
#include <stdio.h>
int main( )
{
    int b[ ] = { 10, 20, 30, 40, 50 } ;
    int i, *k ;
    k = &b[4] - 4 ;
    for ( i = 0 ; i <= 4 ; i++ )
    {
        printf ( "%d ", *k ) ;
        k++ ;
    }
    return 0 ;
}
```

Output

10 20 30 40 50

Explanation

First look at Figure 2.6. The array elements are stored in contiguous memory locations and each element is an integer, hence is occupying 4 locations.

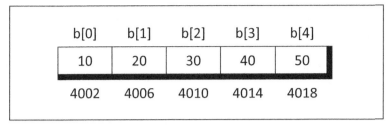

Figure 2.6

The expression **&b[4]** gives the address of **b[4]** (4018 in this case). From this address if we subtract 4, we get 4002. Or did you expect to get 4014? Remember that by subtracting 4 from 4018 what we mean is get the address of an integer, which is 4 integers to the left of the integer whose address is 4018. Now, address of the integer, which is 4 integers to the left of the integer whose address is 4018, is the address 4002. This address, 4002, is stored in **k**, which has been declared as a variable capable of holding an integer's address. First time through the **for** loop ***k** would result into 10, i.e. value at the address contained in **k**. **k++** then increments **k** such that it contains the address of the next integer, i.e. 4006. Next time through the **for** loop ***k** would yield the value at address contained in **k**, i.e. value at the address 4006, which is 20. Similarly, the loop prints out the rest of the elements of the array.

(5)
```c
#include <stdio.h>
int main( )
{
    char a[ ] = "Visual C++" ;
    char *b = "Visual C++" ;
    printf ( "%d  %d\n", sizeof ( a ), sizeof ( b ) ) ;
    printf ( "%d  %d\n", sizeof ( *a ), sizeof ( *b ) ) ;
    return 0 ;
}
```

Output   .

```
11  4
1  1
```

Explanation

sizeof reports the number of bytes occupied by an entity in memory. The array **a** is reported to be of 11 bytes because there is a '\0' sitting at the end. **b** is a pointer hence its size is 4 bytes. ***a** and ***b** both yield a character 'V', whose size is one byte.

(6)
```
#include <stdio.h>
int main( )
{
/* Assume array begins at address 1200 */
int arr[ ] = { 2, 3, 4, 1, 6 } ;
printf ( "%u  %d\n", arr, sizeof ( arr ) ) ;
return 0 ;
}
```

Output

1200 20

Explanation

Mentioning the name of an array yields its base address. Hence, **arr** would give 1200. Since the array contains five elements, each of 4 bytes, size of the array is reported as 20 bytes. Note that except when used with **sizeof( )**, name of the array yields its base address.

(7)
```
#include <stdio.h>
int main( )
{
/* Assume array begins at address 65486 */
int arr[ ] = { 12, 14, 15, 23, 45 } ;
printf ( "%u  %u\n", arr, &arr ) ;
printf ( "%u  %u\n", arr + 1, &arr + 1 ) ;
return 0 ;
}
```

Output

65486 65486
65490 65506

Explanation

Both **arr** and **&arr** yield the base address of the array. However, **arr + 1** gives 65490, i.e. the address of the next integer. However, **&arr + 1** gives 65506, i.e. the address of the next array of 5 integers.

(8) ```
#include <stdio.h>
int main( )
{
    /* Assume array begins at address 65472 */
    int a[3][4] = {
                    1, 2, 3, 4,
                    4, 3, 2, 1,
                    7, 8, 9, 0
                  } ;
    printf ("%u %u\n", a + 1, &a + 1) ;
    return 0 ;
}
```

*Output*

65488  65520

*Explanation*

Name of a 2-D array always acts as pointer to the zeroth element of the array. Since the zeroth element of our 2-D array is 1-D array of 4 integers, **a** acts as pointer to this zeroth 1-D array. Hence **a + 1** gives us the address of the next 1-D array, i.e. 65488.

The expression **&a + 1** yields 65520, i.e. the address of the next 2-D array of 3 rows and 4 columns.

(9)  ```
#include <stdio.h>
int main( )
{
    /* Assume array begins at location 1002 */
    int a[3][4] = {
                    1, 2, 3, 4,
                    5, 6, 7, 8,
                    9,10,11,12
                  } ;
    printf( "%u %u %u\n", a[0] + 1, * ( a[0] + 1 ), * ( * ( a + 0 ) + 1 ) );
    return 0 ;
}
```

Output

1006 2 2

Explanation

A 2-D array is a collection of several 1-D arrays. Name of a 2-D array always acts as pointer to zeroth element of the array. Hence, **a** acts as pointer to the zeroth 1-D array.

The expression **a[0] + 1** is interpreted by the compiler as ***(a + 0) + 1**. This is same as ***a + 1**. The expression ***a** gives 1002. Therefore, ***a + 1** would give the address of the next integer, i.e. 1006. Since **a[0] + 1** yields 1006, ***(a[0] + 1)** would yield the value at address 1006, i.e. ***(a[0] + 1)** can be expanded as ***(*(a + 0) + 1)**. Hence, both the expressions would yield the same result, i.e. 2.

(10)
```
#include <stdio.h>
void fun ( int ** ) ;
int main( )
{
    int a[3][4] = {
                        1, 2 ,3 ,4,
                        4, 3, 2, 8,
                        7, 8, 9, 0
                    } ;
    int *ptr ;
    ptr = &a[0][0] ;
    fun ( &ptr ) ;
    return 0 ;
}
void fun( int **p )
{
    printf ( "%d\n", **p ) ;
}
```

Output

1

Explanation

Here, in **ptr** we have stored address of 1. Then we have passed address of **ptr** to **fun( )** and collected it in a pointer to an **int** pointer. Dereferencing this pointer yields 1.

(11) #include <stdio.h>
    int main( )
    {
        /* Assume array begins at location 1002 */
        int a[2][3][4] = {
                {
                    1, 2, 3, 4,
                    5, 6, 7, 8,
                    9, 1, 1, 2
                },
                {
                    2, 1, 4, 7,
                    6, 7, 8, 9,
                    0, 0, 0, 0
                }
              };
        printf ("%u %u %u %d\n", a, *a, **a, ***a) ;
        return 0 ;
    }

Output

1002 1002 1002 1

Explanation

The expressions **a**, ***a**, ****a**, would give the base address, i.e. 1002, whereas the expression *****a** would give the value at address 1002, i.e. 1. Note that the expression **a[0][0][0]** is expanded into ***(*(*(a + 0) + 0) + 0)**. This is same as *****a**.

(12) #include <stdio.h>
    int main( )
    {
        int a[ ] = { 2, 4, 6, 8, 10 } ;
        int i ;
        for (i = 0 ; i <= 4 ; i++)
        {

```
            *( a + i ) = a[i] + i[a] ;
            printf ( "%d ", *( i + a ) ) ;
        }
        return 0 ;
    }
```

Output

4 8 12 16 20

Explanation

Imbibe the following three facts and the program becomes very simple to understand:

- Mentioning the name of the array gives the base address of the array.
- Array elements are stored in contiguous memory locations.
- On adding 1 to the address of an integer, we get the address of the next integer.

With those facts clearly laid out, let us now try to understand the program. Remember that internally C always accesses array elements using pointers. Thus, when we say **a[i]**, internally C converts it to ***(a + i)**, which means value of ith integer from the base address. Now, if the expression **a[i]** is same as ***(a + i)** then ***(i + a)** must be same as **i[a]**. But ***(a + i)** is same as ***(i + a)**. Therefore **a[i]** must be same as **i[a]**.

Thus **a[i]**, ***(a + i)**, ***(i + a)** and **i[a]** refer to the same element— the ith element from the base address.

Therefore, the expression used in the **for** loop, ***(a + i) = a[i] + i[a]** is nothing but **a[i] = a[i] + a[i]**. Thus all that is done in the **for** loop is, each array element is doubled and then printed out.

```
(13) #include <stdio.h>
     void f ( int, int * ) ;
     int main( )
     {
         int a[5] = { 2, 4, 6, 8, 10 } ;
         int i, b = 5 ;
         for ( i = 0 ; i < 5 ; i++ )
```

```
    {
        f ( a[i], &b ) ;
        printf ( "%d  %d\n", a[i], b ) ;
    }
    return 0 ;
}
void f ( int x, int *y )
{
    x = *( y ) += 2 ;
}
```

Output

```
2 7
4 9
6 11
8 13
10 15
```

Explanation

After initializing the array when the control enters the **for** loop, the function **f( )** gets called with value of **a[i]** and address of **b**. In **f( )** these are collected in variables **x** and **y**. Then comes the expression **x = *(y) += 2**. Here ***(y) += 2** is evaluated first and then the result of this expression is assigned to **x**. The first time through the **for** loop ***(y)** gives 5, to which 2 is added and the result is stored at ***(y)**. It means 7 is assigned to **b**. Finally, the = operator assigns 7 to **x**. However, on assigning a new value to **x**, the array element **a[0]** in **main( )** remains unchanged. Thus, during every call to **f( )**, **b**'s value keeps getting updated, whereas there is no change in the values of the array elements.

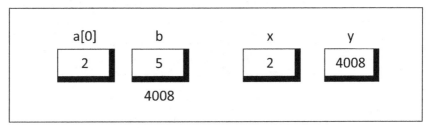

Figure 2.7

(14)
```
#include <stdio.h>
void change ( int * ) ;
int main( )
{
    int a[5] = { 2, 3, 4, 5, 6 } ;
    int i ;
    change ( a ) ;
    for ( i = 4 ; i >= 0 ; i-- )
        printf ( "%d ", a[i] ) ;
    return 0 ;
}
void change ( int *b )
{
    int i ;
    for ( i = 0 ; i <= 4 ; i++ )
    {
        *b = *b + 1 ;
        b++ ;
    }
}
```

Output

7 6 5 4 3

Explanation

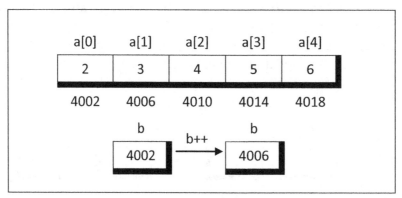

Figure 2.8

While calling **change( )** we are passing the base address of the array, which as per Figure 2.8 is 4002. This address is collected in **b** in the function **change( )**. Then the control enters the **for** loop, where we meet the expression ***b = *b + 1**. This means replace the value at the address contained in **b**, with value at the address contained in **b** plus 1. Every time **b++** is executed, the address of the next integer gets stored in **b**. Thus, using the address stored in **b**, we get an access to array elements that are now changed to 3, 4, 5, 6 and 7. Once the control comes back from **change( )**, the current array contents are then printed out from end to beginning through the **for** loop.

(15) #include <stdio.h>
    int main( )
    {
        int arr[ ] = { 0, 1, 2, 3, 4 } ;
        int *ptr ;
        for (ptr = &arr[0] ; ptr <= &arr[4] ; ptr++)
            printf ("%d ", *ptr) ;
        return 0 ;
    }

Output

0 1 2 3 4

Explanation

Refer Figure 2.9 for a better understanding of the program.

Here **ptr** has been declared as an integer pointer, i.e. a variable capable of holding the address of an integer. In the **for** loop, in the initialization part, this **ptr** is assigned the address of the zeroth element of the integer array. Suppose this address turns out to be 6004. Then address of the first element of the array would be 6008, address of the second element would be 6012, and so on. In the condition part of the **for** loop, the address stored in **ptr** is compared with the address of the fourth array element, i.e. 6020. Since for the first time the condition is satisfied (since 6004 is less than 6020), the control reaches **printf( )** where the value at address 6004, i.e. 0 gets printed. After executing **printf( )** the control reaches **ptr++**, where **ptr** is incremented such that it contains the address of the next integer. Since the next integer is stored at 6008, **ptr** now contains 6008. Once again the condition is tested. Since 6008 is also smaller than 6020, the condition is satisfied hence the

printf( ) prints out the value at 6008, i.e. 1 . And then **ptr++** is executed again so that it contains the address of the next integer, i.e. 6012. This process continues till all the array elements have been printed.

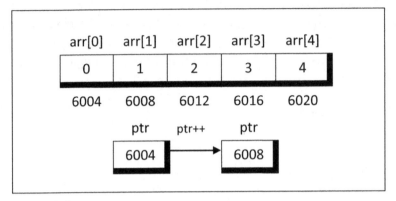

Figure 2.9

(16) #include <stdio.h>
```
int main( )
{
    int arr[ ] = { 0, 1, 2, 3, 4 };
    int i, *ptr ;
    for ( ptr = &arr[0], i = 0 ; i <= 4 ; i++ )
        printf ( "%d ", ptr[i] ) ;
    return 0 ;
}
```

Output

0 1 2 3 4

Explanation

In the initialization part of the **for** loop, multiple initializations are being done. Firstly, **ptr** is set up with the base address of the array and then **i** is set to 0. Since 0 is less than 4, the condition is satisfied for the first time and the control reaches **printf( )**. Here the value of the expression **ptr[i]** gets printed. Now **ptr[i]** is nothing but ***(ptr + i)**. Since **ptr** contains the base address of the array, **(ptr + i)** would give the address of the ith integer from the base address. Since **i** is going to vary from 0 to 4, this would give addresses of 0th, 1st, 2nd, 3rd and 4th integers from the base address of the array. Naturally, the expression ***(ptr + i)** would give values at these addresses. Thus, the **for** loop would print out all the array elements.

(17) #include <stdio.h>
     int main( )
     {
         int arr[ ] = { 0, 1, 2, 3, 4 } ;
         int i, *p ;
         for (p = arr, i = 0 ; p + i <= arr + 4 ; p++, i++)
             printf ("%d ", *(p + i)) ;
         return 0 ;
     }

Output

0 2 4

Explanation

The following figure would help in understanding the program.

arr[0]	arr[1]	arr[2]	arr[3]	arr[4]
0	1	2	3	4
6004	6008	6012	6016	6020

Figure 2.10

In the **for** loop there are multiple initializations and multiple incrementations, each separated by the comma operator. In the initialization part, **p** is initialized to the base address of the array, whereas **i** is initialized to 0. After these initializations the control reaches the condition. The condition is a little complicated so let us isolate it for a clearer understanding.

p + i <= arr + 4

Here **+** enjoys a higher priority than **<=**. Therefore, first **p + i** and **arr + 4** are performed and then the **<=** goes to work. **p + i** yields 6004, whereas **arr + 4** evaluates to 6020. Since 6004 is less than 6020, the condition is satisfied and the control reaches **printf( )**, where value at (**p + i**), i.e. 0 gets printed. Then the control reaches the incrementation part of the **for** loop, where **p++** increments **p** to 6008, and **i++** increments **i** to 1. Next, once again the condition is tested. This time **p + i** gives 6012 (since **p** is 6008 and **i** is 1) and **arr + 4** gives 6020. Since the condition once again gets satisfied, the **printf( )** prints out the value at (**p + i**), i.e. 2. Similarly, next time around 4 gets printed and then the condition fails therefore the execution is terminated.

(18)
```
#include <stdio.h>
int main( )
{
    int arr[ ] = { 0, 1, 2, 3, 4 };
    int *ptr ;
    for ( ptr = arr + 4 ; ptr >= arr ; ptr-- )
        printf ( "%d ", arr [ptr - arr] ) ;
    printf ( "\n" ) ;
    return 0 ;
}
```

Output

4 3 2 1 0

Explanation

The following figure would lead to a better understanding of the program.

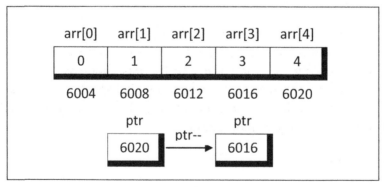

Figure 2.11

In the initialization part, **ptr** is assigned the address of the last element in the array. This is because **arr + 4** gives the address of the fourth integer from the base address. First time through the loop the condition evaluates to true, since the address of the fourth element (6020) would certainly be bigger than the base address (6004) of the array. Next, the control reaches **printf( )**, which prints out the value at address contained in **ptr**, i.e. value at address 6020. Next, the statement **ptr--** gets executed which reduces **ptr** to 6016. Since 6016 is also bigger than 6004, the condition is satisfied once again, and the value at 6016 gets printed through the **printf( )**. This process is repeated for all the array elements.

(19) ```c
#include <stdio.h>
int main( )
{
    int arr[ ] = { 0, 1, 2, 3, 4 } ;
    int i, *ptr ;
    for (ptr = arr + 4, i = 0 ; i <= 4 ; i++)
        printf ("%d ", ptr[-i]) ;
    return 0 ;
}
```

*Output*

4 3 2 1 0

*Explanation*

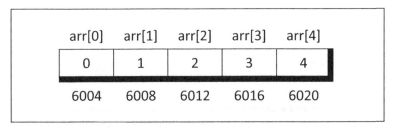

Figure 2.12

The above figure shows the arrangement of array elements in memory.

In the initialization part of the **for** loop, **ptr** is assigned a value 6020, since **arr + 4** gives the address of the fourth integer from the base address of the array. Here, the variable **i** is also initialized to 0. Since the condition is satisfied for the first time (**i** being 0), the **printf( )** prints out the value of **ptr[-i]**. But what is **ptr[-i]**? Nothing but *( **ptr** - i ). And since i is 0, *( **ptr** - i ) evaluates to *( **6020 - 0** ), i.e. 4. Then
```

the control reaches **i++** where **i** is incremented to 1. Next, the condition is checked and since it evaluates to true, the **printf( )** prints out the value of **ptr[-i]**. Since this time **i** is 1, **ptr[-i]** becomes *(ptr - 1), i.e. *(6020 - 1), i.e. * (6016). Thus the value 3 gets printed. Likewise, 2, 1 and 0 also get printed subsequent times through the **for** loop.

(20) #include <stdio.h>
```
int main( )
{
    int arr[ ] = { 0, 1, 2, 3, 4 } ;
    int *ptr ;
    for ( ptr = arr + 4 ; ptr >= arr ; ptr-- )
        printf ( "%d ", arr[ptr - arr] ) ;
    return 0 ;
}
```

Output

4 3 2 1 0

Explanation

A picture is worth a thousand words. Going by this dictum, the following figure should add clarity to your understanding of the program.

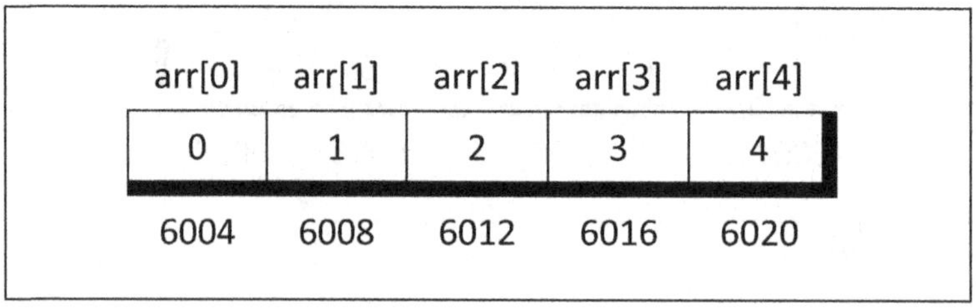

arr[0]	arr[1]	arr[2]	arr[3]	arr[4]
0	1	2	3	4
6004	6008	6012	6016	6020

Figure 2.13

Now things are getting really complicated, as the **printf( )** would justify. Let us begin with the **for** loop. Firstly **ptr** is assigned the address 6020, the address of the fourth integer from the base address. Since this address is greater than the base address, the condition is satisfied and the control reaches **printf( )**. What does **arr [ptr - arr]** evaluate to? **ptr - arr** means 6020 - 6004, which yields 4, and hence **arr[4]** prints out the fourth element of the array. Then

ptr-- reduces **ptr** to 6016. Since 6016 is greater than the base address 6004, the condition is satisfied and once again the control reaches the **printf( )**. This time **ptr - arr** becomes 6016 - 6004, i.e. 3. Thus **arr[3]** prints out 3. This process is repeated till all the integers in the array have been printed out.

Possibly an easier way of understanding the expression **ptr -arr** would be as follows. Suppose **ptr** contains 6020 and **arr** contains 6004. We can then view the subtraction as **(arr + 4 -arr)**, since **ptr** is nothing but **arr + 4**. Now I suppose it is quite logical to expect the result of the subtraction as 4.

(21)
```
#include <stdio.h>
int main( )
{
    static int a[ ] = { 0, 1, 2, 3, 4 } ;
    static int *p[ ] = { a, a + 1 , a + 2, a + 3, a + 4 } ;
    int **ptr = p ;
    printf ( "%u %d\n", a,*a ) ;
    printf ( "%u %u %d\n", p, *p,**p ) ;
    printf ( "%u %u %d\n", ptr, *ptr, **ptr ) ;
    return 0 ;
}
```

Output

```
6004 0
9016 6004 0
9016 6004 0
```

Explanation

Look at the initialization of the array **p[ ]**. During initialization, the addresses of various elements of the array **a[ ]** are stored in the array **p[ ]**. Since the array **p[ ]** contains addresses of integers, it has been declared as an array of pointers to integers. Figure 2.14 shows the contents of arrays **a[ ]** and **p[ ]**. In the variable **ptr**, the base address of the array **p[ ]**, i.e. 9016 is stored. Since this address is the address of **p[0]**, which itself is a pointer, **ptr** has been declared as pointer to an integer pointer.

Let us understand the first **printf( )** now.

printf ("%u %d\n", a, *a) ;

It prints out the base address of the array **a[ ]** and the value at this base address.

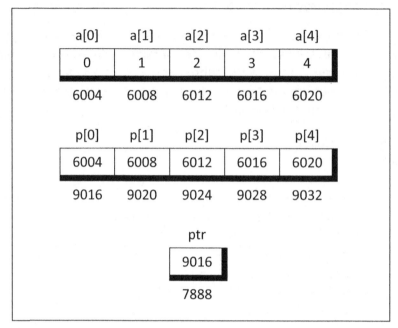

Figure 2.14

Looking at the figure, this would turn out to be 6004 and 0. When you execute the program, the address may turn out to be something other than 6004, but the value at the address would be surely 0.

Now look at the second **printf( )**.

printf ("%u %u %d\n", p, *p, **p) ;

Here **p** would give the base address of the array **p[ ]**, i.e. 9016; ***p** would give the value at this address, i.e. 6004; ****p** would give the value at the address given by ***p**, i.e. value at address 6004, which is 0.

Now onto the last **printf( )**.

printf ("%u %u %d", ptr, *ptr, **ptr) ;

Here **ptr** contains the base address of the array **p[ ]**, i.e. 9016; ***ptr** would give the value at this address, i.e. 6004; ****ptr** would give the value at the address given by ***ptr**, i.e. value at address 6004, which is 0.

(22) #include <stdio.h>
```
int main( )
{
    static int a[ ] = { 0, 1, 2, 3, 4 } ;
    static int *p[ ] = { a, a + 1, a + 2, a + 3, a + 4 } ;
    int **ptr = p ;
    ptr++ ;
    printf ( "%d %d %d\n", ptr - p, *ptr - a, **ptr ) ;
    *ptr++ ;
    printf ( "%d %d %d\n", ptr - p, *ptr - a, **ptr ) ;
    *++ptr ;
    printf ( "%d %d %d\n", ptr - p, *ptr - a, **ptr ) ;
    ++*ptr ;
    printf ( "%d %d %d\n", ptr - p, *ptr - a, **ptr ) ;
    return 0 ;
}
```

Output

```
1 1 1
2 2 2
3 3 3
3 4 4
```

Explanation

Figure 2.15 would go a long way in helping us to understand this program.

Here **ptr** has been declared as a pointer to an integer pointer and assigned the base address of the array **p[ ]**, which has been declared as an array of integer pointers. What happens when **ptr++** gets executed? **ptr** points to the next integer pointer in the array **p[ ]**. In other words, now **ptr** contains the address 9020. Now let us analyze the meaning of **ptr - p**, ***ptr – a** and ****ptr**.

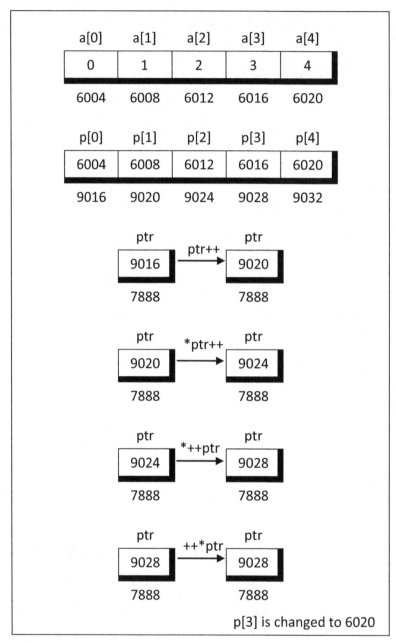

Figure 2.15

ptr - p

Since **ptr** is containing the address 9020, we can as well say that **ptr** is containing the address given by **p + 1**. Then **ptr - p** is reduced to (**p + 1 - p**), which yields 1.

*ptr - a

*ptr means value at the address contained in **ptr**. Since **ptr** contains 9020, the value at this address would be 6008. Now 6008 can be imagined as **(a + 1)**. Thus the expression becomes **(a + 1 - a)**, which is nothing but 1.

**ptr

ptr contains 9020, so ***ptr** yields 6008, and hence ****ptr** becomes ***(6008)**, which yields 1.

Thus the output of the first **printf( )** becomes 1 1 1.

Take a deep breath and then begin with the analysis of ***ptr++**. Here ***** and **++** both are unary operators. Since **++** occurs after the variable, **++** would be done later. Firstly ***(9020)** is performed, but since this value is not being assigned to any variable it gets ignored. Next, **++** goes to work and increments value in **ptr** to 9024. Now with **ptr** containing 9024, let us once again analyze the expressions **ptr - p**, ***ptr - a** and ****ptr**.

ptr - p

Since **ptr** contains 9024, it can be visualized as **(p + 2)**. Thus **ptr - p** would become **(p + 2 - p)**, which gives 2.

*ptr-a

*ptr would give value at address 9024, i.e. 6012, which is nothing but the address given by **a + 2**. Thus the expression becomes **(a + 2 – a)**, which gives 2.

**ptr

*ptr gives the value at address 9024, i.e. 6012, and ***(6012)** gives the value at 6012, i.e. 2.

I hope your confidence is building and you are ready to meet head on the expression ***++ptr**. Here, since **++** precedes **ptr**, firstly **ptr** is incremented such that it contains the address 9028, and then the value at this address is obtained. Since the value is not collected in any variable, it gets ignored. Now having cooked enough pointer stew you can easily imagine that the output of the third **printf( )** would be 3 3 3.

Finally, let us understand the expression **++*ptr**. Here obviously, the priority goes to the *****. Thus, this expression increments the value given by ***ptr**. Since **ptr** contains 9028, ***ptr** gives value at 9028, i.e. 6016. This value is incremented to 6020. So **p[3]** now contains 6020, whereas value of **ptr** remains stationary at 9028. Let us now analyze the expressions **ptr - p**, ***ptr - a** and ****ptr**.

ptr - p

ptr contains 9028, therefore **ptr** can be imagined as **(p + 3)**. Thus **(ptr – p)** becomes **(p + 3 - p)**, which yields 3.

*ptr - a

 *ptr yields 6020 which can be thought of as **(a + 4)**. Thus the expression is reduced to **(a + 4 – a)**, which yields 4.

**ptr

*ptr yields 6020, therefore ****ptr** would yield the value at ***ptr**, or the value at 6020, which is 4.

(23) #include <stdio.h>
```
int main( )
{
    static int a[ ] = { 0, 1, 2, 3, 4 } ;
    static int *p[ ] = { a, a + 1, a + 2, a + 3, a + 4 } ;
    int **ptr ;
    ptr = p ;
    **ptr++ ;
    printf ( "%d %d %d\n", ptr - p, *ptr - a, **ptr ) ;
    *++*ptr ;
    printf ( "%d %d %d\n", ptr - p, *ptr - a, **ptr ) ;
    ++**ptr ;
    printf ( "%d %d %d\n", ptr - p, *ptr - a, **ptr ) ;
    return 0 ;
}
```

Output

1 1 1
1 2 2
1 2 3

Explanation

To begin with, the array **a[ ]** is initialized and the array **p[ ]** is set such that it contains the addresses of elements of array **a[ ]**. Thus array **p[ ]** becomes an array of pointers. The base address of this array of pointers is then assigned to **ptr**, which is rightly called a pointer to a pointer. The possible arrangement of the array elements in memory is shown in the following figure.

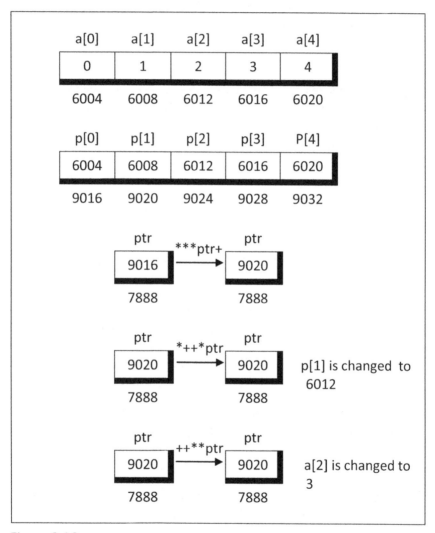

Figure 2.16

Let us now analyze the expression ****ptr++**. **ptr** contains the address 9016, therefore ***ptr** would yield the address 6004. ****ptr** would give the value at this address. This value turns out to be 0. However, this value is not assigned to any variable. Lastly **ptr++**

goes to work. This increments the value stored in **ptr** to 9020. Once you are sure that **ptr** contains 9020, let us now proceed to find out what the output of **printf( )** is. Let us take one expression at a time and analyze it step by careful step.

ptr - p

Since **ptr** is containing the address 9020, we can as well say that **ptr** is containing the address given by **p + 1**. Thus **ptr - p** is reduced to (**p + 1 - p**), which yields 1.

*ptr - a

*ptr means value at the address contained in **ptr**. Since **ptr** contains 9020, the value at this address would be 6008. Now 6008 can be imagined as (**a + 1**). Thus the expression becomes (**a + 1 - a**), which is nothing but 1.

**ptr

ptr contains 9020, so ***ptr** would yield 6008, and hence ****ptr** becomes ***(6008)**, which would yield 1.

Thus the output of the first **printf( )** turns out to be 1 1 1.

The next statement needs a closer look. In ***++*ptr**, the order of evaluation would be ***(++(*ptr))**. Since **ptr** contains 9020, ***(ptr)** would yield the value at 9020, i.e. 6008. Then **++** goes to work on 6008 and increments it such that it is now 6012. Thus **p[1]** would now contain 6012. And finally ***(6012)** would give 2, which is ignored since it is not assigned to any variable.

Now, with **ptr** containing 9020, let us once again analyze the expressions **ptr - p**, ***ptr - a** and ****ptr**.

ptr - p

Since **ptr** contains 9020, it can be visualized as (**p + 1**), thus **ptr - p** would become (**p + 1 − p**), which would be 1.

*ptr - a

*ptr would give value at address 9020, i.e. 6012, which is nothing but the address given by **a + 2**. Thus the expression becomes (**a + 2 - a**), which gives 2.

**ptr

*ptr gives the value at address 9020, i.e. 6012, and *(6012) gives the value at 6012, i.e. 2.

Thus the output of the second **printf( )** would be 1 2 2.

Finally, we reach the third expression ++**ptr. As the unary operators are evaluated from right to left, the order of evaluation of the above expression becomes: (++(*(*ptr))). Since **ptr** contains 9020, *ptr yields 6012. *(6012) results into 2. This value at the address 6012 is then incremented from 2 to 3.

ptr - p

Since **ptr** contains 9020, it can be visualized as (p + 1), thus **ptr - p** would become (p + 1 - p), which would be 1.

*ptr - a

*ptr would give value at address 9020, i.e. 6012, which is nothing but the address given by a + 2. Thus the expression becomes (a + 2 − a), which gives 2.

**ptr

*ptr gives the value at address 9020, i.e. 6012, and *(6012) gives the value at 6012, i.e. 3.

Thus the output of the third **printf( )** is 1 2 3.

(24) #include <stdio.h>
    int main( )
    {
        int n[3][3]= {
                        2, 4, 3,
                        6, 8, 5,
                        3, 5, 1
                    } ;
        /* Assume that array begins at address 404 */
        printf ("%u %u %d\n", n, n[2], n[2][2]) ;
        return 0 ;
    }

Output

404 428 1

Explanation

n[ ][ ], to begin with, is declared as a two-dimensional array. Whenever we mention the name of the array, we get its base address. Therefore in **printf( )**, the first output would be the base address of the array. In our case it turned out to be 404. The array elements are arranged in memory as shown in Figure 2.17. Remember that there are no rows and columns in memory.

A two-dimensional array is nothing but an array of several one-dimensional arrays. The 2-D array contains addresses of these 1-D arrays. Thus **n[0]**, **n[1]** and **n[2]** contain the addresses 404, 416 and 428 respectively. Hence the second output of **printf( )**. The third output is quite straightforward. **n[2][2]** prints out the element in the second row and second column of the array.

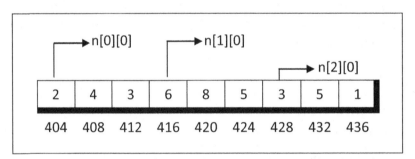

Figure 2.17

```
(25) #include <stdio.h>
     int main( )
     {
         int n[3][3] = {
                             2, 4, 3,
                             6, 8, 5,
                             3, 5, 1
                       };
         int *ptr ;
         ptr = ( int * ) n ;
         printf ( "%u ", n[2] );
         printf ( "%d ", ptr[2] );
```

```
        printf ( "%d\n", *( ptr + 2 ) ) ;
        return 0 ;
}
```

Output

428 3 3

Explanation

ptr has been declared as an integer pointer, and to begin with is assigned the base address of the array, i.e. 404.

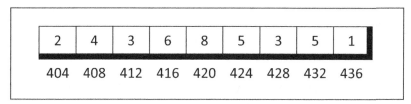

2	4	3	6	8	5	3	5	1
404	408	412	416	420	424	428	432	436

Figure 2.18

n[2] gives the base address of the second one-dimensional array, that is 428. Next comes the expression **ptr[2]**. Can we use such an expression? Yes, because ultimately **ptr[2]** is nothing but ***(ptr + 2)**. Thus, even though **ptr** has not been declared as an array, we are perfectly justified in using the expression **ptr[2]**. **ptr** stores the address 404, so ***(ptr + 2)** gives the value of the second integer from 404, which in this program happens to be 3.

```
(26) #include <stdio.h>
     int main( )
     {
         int n[3][3] = {
                         2, 4, 3,
                         6, 8, 5,
                         3, 5, 1
                      } ;
         int i, j ;
         for ( i = 2 ; i >= 0 ; i-- )
         {
             for ( j = 2 ; j >= 0 ; j-- )
                 printf ( "%d %d\n", n[i][j], *( *( n + i ) + j ) ) ;
         }
```

```
        return 0 ;
}
```

Output

```
1 1
5 5
3 3
5 5
8 8
6 6
3 3
4 4
2 2
```

Explanation

The output of **n[i][j]** is as per the expectations, I believe. All that is done is, using the **for** loops, rows and columns are varied, **i** controlling the row and **j** controlling the column. What is definitely difficult to comprehend is the second expression in **printf( )**, ***(*(n + i) + j)**. Let us try to understand it. The following figure should prove helpful in doing so.

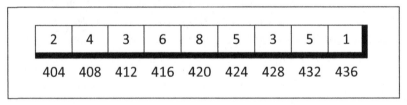

Figure 2.19

Imagine a 2-D array as a collection of several 1-D arrays. The only thing that the compiler needs to remember about a 1-D array is its base address. Thus, if three 1-D arrays are to be remembered, the compiler should store somewhere the base addresses of these arrays. These base addresses are stored in **n[0]**, **n[1]** and **n[2]**. Now if **n[1]** gives the base address of the first array, then **n[1] + 2** would give the address of the second integer from this base address. In this case it turns out to be 424. The value at this address, that is 5, can be obtained through the expression ***(n[1] + 2)**. We know all too well that **n[1]** can also be expressed as ***(n + 1)**. Thus, the expression ***(n[1] + 2)** is same as ***(*(n + 1) + 2)**, which is same as

n[1][2]. Therefore in general, we can say that **n[i][j]** is same as ***(*(n + i) + j)**. With that I suppose, the output of the above program is quite simple.

```c
(27) #include <stdio.h>
     int main( )
     {
         static int a[3][3] = {
                                 1, 2, 3,
                                 4, 5, 6,
                                 7, 8, 9
                              } ;
         static int *ptr[3] = { a[0], a[1], a[2] } ;
         int **ptr1 = ptr ;
         int i ;
         printf ( "\n" ) ;
         for ( i = 0 ; i <= 2 ; i++ )
             printf ( "%d ", *ptr[i] ) ;
         printf ( "\n" ) ;
         for ( i = 0 ; i <= 2 ; i++ )
             printf ( "%d ", *a[i] ) ;
         printf ( "\n" ) ;
         for ( i = 0 ; i <= 2 ; i++ )
         {
             printf ( "%d ", **ptr1 ) ;
             ptr1++ ;
         }
         return 0 ;
     }
```

Output

```
1 4 7
1 4 7
1 4 7
```

Explanation

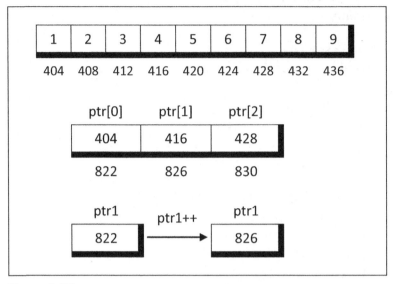

Figure 2.20

ptr[ ] has been declared as an array of pointers containing the base addresses of the three 1-D arrays as shown in Figure 2.20. Once past the declarations, the control reaches the first **for** loop. In this loop the **printf( )** prints the values at addresses stored in **ptr[0]**, **ptr[1]** and **ptr[2]**, which turn out to be 1, 4 and 7.

In the next **for** loop, the values at base addresses stored in the array **a[ ]** are printed, which once again turn out to be 1, 4 and 7. The third **for** loop is also simple.

Since **ptr1** has been initialized to the base address of the array **ptr[ ]**, it contains the address 822. Therefore ***ptr1** would give the value at address 822, i.e. 404, and ****ptr1** would give the value at address given by ***ptr1**, i.e. value at 404, which is 1. On incrementing **ptr1** it points to the next location after 822, i.e. 826. Therefore, next time through the **for** loop, ****ptr1** gives value at 416 (which is obtained through ***ptr1**), i.e. 4. Similarly, last time through the loop, the value 7 gets printed.

```
(28) #include <stdio.h>
    int main( )
    {
        int t[3][2][4] = {
                        {
```

                              2, 4, 3, 6,
                              1, 6, 7, 9
                    },
                    {
                              8, 2, 1, 1,
                              2, 3, 7, 3
                    },
                    {
                              1, 6, 2, 4,
                              0, 7, 9, 5
                    }
              } ;
    printf ("%d %d\n", t[2][1][3], *(*(*(t + 2) + 1) + 3)) ;
    return 0 ;
    }

Output

5 5

Explanation

In memory the 3-D array elements are arranged as shown in Figure
2.21.

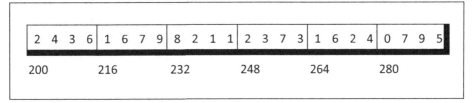

| 2 | 4 | 3 | 6 | 1 | 6 | 7 | 9 | 8 | 2 | 1 | 1 | 2 | 3 | 7 | 3 | 1 | 6 | 2 | 4 | 0 | 7 | 9 | 5 |

200   216   232   248   264   280

Figure 2.21

Here **t[ ][ ][ ]** has been declared as a three-dimensional array. A 3-D
array can be considered as a collection of a number of 2-D arrays.
Thus, the first expression in the **printf( )**, **t[2][1][3]** refers to the
element in 1st row, 3rd column of the 2nd 2-D array. This turns out to
be 5, which is printed through **printf( )**.

The next expression in **printf( )** is a little complicated. Since the only
thing that the compiler needs to remember about the three 2-D
arrays is their base addresses, these addresses are stored in **t[0]**,
t[1] and **t[2]**. Therefore, the expression **t[2][1]** would give the

address of the first row of the second 2-D array. Referring to the figure, this address turns out to be 280. To this address if we add 3, we would get the address of the third integer from this address. This address would be 292. Naturally, the value at this address (i.e. 5) can be obtained through the expression ***(t[2][1] + 3)**. But **t[2][1]** itself can be expressed as ***(t[2] + 1)**. And in this expression **t[2]** can be expressed as ***(t + 2)**. Thus the expression ***(t[2][1] + 3)** can be expressed as ***(*(*(t + 2) + 1) + 3)**.

[B] Answer the following:

(1) For the following statements would **arr[3]** and **ptr[3]** fetch the same character? [Yes/No]:

```
char arr[ ] = "Surprised" ;
char *ptr = "Surprised" ;
```

Explanation

Yes

(2) For the statements in (1) does the compiler fetch the character **arr[3]** and **ptr[3]** in the same manner?

Explanation

No. For **arr[3]** the compiler generates code to start at location **arr**, move three past it, and fetch the character there. When it sees the expression **ptr[3]** it generates the code to start at location stored in **ptr**, add three to the pointer, and finally fetch the character pointed to.

In other words, **arr[3]** is three places past the start of the object named **arr**, whereas **ptr[3]** is three places past the object pointed to by **ptr**.

(3) Can you combine the following two statements into one?

```
char *p ;
p = malloc ( 100 ) ;
```

Explanation

```
char *p = malloc ( 100 )
```

(4) Does mentioning the array name gives the base address in all the contexts?

Explanation

No. Whenever mentioning the array name gives its base address it is said that the array has decayed into a pointer. This decaying doesn't take place in two situations:

— When array name is used with **sizeof** operator.
— When the array name is an operand of the **&** operator.

(5) Are the expressions **arr** and **&arr** same for an array of 10 integers?

Explanation

No. Even though both may give the same addresses they mean two different things. **arr** gives the address of the first **int**, whereas **&arr** gives the address of array of **int**s. Since these addresses happen to be same the results of the expressions are same.

(6) When **char a[ ]** and **char *a** are treated as same by the compiler?

Explanation

When using them as formal parameters while defining a function.

(7) Would the following program compile successfully?

```c
#include <stdio.h>
int main( )
{
    char a[ ] = "Sunstroke" ;
    char *p = "Coldwave" ;
    a = "Coldwave" ;
    p = "Sunstroke" ;
    printf ( "%s %s\n", a, p ) ;
    return 0 ;
}
```

Explanation

No, because we may assign a new string to a pointer but not to an array.

(8) A pointer to a block of memory is effectively same as an array. [True/False]

Explanation

True

(9) What does the following declaration mean:

int (*ptr)[10] ;

Explanation

ptr is a pointer to an array of 10 integers.

(10) If we pass the name of a 1-D **int** array to a function it decays into a pointer to an **int**. If we pass the name of a 2-D array of integers to function what would it decay into?

Explanation

It decays into a pointer to an array and not a pointer to a pointer.

(11) Are the three declarations **char **apple, char *orange[ ]**, and **char cherry[ ][ ]** same? [Yes/No]

Explanation

No

(12) What would be the equivalent pointer expression for referring the element **a[i][j][k][l]**?

Explanation

* (* (* (* (a + i) + j) + k) + l)

(13) In the following program how would you print 50 using **p**?

```
#include <stdio.h>
int main( )
{
    int a[ ] = { 10, 20, 30, 40, 50 } ;
    char *p ;
    p = ( char * ) a ;
```

```
        return 0 ;
    }
```

Explanation

```
printf ( "%d\n", * ( ( int * ) p + 4 ) ) ;
```

(14) How would you define the function **fun( )** in the following program?

```
int arr[MAXROW][MAXCOL] ;
fun ( arr ) ;
```

Explanation

```
fun ( int a[ ][MAXCOL] )
{
}
```

or

```
fun ( int ( *ptr )[MAXCOL] )     /* ptr is pointer to an array */
{
}
```

Exercise

[A] What will be the output of the following programs:

(1) ```c
     #include <stdio.h>
     int main( )
     {
         int arr[3][3][3] ;
         /* Assume base address of arr to be 1000 */
         printf ("%u %u %u\n", arr, arr + 1 , arr + 2) ;
         printf ("%u %u %u\n", arr[0], arr[0] + 1, arr[1]) ;
         printf ("%u %u %u\n", arr[1][1], arr[1][0] + 1, arr[0][1]) ;
         return 0 ;
     }
     ```

(2)  ```c
     #include <stdio.h>
     int main( )
     {
         static int a[3][3][3] = {
                                 {
                                     1, 2, 3,
                                     4, 5, 6,
                                     7, 8, 9
                                 },
                                 {
                                     2, 4, 6,
                                     8, 10, 12,
                                     14, 16, 18
                                 },
                                 {
                                     3, 6, 9,
                                     12, 15, 18,
                                     21, 24, 27
                                 }
                                 } ;
         static int *ptr[ ] = {
                                 a[0][0], a[0][1], a[0][2],
                                 a[1][0], a[1][1], a[1][2],
                                 a[2][0], a[2][1], a[2][2]
                              } ;
         int *ptr1[ ] = { a[0], a[1], a[2] } ;
         int **ptr2 = ptr, i ;
     ```

```
        printf ( "\n" ) ;
        for ( i = 0 ; i <= 8 ; i++ )
        {
            printf ( "%d ", *ptr2 ) ;
            ptr2++ ;
        }
        printf ( "\n" ) ;
        for ( i = 0 ; i <= 2 ; i++ )
            printf ( "%d ", *( ptr1[i] ) ) ;
        printf ( "\n" ) ;
        for ( i = 0 ; i <= 8 ; i++ )
            printf ( "%d ", *ptr[i] ) ;
        return 0 ;
    }

(3)  #include <stdio.h>
     void print ( int *, int *, int *, int *, int * ) ;
     int main( )
     {
         static int arr[ ] = { 97, 98, 99, 100, 101, 102, 103, 104 } ;
         int  *ptr = arr + 1 ;
         print ( ++ptr, ptr--, ptr, ptr++, ++ptr ) ;
         return 0 ;
     }
     void print ( int *a, int *b, int *c, int *d, int *e )
     {
         printf ( "%d %d %d %d %d\n", *a, *b, *c, *d, *e ) ;
     }

(4)  #include <stdio.h>
     int main( )
     {
         int a[3][3][2] = {
                             {
                                 1, 2,
                                 3, 4,
                                 5, 6
                             },
                             {
                                 3, 4,
                                 1, 2,
                                 5, 6
```

```
                          },
                          {
                                5, 6,
                                3, 4,
                                1, 2
                          }
                    };
          printf ( "%d %d %d\n", * ( * ( a[0] + 2 ) + 1 ),
                    * ( * ( * ( a + 2 ) + 1 ) + 1 ), * ( a[1][2] + 1 ) ) ;
          return 0 ;
      }

(5)  #include <stdio.h>
     int main( )
     {
          static int a[ ] = { 0, 1 ,2 ,3 ,4 } ;
          static int *p[ ] = { a, a + 2, a + 1 , a + 4, a + 3 } ;
          int **ptr ;
          ptr = p ;
          **++ptr ;
          printf ( "%d %d %d\n", **ptr, ptr - p, *ptr - a ) ;
          return 0 ;
      }
```

Understanding
Pointers in
C & C++

Pointers and
Strings

If arrays are related to pointers, can strings be far behind? Experience the close relationship between strings and pointers in this chapter...

S trings, simply put, are a special kind of array. Strings, the ways to manipulate them, and how pointers are related to strings are going to be the topics of discussion in this chapter.

What are Strings

The way a group of integers can be stored in an integer array, similarly a group of characters can be stored in a character array. They are used to manipulate text, such as words and sentences.

A string is a 1-D array of characters terminated by a null ('\0'). For example,

char name[ ] = { 'H', 'A', 'E', 'S', 'L', 'E', 'R', '\0' } ;

'\0' is called null character. Note that '\0' and '0' are not same. ASCII value of '\0' is 0, whereas ASCII value of '0' is 48. Figure 3.1 shows the way a string is stored in memory. Note that the elements of the string are stored in contiguous memory locations.

The terminating null ('\0') is important, because it is the only way the functions that work with a string can know where the string ends. In fact, a string not terminated by a '\0' is not really a string, but merely a collection of characters.

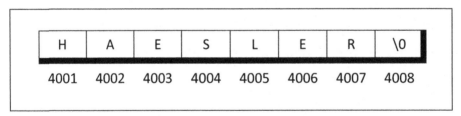

Figure 3.1

C concedes the fact that you would use strings very often and hence provides a shortcut for initializing strings. For example, the string used above can also be initialized as,

char name[ ] = "HAESLER" ;

Note that, in this declaration '\0' is not necessary. C inserts the null automatically. The '\0' comes very handy in printing strings. This is illustrated in the following program.

/* Program 27 */
#include <stdio.h>

```
int main( )
{
    char name[ ] = "Klinsman" ;
    int i ;
    i = 0 ;
    while ( name[i] )
    {
        printf ( "%c %c %c %c\n", name[i], * ( name + i ),
                            *( i + name ), i[name] ) ;
        i++ ;
    }
    return 0 ;
}
```

And here is the output...

```
K K K K
I I I I
i i i i
n n n n
s s s s
m m m m
a a a a
n n n n
```

This program doesn't rely on the length of the string (number of characters in string) to print out its contents and hence is generic. Here is another version of the same program; this one uses pointers to access the array elements.

```
/* Program 28 */
/* Program to print string elements using pointer notation */
#include <stdio.h>
int main( )
{
    char name[ ] = "Klinsman" ;
    char *ptr ;
    ptr = name ;  /* store base address of string */
    while ( *ptr != '\0' )
    {
        printf ( "%c", *ptr ) ;
        ptr++ ;
```

```
    }
    return 0 ;
}
```

As with the integer array, by mentioning the name of the array, we get the base address (address of the zeroth element) of the array. This base address is stored in the variable **ptr**. Once the base address is obtained in **ptr**, ***ptr** would yield the value at this address, which gets printed promptly through,

printf ("%c", *ptr) ;

Then, **ptr** is incremented to point to the next character in the string. This derives from two facts: array elements are stored in contiguous memory locations and on incrementing a pointer, it points to the immediately next location of its type. This process is carried out until **ptr** points to the last character in the string, that is, '\0'.

Even though there are so many ways (as shown above) to refer to the elements of a character array, rarely is any one of them used. This is because **printf( )** function has got a sweet and simple way of doing it, as shown below. Note that **printf( )** doesn't print the '\0'.

```
/* Program 29 */
#include <stdio.h>
int main( )
{
    char name[ ] = "Klinsman" ;
    printf ( "%s\n", name ) ;
    return 0 ;
}
```

The **%s** is a format specification for printing out a string. The same specification can be used to receive a string from the keyboard, as shown below.

```
/* Program 30 */
#include <stdio.h>
int main( )
{
    char name[25] ;
    printf ( "Enter your name:\n" ) ;
    scanf ( "%s", name ) ;
```

```
        printf ( "Hello %s!\n", name ) ;
        return 0 ;
}
```

And here is the sample run of this program...

Enter your name:
Debashish
Hello Debashish!

Note that the declaration **char name[25]** sets aside 25 bytes under the
array **name[ ]**, whereas the **scanf( )** function fills in the characters typed
at keyboard into this array until the Enter key is hit. Once enter is hit,
scanf( ) places a '\0' in the array. Naturally, we should pass the base
address of the array to the **scanf( )** function.

Standard Library String Functions

C has a large set of useful string handling library functions. Here, we
would illustrate the usage of most commonly used functions **(strlen( ),
strcpy( ), strcat( )** and **strcmp( ))** through a program.

```
/* Program 31 */
#include <string.h>
#include <stdio.h>
int main( )
{
    char str1[20] = "Bamboozled" ;
    char str2[ ] = "Chap" ;
    char str3[20] ;
    int l, k ;
    l = strlen ( str1) ;
    printf ( "length of string = %d\n", l ) ;
    strcpy ( str3, str1 ) ;
    printf ( "after copying, string str3 = %s\n", str3 ) ;
    k = strcmp( str1, str2) ;
    printf ( "on comparing str1 and str2, k = %d\n", k ) ;
    k = strcmp ( str3, str1 ) ;
    printf ( "on comparing str3 and str1, k = %d\n", k ) ;
    strcat ( str1,str2 ) ;
    printf ( "on concatenation str1 = %s\n", str1 ) ;
    return 0 ;
}
```

The output would be...

length of string = 10
after copying, string str3 = Bamboozled
on comparing str1 and str2, k = -1
on comparing str3 and str1, k = 0
on concatenation str1 = BamboozledChap

Note that in the call to the function **strlen( )**, we are passing the base address of the string, and the function in turn returns the length of the string. While calculating the length it doesn't count '\0'. Can we not write a function **xstrlen( )** which imitates the standard library function **strlen( )**? Let us give it a try...

```
/* Program 32 */
#include <stdio.h>
int  xstrlen ( char * ) ;
int  main( )
{
    char arr[ ] = "Bamboozled" ;
    int len1, len2 ;
    len1 = xstrlen ( arr ) ;
    len2 = xstrlen ( "HumptyDumpty" ) ;
    printf ( "string = %s length = %d\n ", arr, len1 ) ;
    printf ( "string = %s length = %d\n ", "HumptyDumpty", len2 ) ;
    return 0 ;
}
int  xstrlen ( char *s )
{
    int length = 0 ;
    while ( *s != '\0' )
    {
        length++ ;
        s++ ;
    }
    return ( length ) ;
}
```

The output would be...

string = Bamboozled length = 10
string = HumptyDumpty length =12

The function **xstrlen( )** is fairly simple. All that it does is it keeps counting the characters till the end of string is not met. Or in other words keeps counting characters till the pointer **s** doesn't point to '\0'.

Another function that we have used in Program 32 is **strcpy( )**. This function copies the contents of one string into another. The base addresses of the source and target strings should be supplied to this function. On supplying the base addresses, **strcpy( )** goes on copying the source string into the target string till it doesn't encounter the end of source string. It is our responsibility to see to it that target string's dimension is big enough to hold the string being copied into it. Thus, a string gets copied into another, piecemeal, character by character. There is no shortcut for this. Let us now attempt to mimic **strcpy( )** via our own string copy function, which we would call **xstrcpy( )**.

```
void xstrcpy ( char *t, char *s )
{
    while ( *s != '\0' )
    {
        *t = *s ;
        s++ ;
        t++ ;
    }
    *t = '\0' ;
}
```

Note that having copied the entire source string into the target string, it is necessary to place a '\0' into the target string to mark its end.

The **strcat( )** function concatenates the source string at the end of the target string. For example, "Bamboozled" and "Chap" on concatenation would result into a string "BamboozledChap". Note that the target string **str1[ ]** has been made big enough to hold the final string. I leave it to you to develop your own **xstrcat( )** on lines of **xstrlen( )** and **xstrcpy( )**.

Another useful string function is **strcmp( )** which compares two strings to find out whether, they are same or different. The two strings are compared letter by letter until there is a mismatch or end of one of the strings is reached, whichever occurs first. If the two strings are identical, **strcmp( )** returns a value zero. If they're not, it returns the numeric difference between the ASCII values of the first non-matching pair of characters.

The exact value of mismatch will rarely concern us. All we usually want to know is whether or not the first string is alphabetically above the second string. If it is, a negative value is returned; if it isn't, a positive value is returned. Any non-zero value means there is a mismatch. Let us try to implement this procedure into a function **xstrcmp( )**, which works similar to the **strcmp( )** function.

```
int  xstrcmp ( char *s1, char *s2 )
{
    while ( *s1 == *s2 )
    {
        if ( *s1 == '\0' )
            return ( 0 ) ;

        s1++ ;
        s2++ ;
    }
    return ( *s1 - *s2 ) ;
}
```

Pointers and Strings

Suppose we wish to store "Hello". We may either store it in a string or we may ask the C compiler to store it at some location in memory and assign the address of the string in a **char** pointer. This is shown below:

```
char str[ ] = "Hello" ;
char *p = "Hello" ;
```

There is a subtle difference in usage of these two forms. For example, we cannot assign a string to another, whereas, we can assign a **char** pointer to another **char** pointer. This is shown in the following program.

```
/* Program 33 */
#include <stdio.h>
int main( )
{
    char str1[ ] = "Hello" ;
    char str2[10] ;
    char *s = "Good Morning" ;
    char *q ;
    str2 = str1 ; /* error */
    q = s ; /* works */
```

```
        return 0 ;
}
```

Also, once a string has been defined it cannot be initialized to another set of characters. Unlike strings, such an operation is perfectly valid with **char** pointers.

```
/* Program 34 */
#include <stdio.h>
int main( )
{
    char str1[ ] = "Hello" ;
    char *p = "Hello" ;
    str1 = "Bye" ; /* error */
    p = "Bye" ; /* works */
    return 0 ;
}
```

The *const* Qualifier

The keyword **const** (for constant), if present, precedes the data type of a variable. It specifies that the value of the variable will not change throughout the program. Any attempt to alter the value of the variable defined with this qualifier will result into an error message from compiler. **const** is usually used to replace #**defined** constants.

const qualifier ensures that your program does not inadvertently alter a variable that you intended to be a constant. It also reminds anybody reading the program listing that the variable is not intended to change. Variables with this qualifier are often named in all uppercase, as a reminder that they are constants. The following program shows the usage of **const.**

```
/* Program 35 */
#include <stdio.h>
int main( )
{
    float r, a ;
    const float PI = 3.14 ;
    printf ( "Enter radius:\n" ) ;
    scanf ( "%f", &r ) ;
    a = PI * r * r ;
    printf ( "Area of circle = %f\n", a ) ;
```

```
    return 0 ;
}
```

const is a better idea as compared to **#define** because its scope of operation can be controlled by placing it appropriately either inside a function or outside all functions. If a **const** is placed inside a function, its effect would be localized to that function, whereas, if it is placed outside all functions then its effect would be global. We cannot exercise such fine control while using a **#define**.

const Pointers

Look at the following program:

```
/* Program 36 */
#include <stdio.h>
void xstrcpy ( char *, char * ) ;
int main( )
{
    char str1[ ] = "Nagpur" ;
    char str2[10] ;
    xstrcpy ( str2, str1 ) ;
    printf ( "%s\n", str2) ;
    return 0 ;
}
void xstrcpy ( char *t, char *s )
{
    while ( *t != '\0' )
    {
        *t = *s ;
        t++ ;
        s++ ;
    }
    *t = '\0' ;
}
```

This program simply copies the contents of **str1[ ]** into **str2[ ]** using the function **xstrcpy( )**. What would happen if we add the following lines beyond the last statement of **xstrcpy( )**?

```
s = s - 6 ;
*s = 'K' ;
```

This would change the source string to "Kagpur". Can we not ensure that the source string doesn't change even accidentally in **xstrcpy( )**? We can, by changing the prototype of the function to

void xstrcpy (char*, const char*) ;

Correspondingly the definition would change to:

```
void xstrcpy ( char *t, const char *s )
{
    /* code */
}
```

The following code fragment would help you to fix your ideas about **const** further.

```
char *p = "Hello" ; /* pointer is variable, string is constant */
*p = 'M' ; /* error */
p = "Bye" ; /* works */
```

```
const char *q = "Hello" ; /* string is constant pointer is not */
*q = 'M' ; /* error */
q = "Bye" ; /* works */
```

```
char const *s = "Hello" ; /* string is constant pointer is not */
*s = 'M' ; /* error */
s = "Bye" ; /* works */
```

```
char * const t = "Hello" ; /* pointer is constant, so is string */
*t = 'M' ; /* error */
t = "Bye" ; /* error */
```

```
const char * const u = "Hello" ; /* string is constant, so is pointer */
*u = 'M' ; /* error */
u = "Bye" ; /* error */
```

Returning *const* Values

A function can return a pointer to a constant string as shown below.

```
/* Program 37 */
#include <stdio.h>
int main( )
{
    const char *fun( ) ;
```

```
        const char *p ;
        p = fun( ) ;
        *p = 'A' ; /* error */
        printf ( "%s\n", p ) ;
        return 0 ;
}
const char *fun( )
{
        return "Rain" ;
}
```

Here since the function **fun( )** is returning a constant string, we cannot use the pointer **p** to modify it. Not only this, the following operations too would be invalid:

(a) **main( )** cannot assign the return value to a pointer to a non-**const** string.

(b) **main( )** cannot pass the return value to a function that is expecting a pointer to a non-**const** string.

Two Dimensional Array of Characters

In the previous chapter we saw several examples of 2-D numeric arrays. Let's now look at a similar phenomenon, but one dealing with characters. The best way to understand this concept is through a program. Our example program asks you to type your name. When you do so, it checks your name against a master list to see if you are worthy of entry to the palace. Here's the program...

```
/* Program 38 */
#include <string.h>
#include <stdio.h>
#define FOUND 1
#define NOTFOUND 0
int main( )
{
    char masterlist[6][10] = {
                                "akshay",
                                "parag",
                                "raman",
                                "srinivas",
                                "gopal",
```

```
                                "rajesh"
                        } ;
    int i, flag, a ;
    char yourname[10] ;
    printf ( "Enter your name: " ) ;
    scanf ( "%s", yourname ) ;
    flag = NOTFOUND ;
    for ( i = 0 ; i <= 5 ; i++ )
    {
        a = strcmp ( &masterlist[i][0], yourname ) ;
        if ( a == 0 )
        {
            printf ( "Welcome, you can enter the palace\n" ) ;
            flag = FOUND ;
            break ;
        }
    }
    if ( flag == NOTFOUND )
        printf ( "Sorry, you are a trespasser\n" ) ;
    return 0 ;
}
```

And here is the output for two sample runs of this program...

Enter your name: dinesh
Sorry, you are a trespasser

Enter your name: raman
Welcome, you can enter the palace

Notice how the two-dimensional character array has been initialized. The order of the subscripts in the array declaration is important. The first subscript gives the number of names in the array, while the second subscript gives the length of each item in the array.

Instead of initializing names, had these names been supplied from the keyboard, the program segment would look like this...

```
for ( i = 0 ; i <= 5 ; i++ )
    scanf ( "%s", &masterlist[i][0] ) ;
```

While comparing the strings through **strcmp( )**, note that the addresses of the strings are being passed to **strcmp( )**. As seen in the last section, if the two strings match, **strcmp( )** would return a value 0, otherwise it would return a non-zero value.

The variable **flag** is used to keep a record of whether the control did reach inside the **if** or not. To begin with, we set this **flag** to NOTFOUND. Later through the loop if the names match this flag is set to FOUND. When the control reaches beyond the **for** loop, if **flag** is still set to NOTFOUND, it means none of the names in the **masterlist[ ][ ]** matched with the one supplied from the keyboard.

The names would be stored in memory as shown in Figure 3.2. Note that each string ends with a '\0'. The arrangement as you can appreciate is similar to that of a two-dimensional numeric array.

akshay\0	parag\0	raman\0	srinivas\0	gopal\0	rajesh\0
1001	1011	1021	1031	1041	1051

Figure 3.2

Here, 1001, 1011, 1021, etc. are the base addresses of successive names. As seen from the above figure, some of the names do not occupy all the bytes reserved for them. For example, even though 10 bytes are reserved for storing the name "akshay", it occupies only 7 bytes. Thus, 3 bytes go waste. Similarly, for each name there is some amount of wastage. In fact, more the number of names more would be the wastage. Can this not be avoided? Yes, it can be... by using a data type called an array of pointers to strings, which is our next topic of discussion.

Array of Pointers to Strings

As we know, a pointer variable always contains an address. Therefore, if we construct an array of pointers it would contain a number of addresses. Let us see how the names in the earlier example can be stored in the array of pointers.

```
char *names[ ] = {
                "akshay",
                "parag",
                "raman",
```

```
            "srinivas",
            "gopal",
            "rajesh"
    };
```

In this declaration **names[ ]** is an array of pointers. It contains base addresses of respective names. That is, base addresses of "akshay" is stored in **names[0]**, base addresses of "parag" is stored in **names[1]** and so on. This is depicted in the Figure 3.3.

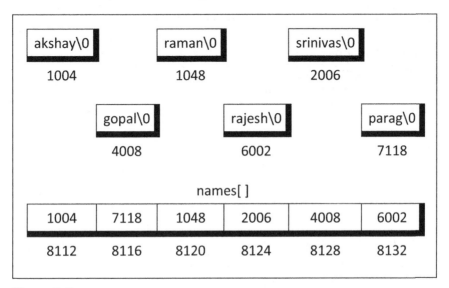

Figure 3.3

In the two-dimensional array of characters, the strings were occupying a total of 60 bytes. As against this by using the array of pointers to strings the same strings can now be stored using 65 bytes, 41 bytes for the actual strings and 24 for the array of pointers.

Thus, one reason to store strings in an array of pointers is to make more efficient use of available memory.

Another reason to use array of pointers to store strings is to obtain greater ease in the manipulation of the strings. The following program shows this. The purpose of the program is very simple. We want to exchange the positions of the names "raman" and "srinivas".

```
/* Program 39 */
#include <stdio.h>
int main( )
{
```

```
    char *names[ ] = {
                        "akshay",
                        "parag",
                        "raman",
                        "srinivas",
                        "gopal",
                        "rajesh"
                } ;
    char *temp ;
    printf ( "Original: %s %s\n", names[2], names[3] ) ;
    temp = names[2] ;
    names[2] = names[3] ;
    names[3] = temp ;
    printf ( "New: %s %s\n", names[2], names[3] ) ;
    return 0 ;
}
```

And here is the output...

Original: raman srinivas
New: srinivas raman

In this program all that we are required to do is exchange the addresses of the names stored in the array of pointers, rather than the names themselves. Thus, by effecting just one exchange we are able to interchange names. This makes managing strings very convenient.

Thus, from the point of view of efficient memory usage and ease of programming, an array of pointers to strings definitely scores over a two-dimensional character array. That is why, even though in principle strings can be stored and handled through a two-dimensional array of characters, in actual practice it is the array of pointers to strings which is more commonly used.

In Program 39 instead of exchanging the names within **main( )** suppose we decide to carry out this exchange through a function **swap( )**. To this function suppose we would pass the addresses given by **(names + 2)** and **(names + 3)**. These addresses would be collected in two variables, which are pointers to pointers (why?). Using these pointers then the names can be exchanged. This is how the **swap( )** function would look like...

```
void swap ( char **s1 , char **s2 )
```

```
{
    char *t ;
    t = *s1 ;
    *s1 = *s2 ;
    *s2 = t ;
}
```

Limitation of Array of Pointers to Strings

When we are using a two-dimensional array of characters we are at liberty to either initialize the strings where we are declaring the array, or receive the strings using **scanf( )** function. However, when we are using an array of pointers to strings we can initialize the strings at the place where we are declaring the array, but we cannot receive the strings from keyboard using **scanf( )**. Thus, the following program would never work out.

```
/* Program 40 */
#include <stdio.h>
int main( )
{
    char *names[6] ;
    int i ;
    for ( i = 0 ; i <= 5 ; i++ )
    {
        printf ( "Enter name: " ) ;
        scanf ( "%s", names[i] ) ;
    }
    return 0 ;
}
```

The program doesn't work because when we are declaring the array it is containing garbage values. And it would be definitely wrong to send these garbage values to **scanf( )** as the addresses where it should keep the strings received from the keyboard.

As a compromise solution we may first allocate space for each name using **malloc( )** and then store the address returned by **malloc( )** in the array of pointers to strings. This is shown in the following program.

```
/* Program 41 */
/* Program to overcome limitation of array of pointers to strings */
#include <stdlib.h>
```

```c
#include <string.h>
#include <stdio.h>
int main( )
{
    char *name[5] ;
    char str[20] ;
    int i ;
    for ( i = 0 ; i < 5 ; i++ )
    {
        printf ( "Enter a String: " ) ;
        gets ( str ) ;
        name[i] = ( char * ) malloc ( strlen ( str ) ) ;
        strcpy ( name[i], str ) ;
    }
    for ( i = 0 ; i < 5 ; i++ )
        printf ( "%s\n", name[i] ) ;
    return 0 ;
}
```

Solved Problems

[A] What will be the output of the following programs:

(1)
```
#include <string.h>
#include <stdio.h>
int main( )
{
    char s[ ] = "Rendezvous !" ;
    printf ( "%d\n", * ( s + strlen ( s ) ) ) ;
    return 0 ;
}
```

Output

0

Explanation

No 'Rendezvous !', but a zero is printed out. Mentioning the name of the string gives the base address of the string. The function **strlen (s)** returns the length of the string **s[ ]**, which in this case is 12. In **printf( )**, using the 'value at address' operator (often called 'contents of' operator), we are trying to print out the contents of the 12th address from the base address of the string. At this address there is a '\0', which is automatically stored to mark the end of the string. The ASCII value of '\0' is 0, which is what is being printed by the **printf( )**.

(2)
```
#include <stdio.h>
int main( )
{
    printf ( 5 + "Fascimile" ) ;
    return 0 ;
}
```

Output

mile

Explanation

When we pass a string to a function, what gets passed is the base address of the string. In this case what is being passed to **printf( )** is the base address plus 5, i.e. address of 'm' in "Fascimile". **printf( )** prints a string starting from the address it receives, up to the end of the string. Hence, in this case 'mile' gets printed.

(3)
```
#include <stdio.h>
int main( )
{
    char ch[20] ;
    int i ;
    for ( i = 0 ; i < 19 ; i ++ )
        *( ch + i ) = 67 ;
    *( ch + i ) = '\0' ;
    printf ( "%s\n", ch ) ;
    return 0 ;
}
```

Output

CCCCCCCCCCCCCCCCCCC

Explanation

Mentioning the name of the array always gives its base address. Therefore (**ch + i**) would give the address of the ith element from the base address, and *(**ch + i**) would give the value at this address, i.e. the value of the ith element. Through the **for** loop we store 67, which is the ASCII value of upper case 'C', in all the locations of the string. Once the control reaches outside the **for** loop the value of **i** would be 19, and in the 19th location from the base address we store a '\0' to mark the end of the string. This is essential, as the compiler has no other way of knowing where the string is terminated. In the **printf( )** that follows, **%s** is the format specification for printing a string, and **ch** gives the base address of the string. Hence starting from the first element, the complete string is printed out.

(4)
```
#include <stdio.h>
int main( )
{
    char str[ ] = { 48, 48, 48, 48, 48, 48, 48, 48, 48, 48 } ;
```

```
        char *s ;
        int i ;
        s = str ;
        for ( i = 0 ; i <= 9 ; i++ )
        {
            if ( *s )
                printf ( "%c ", *s ) ;
            s++ ;
        }
        return 0 ;
}
```

Output

0 0 0 0 0 0 0 0 0 0

Explanation

In all 10 elements of **str[ ]**, an integer, 48 is stored. Wondering whether a **char** string can hold **int**s? The answer is yes, as 48 does not get stored literally in the elements. 48 is interpreted as the ASCII value of the character to be stored in the string. The character corresponding to ASCII 48 happens to be 0, which is assigned to all the locations of the string.

s, a character pointer, is assigned the base address of the string **str[ ]**. Next, in the **if** condition, the value at address contained in **s** is checked for truth/falsity. As 0 represents ASCII 48, the condition evaluates to true every time. Irrespective of whether the condition is satisfied or not, **s** is incremented so that each time it points to the subsequent array element. This entire logic is repeated in the **for** loop, printing out 10 zeros in the process.

(5)
```c
#include <stdio.h>
int main( )
{
    char str1[ ] = "Hello" ;
    char str2[ ] = "Hello" ;
    if ( str1 == str2 )
        printf ( "Equal\n" ) ;
    else
        printf ( "Unequal\n" ) ;
    return 0 ;
```

}

Output

Unequal

Explanation

When we mention the name of the array we get its base address. Since **str1** and **str2** are two different arrays, their base addresses would always be different. Hence, the condition in **if** is never going to get satisfied. If we are to compare the contents of two **char** arrays, we should compare them on a character by character basis or use **strcmp( )**.

(6)
```c
#include <stdio.h>
int main( )
{
    char str[10] = { 0, 0, 0, 0, 0, 0, 0, 0, 0, 0 } ;
    char *s ;
    int i ;
    s = str ;
    for ( i = 0 ; i <= 9 ; i++ )
    {
        if ( *s )
            printf ( "%c", *s) ;
        s++ ;
    }
    return 0 ;
}
```

Output

No output

Explanation

Though you may not have expected zeroes to be outputted this time, you surely did expect some output! We stored the character corresponding to ASCII 0 in all 10 elements of the string. Next, we assign **s**, a **char** pointer, the base address of the string. Through the **for** loop, we are attempting to print out all elements one by one, but not before imposing the **if** condition.

The **if** is made to test the value at address contained in **s** before the execution of **printf( )**. First time through the loop, *****s** yields ASCII 0. Therefore the **if** statement reduces to **if (0)**, and as 0 stands for falsity, the condition fails. Hence, **s** is incremented and control loops back to **for** without executing the **printf( )**. The same thing happens the next time around, and the next, and so on, till the **for** loop ends, resulting in no output at all.

(7) #include <stdio.h>
   int main( )
   {
       printf ("%c", "abcdefgh"[4]) ;
       return 0 ;
   }

Output

e

Explanation

We know that expression **a[4]** gets converted to *****(a + 4)**, where **a** gives the base address of the array. On similar lines **"abcdefgh"[4]** becomes *****("abcdefgh" + 4)**. This is same as *****(base address + 4)**. (**base address + 4)** yields address of 'e'. Thus, what gets passed to **printf( )** is the character 'e', which is promptly printed out.

(8) #include <stdio.h>
   int main( )
   {
       char str[7] = "Strings" ;
       printf ("%s\n", str) ;
       return 0 ;
   }

Output

Error: 'str' array bounds overflow

Explanation

The code reports an error as 'str' array bounds overflow because here **str[ ]** has been declared as a 7 character array and into it a 8 character string has been stored.

(9) ```c
     #include <stdio.h>
     int main( )
     {
         char *str[ ] = { "Frogs", "Do", "Not", "Die.", "They", "Croak!" } ;
         printf ("%d %d\n", sizeof (str), sizeof (str[0])) ;
         return 0 ;
     }
     ```

*Output*

24 4

*Explanation*

Mentioning the name of the array gives its base address. However, when used with **sizeof( )** it yields the number of bytes occupied by the array in memory. Since **str** is holding six addresses, of 4 bytes each, **sizeof ( str )** gives 24.

**str[0]** yields address of "Frogs". This address is reported as 4 bytes big.

(10) ```c
     #include <stdio.h>
     int main( )
     {
         char s[ ] = "C smart!" ;
         int i ;
         for ( i = 0 ; s[i] ; i++ )
             printf ( "%c %c %c %c\n", s[i], *( s + i ) , i[s], *( i + s ) ) ;
         return 0 ;
     }
     ```

Output

C C C C

s s s s
m m m m
a a a a

```
r r r r
t t t t
! ! ! !
```

Explanation

The above program rubs in the point that **s[i]**, **i[s]**, ***(s + i)** and ***(i + s)** are various ways of referring to the same element, that is the ith element of the string **s**. Each element of the string is printed out four times, till the end of the string is encountered. Note that in the **for** loop there is an expression **s[i]** in the condition part. This means the loop would continue to get executed till **s[i]** is not equal to zero. We can afford to say this because a string always ends with a '\0', whose ASCII value is 0. Thus the **for** loop will be terminated when the expression **s[i]** yields a '\0'.

```
(11) #include <stdio.h>
     int main( )
     {
         char s[ ] = "Oinks Grunts and Guffaws" ;
         printf ( "%c\n", *( &s[2] ) ) ;
         printf ( "%s\n", s + 5 ) ;
         printf ( "%s\n", s ) ;
         printf ( "%c\n", *( s + 2 ) ) ;
         printf ( "%u\n", s ) ;
         return 0 ;
     }
```

Output

```
n
<space>Grunts and Guffaws
Oinks Grunts and Guffaws
n
4040
```

Explanation

In the first **printf( )** the 'address of' operator, **&**, gives the address of the second element of the string. Value at this address is 'n', which is printed out by the **printf( )** using **%c**.

Since **s** gives the base address of the array, (**s + 5**) would give the address of the fifth element from the base address.

This address is passed to the second **printf( )**. Using the format specification **%s**, the contents of the string are printed out the 5th element onwards.

The third **printf( )** prints the entire string, as the base address of the string is being passed to it.

The fourth **printf( )** is made to print the second character of the string, as *(**s + 2**) is nothing but **s[2]**. Thus 'n' gets printed.

Does the output of the final **printf( )** surprise you by printing out a number, 4040? Note that the format specification **%u** is used with **s**, which gives the base address of the string. It happened to be 4040 when we executed the program, which got printed out. On executing the same yourself, you may get any other address, depending on what address is allotted to the string by the compiler.

(12)
```c
#include <stdio.h>
int main( )
{
    char arr[ ] = "Pickpocketing my peace of mind.." ;
    int i ;
    printf ( "%c\n", *arr ) ;
    arr++ ;
    printf ( "%c\n", *arr ) ;
    return 0 ;
}
```

Output

Error message: Lvalue required in function main

Explanation

Though everything seems to be in order at first glance, there lies a fundamental error in our program. When we say **arr**, we are referring to the base address of the string. This is the only information that helps the C compiler keep track of the string **arr[ ]**. If this information is lost, there is no way the compiler can access the string. So, this particular address is given a favored status, that of a constant. The statement **arr++** is essentially wrong because a constant can't be incremented and hence the compiler asks for an Lvalue, which is a value that can be changed.

```
(13) #include <stdio.h>
     int main( )
     {
         char str[ ] = "Limericks" ;
         char *s ;
         s = &str[6] - 6 ;
         while ( *s )
                 printf ( "%c", *s++ ) ;
         return 0 ;
     }
```

Output

Limericks

Explanation

The following figure would help in analyzing this program.

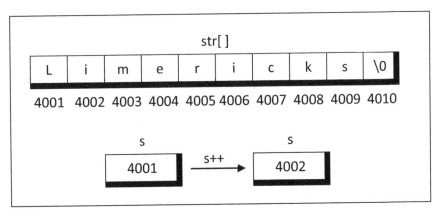

Figure 3.4

s has been declared as a pointer to a **char**, whereas **str[ ]** has been declared as a character string. Let us now evaluate the expression **&str[6] - 6**. Here **&str[6]** gives the address of the sixth element of the string. This address can also be obtained by the expression **str + 6**. On subtracting 6 from this, we end up with good old **str**, the address of the zeroth element, which is assigned to **s**.

In the **printf( )**, the value at address contained in **s** is printed, and then **s** gets incremented so that it points to the next character in the string. The **while** loop continues till **s** doesn't point to '\0', which marks the end of the string. When **s** points to '\0', the value of ***s** would be 0, a falsity. Hence the **while** loop will be terminated.

(14)
```c
#include <stdio.h>
int main( )
{
    static char *s[ ] = {
                            "ice",
                            "green",
                            "cone",
                            "please"
                        };
    static char **ptr[ ] = { s + 3, s + 2, s + 1, s };
    char ***p = ptr ;
    printf ( "%s\n", **++p ) ;
    printf ( "%s\n", *--*++p + 3 ) ;
    printf ( "%s\n", *p[-2] + 3 ) ;
    printf ( "%s\n", p[-1][-1] + 1 ) ;
    return 0 ;
}
```

Output

cone

ase
reen

Explanation

This time we seem to be faced with a galaxy of stars! We would do well to take the help of a figure in crossing them one by one. At the outset, **s[ ]** has been declared and initialized as an array of pointers. Simply saying **s** gives us the base address of this array, 4006 as can be seen from Figure 3.5. **ptr[ ]** stores the addresses of the locations where the base addresses of strings comprising **s[ ]** have been stored, starting with the last string. To put it more clearly, **ptr[0]** stores the address 4018, which is the address at which base address of the string "please" is stored. Similarly, **ptr[1]** stores the address

4014, which is where the base address of the string "cone" is stored, and so on. Since **ptr[ ]** essentially stores addresses of addresses, each element of it is a pointer to a pointer, and has been declared as such using ******.

Finally, the base address of **ptr[ ]** is assigned to a pointer to a pointer to a pointer, **p**. Reeling?! Going through the figure would decidedly aid you to get disentangled. Thus, **p** is assigned the address 6020.

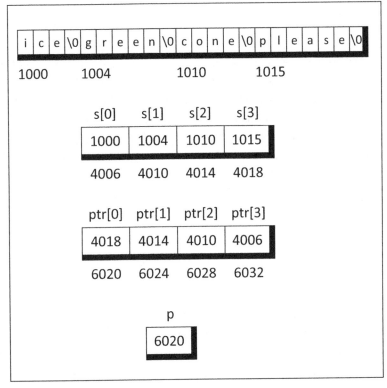

Figure 3.5

Having sorted out what is present where, we now proceed to the **printf( )**s. Let us tackle the expressions one by one.

**++p

The first one prints out the string starting from the address ****++p**. The **++** goes to work first and increments **p** to 6024. The C compiler has been made to understand that on incrementing a pointer variable, it is to point to the next location of its type. The words 'of its type' hold significance here. A pointer to a **char** on incrementing goes one byte further, since a **char** is a 1-byte entity. A pointer to an **int** points 4 bytes further, as an **int** is a 4-byte entity. Also, a pointer by itself is always a 4-byte entity, so incrementing a pointer to a pointer would advance you by 4 bytes.

Having convinced ourselves that **p** now stores 6024, we go on to evaluate the expression further. ***p** signifies contents of 6024, i.e. 4014. ****p** means value at this address, i.e. value at 4014, which is the address 1010. The **printf( )** prints the string at this address, which is "cone".

--++p + 3

p, presently contains 6024, which on incrementing becomes 6028. Value at this address is the address 4010, or in terms of **s**, **s + 1**. On this the decrement operator -- works to give 4006, i.e. **s**. Value at 4006, or ***(s)** is 1000. Thus the expression is now reduced to (1000 + 3), and what finally gets passed to **printf( )** is the address 1003. Value at this address is a '\0', as at the end of every string a '\0' is inserted automatically. This '\0' is printed out as a blank by **printf( )**.

*p[-2] + 3

The current address in **p** is 6028. ***p[-2]** can be thought of as ***(*(p - 2))**, as **num[i]** is same as ***(num + i)**. This in turn evaluates as ***(*(6028 - 2))**, i.e. ***(*(6020))**, as **p** is a pointer to a pointer. This is equal to ***(4018)**, as at 6020 the address 4018 is present. Value at 4018 is 1015, i.e. the base address of the fourth string, "please". Having reached the address of letter 'p', 3 is added, which yields the address 1018. The string starting from 1018 is printed out, which comprises of the last three letters of "please", i.e. 'ase'.

p[-1][-1] + 1

The above expression can be thought of as ***(p[-1] - 1) + 1**, as **num[i]** and ***(num + i)** amounts to the same thing. Further, **p[-1]** can itself be simplified to ***(p - 1)**. Hence we can interpret the given expression as ***(*(p - 1) - 1) + 1**. Now let us evaluate this expression.

After the execution of the third **printf( )**, **p** still holds the address 6028. ***(6028 - 1)** gives ***(6024)**, i.e. address 4014. Therefore the expression now becomes ***(4014 - 1) + 1**. Looking at the figure you would agree that 4014 can be expressed as **s + 2**. So now the expression becomes ***(s + 2 - 1) + 1** or ***(s + 1) + 1**. Once again the figure would confirm that ***(s + 1)** evaluates to ***(4010)** and ***(4010)** yields 1004, which is the base address of the second string "green". To this, 1 is added to yield the address of the first element, 'r'. With this as the starting address, **printf( )** prints out what is remaining of the string "green".

(15) ```
#include <stdio.h>
#include <string.h>
int main( )
{
    char str[ ] = "For your eyes only" ;
    int i ;
    char *p ;
    for (p = str, i = 0 ; p + i <= str + strlen (str) ; p++, i++)
        printf ("%c", *(p + i)) ;
    return 0 ;
}
```

*Output*

Fryu ysol<space>

*Explanation*

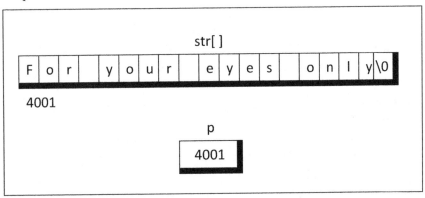

Figure 3.6

The **for** loop here hosts two initializations and two incrementations, which is perfectly acceptable. However, there must always be a unique test condition.
```

In the initialization part, **p** is assigned the base address of the string, and **i** is set to 0. Next the condition is tested. Let us isolate this condition for closer examination.

p + i <= str + strlen (str)

Since length of **str[ ]** is 18, **str + strlen (str)** would give the address of '\0' present at the end of the string. If we assume that the base address of the string is 4001, then the address of '\0' would be 4019. Since **p** has been assigned the base address of the string, in the first go, **p + 0** would yield 4001. Since this is less than 4019, the condition holds good, and the character present at the address (**p + 0**), i.e. 'F', is printed out. This can be understood better with the aid of the Figure 3.6.

After this, both **p** and **i** are incremented, so that **p** contains 4002 and **i** contains 1, and once again the condition in the **for** loop is tested. This time (**p + i**) yields 4003, whereas the expression **str + strlen (str)** continues to yield 4019. Therefore, again the condition is satisfied and the character at address 4003, i.e. 'r' gets printed. Likewise, alternate elements of the string are outputted till **i** is 8, corresponding to which 'l' is printed. Now, when **p** and **i** are incremented one more time, the test condition evaluates to:

p + i <= str + strlen (str)
4019 <= 4019

The 18th element of **str** is of course the '\0', which is also printed out as a blank. On further incrementation of **p** and **i**, control snaps out of the **for** and the program execution is terminated.

```
(16) #include <stdio.h>
     int main( )
     {
         char str[ ] = "MalayalaM" ;
         char *s ;
         s = str + 8 ;
         while ( s >= str )
         {
             printf ( "%c", *s ) ;
             s-- ;
         }
         return 0 ;
```

```
}
```

Output

MalayalaM

Explanation

s, a pointer to a **char**, is assigned an address 8 locations ahead of the base address of the string. That means **s** is currently pointing to the last element 'M' of the string. If we assume the base address to be 4001, then **s** would contain the address 4009. Since this address is greater than the base address, first time through the loop the condition is satisfied. Next the value of the expression ***s** is printed. Since **s** contains the address 4009, the value at this address, i.e. 'M', gets printed. Then **s** is decremented to point to the preceding element, i.e. the element at address 4008.

This way one by one, the elements of the string are printed out in the reverse order, till **s** equals **str**, the address of the zeroth element. That the output is indeed the reverse of the original string can be verified if you read "MalayalaM" backwards. You have been presented with a string that reads the same from either end. Such strings, incidentally, go by the name 'Palindrome'.

```
(17) #include <stdio.h>
     #include <string.h>
     int main( )
     {
         char a[ ] = "Able was I ere I saw elbA" ;
         char *t, *s,*b ;
         s = a ;
         b = a + strlen ( a ) - 1 ;
         t = b ;
         while ( s != t )
         {
             printf ( "%c", *s ) ;
             s++ ;
             printf ( "%c", *t ) ;
             t-- ;
         }
         return 0 ;
     }
```

Output

AAbbllee wwaass ll ee

Explanation

The **char** pointer **s** is assigned the base address of string **a[ ]**. The **char** pointer **b** is assigned the address 24 elements ahead of the base address. Why 24? Because the function **strlen (a)** yields the length of the string **a[ ]**, which in this case turns out to be 25. Thus **b** points to 'A' present at the end of the string. Another character pointer, **t**, is also initialized to the same value as **b**. Assuming the base address of the string to be 5001, **s** would be assigned 5001 and **b** and **t** would be assigned the address 5025.

Naturally, first time through the **while** loop since **s** and **t** are not equal, the condition is satisfied. Hence the **printf( )** prints out the character at which **s** is pointing. Thus the character 'A' gets printed. Now **s** is incremented, so that it points to the character 'b'. The next **printf( )** prints the value at the address contained in **t**. Therefore another 'A' appears on the screen. After printing, **t** is decremented so that it starts pointing to 'b'. This goes on till **s** and **t** meet each other, whence the **while** ends. At this instance, **s** and **t** both are pointing to 'r', the middle character of the entire string.

(18)
```
#include <stdio.h>
int main( )
{
    char s[ ] = "C is a philosophy of life" ;
    char t[40] ;
    char *ss, *tt ;
    ss = s ;
    tt = t ;
    while ( *ss )
        *tt++ = *ss++ ;
    *tt = '\0' ;
    printf ( "%s\n", t ) ;
    return 0 ;
}
```

Output

C is a philosophy of life

Explanation

To begin with, **ss** and **tt** are assigned the base addresses of the two strings **s[ ]** and **t[ ]**. In the **while**, the value at address contained in **ss** is tested for operating the loop. The first time through the loop **ss** contains the base address of the string. Hence ***ss** gives 'C', whose ASCII value is 67. As any non-zero value is a truth value, the condition evaluates to true, and this value is stored at the address contained in **tt**, i.e. at the base address of the string **t[ ]**. Note that the **++** operator occurs after the variables, so after 'C' has been stored in the first location of the string **t[ ]**, both **ss** and **tt** are incremented, so that both now point to the first elements of **s[ ]** and **t[ ]** respectively. In the second go, value at the address contained in **ss** is tested in the **while**, and this time a blank is encountered, whose ASCII value is 32. The condition again holds good, therefore the blank is stored in string **t[ ]**, and **ss** and **tt** are incremented. This goes on till the end of the string is encountered. At the end of any string, a '\0' is stored. ASCII value of '\0' is 0, which when tested in the **while**, evaluates to falsity, and the control comes out of the loop.

Note that the '\0' has not been stored into string **t[ ]**, hence the compiler does not know where the string ends. We do so by inserting a '\0' on leaving the **while**. Finally, the contents of the string **t[ ]** are printed out.

(19)
```c
#include <stdio.h>
int main( )
{
    char s[ ]= "Lumps, bumps, swollen veins, new pains" ;
    char t[40] ;
    char *ss, *tt ;
    tt = t ;
    ss = s ;
    while ( *tt++ = *ss++ );
    printf ( "%s\n", t );
    return 0 ;
}
```

Output

Lumps, bumps, swollen veins, new pains

Explanation

The program begins by assigning the base addresses of strings **s[ ]** and **t[ ]** to the character pointers **ss** and **tt**. The **while** loop that follows next may raise a few eyebrows. We have made it compact by combining the assignment, test condition and the incrementation in the **while** loop itself. In effect, the **while** has been reduced to:

while (*tt++ = *ss++)
    ;

Here the null statement is executed so long as the condition remains true. How the condition is evaluated is like this...

In the **while** the value at the address stored in **ss** replaces the value at the address stored in **tt**. After assignment the test is carried out to decide whether the **while** loop should continue or not. This is done by testing the expression ***tt** for truth/falsity. Since currently **tt** is pointing to 'l' of 'lumps', ***tt** gives 'l' which is a truth-value. Following this **ss** and **tt** both are incremented, so that they have the addresses of the first elements of strings **s[ ]** and **t[ ]** respectively. Since the condition has been satisfied the null statement is executed. This goes on till the end of the string **s[ ]** is encountered, which is marked by the presence of a '\0', having ASCII value 0. When this character is stored in **t[ ]**, ***tt** would give '\0'. This time when the condition is tested, it evaluates to false since ***tt** yields a 0 (ASCII value of '\0'). Thus, all elements of the first string are faithfully copied into the second one, including the '\0'. On printing out string **t[ ]**, we get the entire, string as it was in **s[ ]**.

(20) #include <stdio.h>
```
int main( )
{
    int arr[12] ;
    printf ( "%d\n", sizeof ( arr ) ) ;
    return 0 ;
}
```

Output

48

Explanation

The **sizeof( )** operator gives the size of its argument. As **arr[ ]** is an integer array of 12 elements, saying **sizeof (arr)** gives us the size of this array. Each integer is 4 bytes long, hence the array **arr[ ]** engages four times the number of elements, i.e. 48 bytes.

(21)
```c
#include <stdio.h>
int main( )
{
    char *mess[ ] = {
                        "Some love one",
                        "Some love two",
                        "I love one",
                        "That is you"
                    };
    printf ( "%d %d\n", sizeof ( mess ), sizeof ( mess [1] ) ) ;
    return 0 ;
}
```

Output

16 4

Explanation

mess[ ] has been declared as an array of pointers to strings. This signifies that the array **mess[ ]** stores the starting addresses of the four strings initialized in the program. **mess[0]** has the starting address of the string "Some love one", **mess[1]** the starting address of the second string "Some love two" and so on. As each address is 4 bytes long, four base addresses need 16 bytes, hence the array **mess[ ]** is 16 bytes long.

The **sizeof( )** operator gives the size of the datatype that is supplied as its argument. Therefore, **sizeof (mess)** is reported as 16.

mess[1], the first element of the array of pointers stores an address, which is invariably 4 bytes long. Therefore **printf( )** reports **sizeof (mess[1])** as 4.

(22) #include <stdio.h>
```
int main( )
{
     char names[3][20] ;
     int i ;
     for ( i = 0 ; i <= 2 ; i++ )
     {
          printf ( "ENTER NAME: " ) ;
          scanf ( "%s", names[i] ) ;
          printf ( "You entered %s\n", names[i] ) ;
     }
     return 0 ;
}
```

Output

ENTER NAME: Parag
You entered Parag
ENTER NAME: Veenu
You entered Veenu
ENTER NAME: Jaina
You entered Jaina

Explanation

names[3][20] has been declared as a two-dimensional array of characters. We can think of it as an array of 3 elements, each element itself being an array of 20 characters.

Let the base address of the 2-D array, i.e. names be 4001. In the **scanf( )** and **printf( )** statements, **names[i]** refers to the address of the ith string in the array. **names[0]** refers to the zeroth element of the 2-D array, or the base address of the string of characters starting from 4001. **names[1]** denotes the address of the first element of the 2-D array, which is 20 bytes ahead, i.e. 4021, and so on.

Assured that **names[i]** stands for the base address of the ith string, we proceed to see what actually is going on in this program.

The first time through the **for** loop, when you are prompted "ENTER NAME: ", say you entered 'Parag'. The **scanf( )** accepts this name and stores it at the address given by **names[0]**. The **printf( )** immediately reads from the same address **name[0]**, and prints the name starting at this address on to the screen. This is repeated by incrementing the value of **i** each time through the loop. When **i** is incremented for the third time, the process is terminated.

(23)
```
#include <stdio.h>
int main( )
{
    char names[5][20] = {
                            "Roshni",
                            "Manish",
                            "Mona",
                            "Baiju",
                            "Ritu"
                        } ;
    int i ;
    char *t ;
    t = names[3] ;
    names[3] = names[4] ;
    names[4] = t ;
    for ( i = 0 ; i <= 4 ; i++ )
        printf ( "%s\n", names[i] ) ;
    return 0 ;
}
```

Output

Error message: Lvalue required in function main

Explanation

Apparently, what the program attempts to do is interchange the addresses stored in **names[3]** and **names[4]** using an auxiliary variable **t**. Sounds straight forward, but is essentially against the very concept of how the C compiler deals with strings. The compiler keeps track of any string by remembering only the base address of the string. So it has its reservations when it comes to changing this information, as it anticipates that there would be no one to blame but itself once this information is waylaid and we demand an access to the string later. And this is what is being attempted in the statement **names[3] = names[4]**. Here we are trying to change the base address stored in **names[3]**. As said earlier, this will not be allowed. Thus the starting address of a string is an indelible entity, in no way an Lvalue, which is a value that can change. Hence the error message.

(24) #include <stdio.h>
```
int main( )
{
    char mess[6][30] = {
                        "Don't walk in front of me ...",
                        "I may not follow ;",
                        "Don't walk behind me ...",
                        "I may not lead ;",
                        "Just walk beside me ...",
                        "And be my friend."
                    } ;
    printf ( "%c %c\n", *( mess[2] + 9 ), *( *( mess + 2 ) + 9 ) ) ;
    return 0 ;
}
```

Output

k k

Explanation

The two-dimensional array comprises of one-dimensional arrays, each of which is 30 characters long. We know, **mess[2][9]** refers to the 9th element of the 2nd 1-D array.

Recall that **mess[2]** would give the base address of the second string. If this address turns out to be 4001, then the expression **mess[2] + 9** would become (4001 + 9), which would give the address of the ninth character from the address 4001. This address happens to be the address of the letter 'k' in the string "Don't walk behind me". Hence this letter 'k' can be accessed by the expression ***(mess[2] + 9)**. But we already know that whenever we use the notation **mess[2]**, it is internally converted to ***(mess + 2)** by the compiler. Therefore ***(mess[2] + 9)** can also be expressed as ***(*(mess + 2) + 9)**.

Thus, **mess[2][9]**, ***(mess[2] + 9)** and ***(*(mess + 2) + 9)** are one and the same, i.e. the 9th element of the 2nd string in the array. The same array element can thus be accessed in any of these three ways. The **printf( )** on execution outputs the letter 'k' twice.

[B] Answer the following:

(1) Is the following program correct? <Yes/No>

```c
#include <stdio.h>
#include <string.h>
int main( )
{
    char *str1 = "United" ;
    char *str2 = "Front" ;
    char *str3 ;
    str3 = strcat ( str1, str2 ) ;
    printf ( "%s\n", str3 ) ;
    return 0 ;
}
```

Explanation

No, since what is present in memory beyond "United" is not known and we are attaching "Front" at the end of "United", thereby overwriting something, which is an unsafe thing to do.

(2) How would you improve the code in [B](1) above?

Explanation

```c
#include <string.h>
#include <stdio.h>
int main( )
{
    char str1[15] = "United" ;
    char *str2 = "Front" ;
    char *str3 ;
    str3 = strcat ( str1, str2 ) ;
    printf ( "%s\n",str3) ;
    return 0 ;
}
```

(3) In the following code which function would get called, the user-defined **strcpy( )** or the one in the standard library?

```
#include <stdio.h>
#include <string.h>
void strcpy ( char *, char * ) ;
int main( )
{
    char str1[ ] = "Keep India Beautiful... emigrate!" ;
    char str2[40] ;
    strcpy ( str2, str1 ) ;
    printf ( "%s\n", str2 ) ;
    return 0 ;
}
void strcpy ( char *t, char *s )
{
    while ( *s )
    {
        *t = *s ;
        t++ ;
        s++ ;
    }
    *t = '\0' ;
}
```

Explanation

User-defined **strcpy( )**

(4) Can you compact the code of **strcpy( )** given in (3) above into one
     line?

Explanation

```
void strcpy ( char *t, char *s )
{
    while ( *t++ = *s++ ) ;
}
```

(5) How would you find the length of each string in the program [A](9)
     above?

Explanation

```
#include <string.h>
#include <stdio.h>
```

```
int main( )
{
    char *str[ ] = { "Frogs", "Do", "Not", "Die.", "They", "Croak!" } ;
    int i ;
    for ( i = 0 ; i <= 5 ; i++ )
        printf ( "%s %d\n", str[i], strlen ( str[i] ) ) ;
    return 0 ;
}
```

(6) Would the following code compile successfully?

```
#include <stdio.h>
int main( )
{
    printf ( "%c", 7[ "Sundaram " ] ) ;
    return 0 ;
}
```

Explanation

Yes. It would print 'm' of "Sundaram".

(7) What is the difference in the following declarations?

```
char *p = "Samuel" ;
char a[ ] = "Samuel" ;
```

Explanation

Here **a** is an array big enough to hold the message and the '\0' following the message. Individual characters within the array can be changed but the address of the array would remain same.

On the other hand, **p** is a pointer, initialized to point to a string constant. The pointer **p** may be modified to point to another string, but if you attempt to modify the string at which **p** is pointing the result is undefined.

(8) While handling a string do we always have to process it character by character or there exists a method to process the entire string as one unit.

Explanation

A string can be processed only on a character by character basis.

Exercise

[A] Attempt the following:

(1) Write a function **xstrchr( )** which scans a string from   beginning to end in search of a character. If the character is found it should return a pointer to the first occurrence of the given character in the string. If the given character is not found in the string, the function should return a NULL. The prototype of the function would be:

char * xstrchr (char *string, char ch) ;

(2) Write a function **xstrstr( )** that will scan a string for the   occurrence of a given sub-string. The prototype of the function would be:

char * xstrstr (char *string1, char *string2) ;

The function should return a pointer to the element in **string1** where **string2** begins. If **string2** doesn't occur in **string1** then **xstrstr( )** should return a NULL.

For example, if **string1** is "somewhere over the rainbow", and **string2** is "over" then **xstrstr( )** should return address of 'o' in **string1**.

(3) Suppose 7 names are stored in an array of pointers **names[ ]** as shown below:

char *names[ ] = {

                      "Santosh",
                      "Amol",
                      "Santosh Jain",
                      "Kishore",
                      "Rahul",
                      "Amolkumar",
                      "Hemant"

        } ;

Write a program to arrange these names in alphabetical order.

(4) Write a program to compress any given string such that the multiple blanks present in it are eliminated. Store the compressed message in another string. Also write a decompressant program to get back the original string with all its spaces restored.

The uncompressed string can be:

"Imperial Palace. Rome.   Attention   Julius Caesar. Dear Caesar,
we have the   clarification you   requested. Details to   follow   by
courier. Meanwhile   stay clear of Brutus."

(5) Write a program to encode any given string such that it gets
     converted into an unrecognizable form. Also write a decode
     function to get back the original string. Try to make the encryption
     scheme as difficult to break as possible.

[B] What will be the output of the following programs:

(1) ```c
     #include <stdio.h>
     int main( )
     {
          char string[ ] = "OddLengthString" ;
          char *ptr1 = string, *ptr2 = string + sizeof (string) - 1 ;
          int i ;
          for (i = 0 ; ptr1 != ptr2 ; i++)
          {
               ++ptr1 ;
               --ptr2 ;
          }
          printf ("%d", i) ;
          return 0 ;
     }
     ```

(2)  ```c
     #include <stdio.h>
     #include <string.h>
     int main( )
     {
          static char str1[ ] = "Good" ;
          static char str2[20] ;
          static char str3[20] = "Day" ;
          int l ;
          l = strcmp ( strcat ( str3, strcpy ( str2, str1 ) ), strcat (
                              str3, "good" ) ) ;
          printf ( "%d", l ) ;
          return 0 ;
     }
     ```

(3) ```c
     #include <stdio.h>
     int main( )
     {
     ```
     ```

```
            char str [ ] = "Way of trouble is out through it" ;
            int i ;
            for ( i = 0 ; i <= 3 ; i++ )
                printf ( "%c", *( str + i ) ) ;
            for ( i = 0 ; i <= 3 ; i++ )
                printf ( "%c", *( str + 18 + i ) ) ;
            for ( i = 0 ; i <= 13 ; i++ )
                printf ( "%c", *( str + 4 + i ) ) ;
            for ( i = 0 ; i <= 9 ; i++ )
                printf ( "%c", *( str + 22 + i ) ) ;
            return 0 ;
        }
(4)  #include <stdio.h>
     int main( )
     {
            char s[ ] = "C a of " ;
            char t[ ] = "is philosophy life" ;
            char u[40] ;
            char *ss = s, *tt = t, *uu = u ;
            while ( *ss || *tt )
            {
                while ( *ss )
                {
                    if ( ( *uu++ = *ss++ ) == ' ' )
                        break ;
                }
                while ( *tt )
                {
                    if ( ( *uu++ = *tt++ ) == ' ' )
                        break ;
                }
            }
            *uu = '\0' ;
            puts ( u ) ;
            return 0 ;
     }
(5)  #include <stdio.h>
     int main( )
     {
            char a[2][2][25] = {
```

```
                    {
                        "Jack and Jill",
                        "Went up the hill"
                    },
                    {
                        "Jack fell down",
                        "And broke his crown"
                    }
                };
        printf ( "%s %s %s %s\n", &a[0][0][9], &a[0][1][12],
                        &a[1][0][10], &a[1][1][14] ) ;
        return 0 ;
    }
```

Understanding
Pointers in
C & C++

Pointers and
Structures

Structures are typically heavy-weight entities.
Passing them amongst functions is a costly affair.
Hence they are used with pointers which are
relatively light-weight. This chapter explores the
interaction between strctures and pointers...

While handling real world data, we usually deal with a collection of ints, chars and floats rather than isolated entities. For example, an entity we call a 'book' is a collection of things like a title, an author, a call number, a publisher, number of pages, date of publication, price, etc. As you can see, all this data is dissimilar; author is a string, price is a **float**, whereas number of pages is an **int**.   For dealing with such collections, C provides a data type called 'structure'. A structure gathers together different atoms of information that form a given entity.

Look at the following program that combines dissimilar data types into an entity called structure.

```
/* Program 42 */
#include <stdio.h>
int main( )
{
    struct account
    {
        int no ;
        char acc_name[15] ;
        float bal ;
    } ;
    struct account a1, a2, a3 ;
    printf ( "Enter account nos., names, and balances\n" ) ;
    scanf ( "%d %s %f", &a1.no, a1.acc_name, &a1.bal ) ;
    scanf ( "%d %s %f", &a2.no, a2.acc_name, &a2.bal ) ;
    scanf ( "%d %s %f", &a3.no, a3.acc_name, &a3.bal ) ;
    printf ( "%d %s %f\n", a1.no, a1.acc_name, a1.bal ) ;
    printf ( "%d %s %f\n", a2.no, a2.acc_name, a2.bal ) ;
    printf ( "%d %s %f\n", a3.no, a3.acc_name, a3.bal ) ;
    return 0 ;
}
```

Now a few tips about the program:

(a) The declaration at the beginning of the program combines dissimilar data types into a single entity called **struct account**. Here **struct** is a keyword, **account** is the structure name, and the dissimilar data types are structure elements.

(b) **a1, a2** and **a3** are structure variables of the type **struct account**.

(c) The structure elements are accessed using a '.' operator. So to refer **no** we use **a1.no** and to refer to **acc_name** we use **a1.acc_name**. Before the dot there must always be a structure variable and after the dot there must always be a structure element.

(d) Since **a1.acc_name** is a string, its base address can be obtained just by mentioning **a1.acc_name**. Hence the 'address of' operator **&** has been dropped while receiving the account name in **scanf( )**.

(e) The structure elements are always arranged in contiguous memory locations. This arrangement is shown in the following figure.

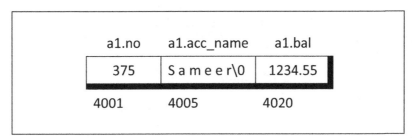

Figure 4.1

Array of Structures

In the above example if we were to store data of 100 accounts, we would be required to use 100 different structure variables from **a1** to **a100**, which is definitely not very convenient. A better approach would be to use an array of structures. The arrangement of the array of structures in memory is shown in the following figure.

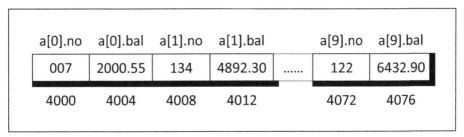

Figure 4.2

Now let us write a program, which puts the array of structures to work.

```
/* Program 43 */
#include <stdio.h>
int main( )
{
```

```
struct account
{
    int no ;
    float bal ;
};
struct account a[10] ;
int i, acc ;
float balance ;
for ( i = 0 ; i <= 9 ; i++ )
{
    printf ( "Enter account no. and balance:\n" ) ;
    scanf ( "%d %f" , &acc, &balance ) ;
    a[i].no = acc ;
    a[i].bal = balance ;
    printf ( "%d %f\n", a[i].no, a[i].bal ) ;
}
return 0 ;
}
```

As you can see the structure elements are still accessed using the '.' operator, and the array elements using the usual subscript notation.

Intricacies of Structures

Let us now explore the intricacies of structures with a view of programming convenience.

(a) The declaration of structure type and the structure variable can be combined in one statement. For example,

```
struct player
{
    char name[20] ;
    int age ;
};
struct player p1 = { "Nick Yates", 30 } ;
```

is same as...

```
struct player
{
    char name[20] ;
    int age ;
```

```
} p1 = { "Nick Yates", 30 } ;
```

or even...

```
struct
{
        char name[20] ;
        int age ;
} p1 = { "Nick Yates", 30 } ;
```

(b) The value of one structure variable can be assigned to another structure variable of the same type using the assignment operator. It is not necessary to copy the structure elements piece-meal. For example,

```
struct player
{
        char name[20] ;
        int age ;
} ;
struct player p2, p1 = { "Nick Yates", 30 } ;
p2 = p1 ;
```

(c) One structure can be nested within another structure as shown below.

```
struct part
{
        char type ;
        int qty ;
} ;
struct vehicle
{
        char maruti[20] ;
        struct part bolt ;
} ;
struct vehicle v ;
v.bolt.qty = 300 ;
```

(d) Like an ordinary variable, a structure variable can also be passed to a function. We may either pass individual structure elements or the entire structure at one go. If need be we can also pass addresses of structure elements or address of a structure variable as shown below.

```
struct player
{
    char nam[20] ;
    int age ;
} ;
struct player p1 = { "Nick Yates", 30 } ;
display ( p1.nam, p1.age ) ; /* passing individual elements */
show ( p1 ) ; /* passing structure variable */
d ( p1.nam, &p1.age ) ; /* passing addresses of structure ele. */
print ( &p1 ) ; /* passing address of structure variable */
```

Structure Pointers

The way we can have a pointer pointing to an **int**, or a pointer pointing to a **char**, similarly we can have a pointer pointing to a **struct**. Such pointers are known as 'structure pointers'. Let us look at a program, which demonstrates the usage of these pointers.

```
/* Program 44 */
#include <stdio.h>
int main( )
{
    struct book
    {
        char name[25] ;
        char author[25] ;
        int callno ;
    } ;
    struct book b1 = { "Let us C", "YPK", 101 } ;
    struct book *ptr ;
    ptr = &b1 ;
    printf ( "%s %s %d\n", b1.name, b1.author, b1.callno ) ;
    printf ( "%s %s %d\n", ptr -> name, ptr -> author, ptr -> callno ) ;
    return 0 ;
}
```

The first **printf( )** is as usual. The second **printf( )** however is peculiar. We can't use **ptr.name** or **ptr.callno** because **ptr** is not a structure variable but a pointer to a structure, and the dot operator requires a structure variable on its left. In such cases C provides an operator ->, called an arrow operator to refer to the structure elements. Remember that on the left hand side of the '.' structure operator, there must always be a structure variable, whereas on the left hand side of the -> operator there must always be a pointer to a structure. The arrangement of the structure variable and pointer to structure in memory is shown in the figure given below.

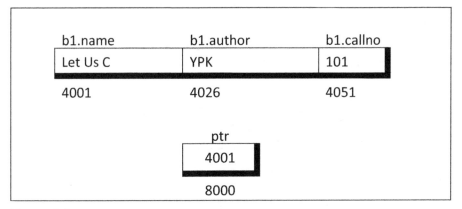

Figure 4.3

Can we not pass the address of a structure variable to a function? We can. The following program demonstrates this.

```
/* Program 45 */
/* Passing address of a structure variable */
#include <stdio.h>
struct book
{
    char name[25] ;
    char author[25] ;
    int callno ;
} ;
int main( )
{
    void display ( struct book * ) ;
    struct book b1 = { "Let us C", "YPK", 101 } ;
    display ( &b1 ) ;
    return 0 ;
}
void display ( struct book *b ) /* b is a pointer to a structure */
{
    printf ( "%s\n%s\n%d\n", b -> name, b -> author, b -> callno ) ;
}
```

And here is the output...

Let us C
YPK
101

Again, note that, to access the structure elements using pointer to a structure we have to use the '->' operator. Also, the structure **struct book** should be declared outside **main( )** such that this data type is available to **display( )** while declaring the variable **b** as a pointer to the structure.

Offsets of Structure Elements

Consider the following structure:

```
struct a
{
    struct b
    {
        int i ;
        float f ;
        char ch ;
    } x ;
    struct c
    {
        int j ;
        float g ;
        char ch ;
    } y ;
} z ;
```

Suppose we make a call to a function as shown below:

```
fun ( &z.y ) ;
```

In the function **fun( )** can we access the elements of structure **b** through the address of **z.y**? We can. For this we need to first find out the offset of **j**. Using this offset we can find out address where **x** begins in memory. Once we get this address we can have an access to elements **i**, **f** and **ch**. This is shown in the following program.

```
/* Program 46 */
#include <stdio.h>
void fun ( struct c * ) ;
```

```
struct a
{
    struct b
    {
        int i ;
        float f ;
        char ch ;
    } x ;
    struct c
    {
        int j ;
        float g ;
        char ch ;
    } y ;
};
int main( )
{
    int *p ;
    struct a z ;
    fun ( &z.y ) ;
    printf ( "%d %f %c\n", z.x.i, z.x.f, z.x.ch ) ;
    return 0 ;
}
void fun ( struct c * p )
{
    int offset ;
    struct b * address ;
    offset = ( char * ) & ( ( struct c * ) ( & ( ( struct a * ) 0 ) -> y ) -> j )
             - ( char * ) ( ( struct a * ) 0 ) ;
    address = ( struct b * ) ( ( char * ) & ( p -> j ) - offset ) ;
    address -> i = 400 ;
    address -> f = 3.14 ;
    address -> ch = 'c' ;
}
```

In the above program structures **b** and **c** having members **i, f, ch** and **j, g, ch** are nested within the structure **a** with structure variables **x** and **y** of structure **b** and **c** respectively. Next we have called the function **fun( )** with the base address of the structure variable **y**. Now from **fun( )**, we wish to access the members of structure variable **x**. But, since **fun( )** has been passed a pointer to structure **c**, we do not have direct access to elements of **x**. The solution is to calculate the offset of the first member of **y**, in our case, **j**. This has been achieved through the statement:

offset = (char *) & ((struct c *) (& ((struct a *) 0) -> y) -> j) -
                (char *) ((struct a *) 0) ;

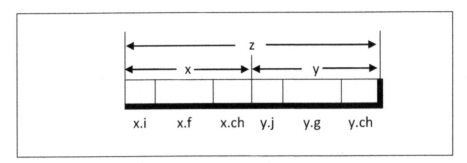

Figure 4.4

Let us understand this statement part by part.

In the expression **((struct a *) 0)**, 0 is being typecasted into pointer to **struct a**. This expression is pretending that there is a variable of type **struct a** at address 0. The expression **& (((struct a *) 0) -> y)** gives the address of structure variable **y**. But this is not the base address of the structure **c**. Hence we have typecasted it using **struct c ***. Using this address we can access the member **j** of the structure variable **y**. Finally, after taking the address of member **j**, we have typecasted it using **char *** to make the subtraction possible. The statement to the right of the '-' operator is straightforward. On subtraction, we get the offset of member **j** of structure variable **y**. Now using offset the base address is calculated through the following statement.

address = (struct b *) ((char *) & (p -> j) – offset) ;

In the above statement **& (p -> j)** gives the address of member **j** of structure variable **y**. Subtracting offset from this yields the address of structure variable **x**. Using this address, we have stored the values in the member variables **i**, **f** and **ch**. Back into **main( )**, we have printed these values using **printf( )**.

Solved Problems

[A] What will be the output of the following programs:

(1)
```c
#include <stdio.h>
void f ( struct s ) ;
void g ( struct s * ) ;
struct s
{
    char ch ;
    int i ;
    float a;
} ;
int main( )
{
    struct s var = { 'C', 100, 12.55 } ;
    f ( var ) ;
    g ( &var ) ;
    return 0 ;
}
void f ( struct s v )
{
    printf ( "%c %d %f\n", v -> ch, v -> i, v -> a ) ;
}
void g ( struct s *v )
{
    printf ( "%c %d %f\n", v.ch, v.i, v.a ) ;
}
```

Output

Error message: Pointer required on left of -> in function f
Error message: Variable required on left of . in function g

Explanation

The function **f( )**, called from **main( )**, is sent the **struct** variable **var**, which is collected in **v**. The **printf( )** in **f( )** attempts to print the structure elements using the arrow operator with **v**, wherein lies the first error. On the left of the arrow operator, there must always be a pointer to a structure. On the other hand, function **g( )** collects a pointer to a structure, which it uses in conjunction with the dot operator. The dot operator must always be preceded by a structure variable, never a pointer. Hence the second error message.

(2) ```c
     #include <stdio.h>
     #include <string.h>
     int main( )
     {
         struct
         {
             int num ;
             float f ;
             char mess[50] ;
         } m ;
         m.num = 1 ;
         m.f = 3.14 ;
         strcpy (m.mess, "Everything looks rosy") ;
         printf ("%u %u %u\n", &m.num, &m.f, m.mess) ;
         printf ("%d %f %s\n", m.num, m.f, m.mess) ;
         return 0 ;
     }
     ```

*Output*

1401 1405 1409
1 3.140000 Everything looks rosy

*Explanation*

In the elements **num** and **f** of the structure, 1 and 3.14 are stored. For assigning contents to the third element of the structure, i.e. the array in **mess[ ]**, **strcpy( )**, the string copy function is used. Why use a string function for this? Could we not have said:

m.mess = "Everything looks rosy" ;

like when we assigned values to **num** and **f**? The answer is an emphatic NO! Unlike **m.num** and **m.f**, **m.mess** signifies an address, and a base address at that. Hence, it can't ever occur on the left-hand side of the assignment operator. In other words, **m.mess** is not a lvalue.

The first **printf( )** prints the addresses of the three elements within the **struct**. The output goes to show that the elements of a **struct**
     ```

are stored in contiguous memory locations. Address of **m.num** is found to be 1401. Since an **int** occupies four bytes in memory, address of the **float**, **m.f**, is 1405. Finally, the address of the array **mess[ ]** is 1409. This is four bytes ahead of the address of **m.f**, as a **float** is a four-byte entity.

The second **printf( )** prints out the three elements of the structure.

(3) ```
     #include <stdio.h>
     int main( )
     {
         struct a
         {
             char arr[10] ;
             int i ;
             float b ;
         } v[2] ;
         /* assume that the first structure begins at address 1004 */
         printf ("%u %u %u\n", v[0].arr, &v[0].i, &v[0].b) ;
         printf ("%u %u %u\n", v[1].arr, &v[1].i, &v[1].b) ;
         return 0 ;
     }
     ```

*Output*

1004 1016 1020
1024 1036 1040

*Explanation*

In Windows, if a structure element is stored at an address which is multiple of 4, then it becomes easier to access the element. Hence even though the char array **arr[ ]** is only 10 bytes big, it occupies 12 bytes.

**v[ ]** has been declared as an array of structures. Understand that though each structure consists of dissimilar data types, more than one similar structures are capable of forming an array. The word 'similar' is important here, as that is the only criterion Dennis Ritchie set for constructing an array of any data type.

The output verifies that elements of an array of structures, in keeping with the tradition of arrays, are stored in contiguous
     ```

memory locations. The address of the zeroth element of the zeroth structure is 1004. Then 12 bytes are used by a **char** array of size 10. Next, at 1016, the **int** of the zeroth structure is stored. After leaving 4 bytes for **v[0].i**, the **float v[0].b** occupies bytes 1020 to 1023. Immediately after this, the next structure of the array is stored, as the outputted addresses 1024, 1036, and 1040, justify.

(4) ```c
     #include <stdio.h>
     int main( )
     {
         struct a
         {
             char ch[7] ;
             char *str ;
         };
         struct a s1 = { "Nagpur", "Bombay" } ;
         printf ("%c %c\n", s1.ch[0], *s1.str) ;
         printf ("%s %s\n", s1.ch, s1.str) ;
         return 0 ;
     }
     ```

*Output*

N B
Nagpur Bombay

*Explanation*

**struct a** comprises of **char** array **ch[ ]** and a **char** pointer **str**. **s1**, a variable of type **struct a**, is initialized next. Here "Nagpur" gets stored in the array **ch[ ]**, and "Bombay" gets stored starting from the address contained in **str**.

In the first **printf( )**, **ch[0]** signifies the zeroth element of the array **ch[ ]**. Since this array is within a **struct**, a dot operator preceded by the structure variable of that type must be used. Thus, **s1.ch[0]** refers to the zeroth element of array **ch[ ]**. As this array has been assigned the string "Nagpur", the first character 'N' is printed out.

Next, **\*s1.str** signifies the value at address contained in **s1.str**. Since this is the address at which 'B' of "Bombay" is stored, the **printf( )** prints out a 'B'.
     ```

The next **printf( )** outputs both "Nagpur" and "Bombay", as **s1.ch** denotes the base address of the former, and **s1.str**, that of the latter string.

(5)
```
#include <stdio.h>
int main( )
{
    struct a
    {
        char ch[7] ;
        char *str ;
    } ;
    struct b
    {
        char *c ;
        struct a ss1 ;
    } ;
    struct b s2 = { "Raipur", "Kanpur", "Jaipur" } ;
    printf ( "%s %s\n", s2.c, s2.ss1.str ) ;
    printf ( "%s %s\n", ++s2.c, ++s2.ss1.str ) ;
    return 0 ;
}
```

Output

Raipur Jaipur
aipur aipur

Explanation

At the outset, **struct a** is declared to comprise a character array **ch[ ]** and a character pointer **str**. Next, **s2** is declared as a variable of type **struct b**, which is made up of a **char** pointer **c** and another variable **ss1** of type **struct a**. While initialising **s2**, the base address of the string "Raipur" is assigned to **s2.c**, "Kanpur" is assigned to **s2.ss1.ch[ ]**, and the base address of "Jaipur" is assigned to **s2.ss1.str**.

Coming to the **printf( )**s now, the first one is supplied **s2.c** and **s2.ss1.str**. **s2.c** gives the base address of "Raipur", and **s2.ss1.str** gives the base address of "Jaipur". Since these base addresses are passed to **printf( )**, it promptly prints out the two strings.

The second **printf( )** uses incremented values of these addresses. On incrementing **s2.c** using the **++** operator, it now points to the next element 'a' of "Raipur". Similarly, on incrementing **s2.ss1.str**, it points to 'a' of "Jaipur". With these as starting addresses, the remaining strings are printed out.

(6)
```c
#include <stdio.h>
int main( )
{
    struct s1
    {
        char *z ;
        int i ;
        struct s1 *p ;
    };
    static struct s1 a[ ] =  {
                                { "Nagpur", 1, a + 1 },
                                { "Raipur", 2, a + 2 },
                                { "Kanpur", 3, a }
                            };
    struct s1 *ptr = a ;
    printf ( "%s %s %s\n", a[0].z, ptr -> z, a[2].p -> z ) ;
    return 0 ;
}
```

Output

Nagpur Nagpur Nagpur

Explanation

The zeroth and first elements of **struct s1** are a character pointer and an **int** respectively. The second element is what's new. It is a pointer to a structure. That is, **p** stores the starting address of a structure variable of the type **struct s1**. Next, **a[ ]**, an array of such structures is declared as well as initialised. During initialisation the base address of "Nagpur" is stored in **a[0].z**, 1 is stored in the element **a[0].i**, and **a + 1** is assigned to **a[0].p**. On similar lines, the remaining two elements of the array are initialised. **a[1].z**, **a[1].i** and **a[1].p** are assigned "Raipur", 2 and **a + 2** in that order, and "Kanpur", 3 and **a** are stored at **a[2].z**, **a[2].i** and **a[2].p** respectively.

What exactly do **a**, **a + 1** and **a + 2** signify? **a**, of course, is the base address of the array **a[ ]**. Let us assume it to be 4000, as shown in Figure 4.15. Locations 4000, 4001, 4002 and 4003 are occupied by the **char** pointer **a[0].z**, since a pointer is always four bytes long. The next four bytes are used to store the integer **a[0].i**, and then 4008, 4009, 4010 and 4011 are used by **a[0].p**. Similarly, the next 12 bytes store the first structure **a[1]**, and the 12 bytes after that contain **a[2]**, the second structure in the array.

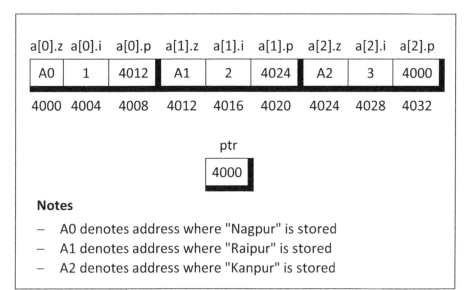

a[0].z	a[0].i	a[0].p	a[1].z	a[1].i	a[1].p	a[2].z	a[2].i	a[2].p
A0	1	4012	A1	2	4024	A2	3	4000
4000	4004	4008	4012	4016	4020	4024	4028	4032

ptr

4000

Notes

- A0 denotes address where "Nagpur" is stored
- A1 denotes address where "Raipur" is stored
- A2 denotes address where "Kanpur" is stored

Figure 4.15

Now, when we say **a + 1**, we do not arrive at 4001, but at 4012. This is because on incrementing any pointer, it points to the next location of its type, **a** points to the zeroth structure in the array, i.e. **a[0]**. Hence, on incrementing **a**, it will point to the immediately next element of its type, i.e. the first structure **a[1]** of the array. Likewise, **a + 2** signifies the address of the second element **a[2]** of the array. Thus, **a[0].p** contains address 4012 (refer figure), **a[1].p** contains 4024, and **a[2].p** stores 4000.

A **struct** pointer **ptr** is now set up, which is assigned **a**, the base address of the array.

In the **printf( )**, **a[0].z** denotes the address where "Nagpur" is stored. Hence "Nagpur" gets printed out.

Since **ptr** contains the address of **a[0]**, **ptr -> z** refers to the contents of element **z** of the array element **a[0]**. Thus **ptr -> z** gives the address A0 (refer figure) and this address happens to be the base address of the string "Nagpur". Hence "Nagpur" gets printed out.

Let us now analyse the expression **a[2].p -> z**. The left side of the arrow operator always represents the base address of a structure. What structure does **a[2].p** point to? Looking at the figure we can confirm that **a[2].p** contains the address 4000, which is the base address of the array **a[ ]**. Hence the expression **a[2].p -> z** can also be written as **a -> z**. Since **a** is the base address of the structure **a[0]**, this expression refers to the element **z** of the zeroth structure. Thus, "Nagpur" gets printed for the third time.

(7)
```
#include <stdio.h>
int main ( )
{
     struct s1
     {
          char *str ;
          int i ;
          struct s1 *ptr ;
     } ;
     static struct s1 a[ ] =  {
                                    { "Nagpur", 1, a + 1 },
                                    { "Raipur",  2, a + 2 },
                                    { "Kanpur", 3, a }
                               } ;
     struct s1 *p = a ;
     int j ;
     for ( j = 0 ; j <= 2 ; j++ )
     {
          printf ( "%d ", --a[j].i ) ;
          printf ( "%s\n", ++a[j].str ) ;
     }
     return 0 ;
}
```

Output

0 agpur
1 aipur
2 anpur

Explanation

The example deals with a structure similar to the one we just encountered. Picking up from the **for** loop, it is executed for 3 values of **j**: 0, 1 and 2. The first time through the **for** loop, **j** is equal to zero, so the first **printf( )** prints **--a[0].i**. Since the dot operator has a higher priority, first **a[0].i** is evaluated, which is 1. As **--** precedes the value to be printed, 1 is first decremented to 0, and then printed out.

The second **printf( )** prints the string at address **++a[0].str**. **a[0].str** gives the starting address of "Nagpur". On incrementing, it points to the next character, 'a' of "Nagpur", so starting from 'a', the remaining string "agpur" is outputted.

A similar procedure is repeated for **j = 1**, and then once again for **j = 2**, following which the execution is terminated.

(8)
```c
#include <stdio.h>
int main( )
{
    struct s1
    {
        char *z ;
        int i ;
        struct s1 *p ;
    };
    static struct s1 a[ ] =  {
                                { "Nagpur", 1, a + 1 },
                                { "Raipur", 2, a + 2 },
                                { "Kanpur", 3, a }
                            };
    struct s1 *ptr = a ;
    printf ( "%s\n", ++( ptr -> z ) ) ;
    printf ( "%s\n", a[ ( ++ptr ) -> i ].z ) ;
    printf ( "%s\n", a[ --( ptr -> p -> i ) ].z ) ;
    return 0 ;
}
```

Output

agpur
Kanpur

Kanpur

Explanation

With a similar set up as in the previous two programs, we try to print some more combinations. Let us tackle them one by one. The following figure should prove helpful in analysing these combinations.

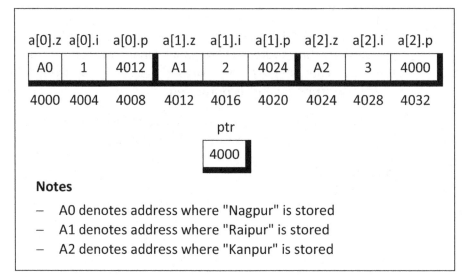

Figure 4.16

++(ptr -> z)

ptr holds the base address of the array of structures. We can also think of this base address as the address of the zeroth structure in the array. **ptr -> z** thus signifies the element **z** of the zeroth structure, which is the starting address of the string "Nagpur". On incrementing this using **++** operator, we get the next address, that of 'a' in "Nagpur". Therefore the string is printed out 'a' onwards.

a[(++ptr) -> i].z

Intimidating? Won't seem so after we have finished dissecting it. Starting from the parentheses, **++ptr** leads to contents of **ptr** being incremented. Currently **ptr** contains the address of the zeroth structure of the array **a[ ]**. This address, as per the figure, turns out to be 4000. Adding 1 to this address takes you 12 bytes further, and not 1, as you might be led to believe. This is so because on incrementing any pointer, it points to the next location of its type. Since **ptr** is a pointer to a structure, it skips as many bytes as the structure comprises of, and points to the following location. Our structure **s1** uses 4 bytes for the **char** pointer **z**, 4 for the **int i**, and 4 for the **struct** pointer **p**. Hence, on incrementing **ptr**, we get that address where **a[1]**, the next structure of the array begins. This address as per the figure is 4012. Now, (**4012**) -> **i** is 2, as has been initialised earlier. Thus the expression **a[(++ptr) -> i].z** reduces to plain and simple **a[2].z**, which yields the base address of the string "Kanpur". The same is printed out by **printf( )**.

Following our strategy of crossing the bridges one at a time, we start with the inner parentheses. Moving from left to right, **ptr -> p** is evaluated first. **ptr**, after getting incremented in the second **printf( )**, points to the first structure, **a[1]** of the array. The element **p** of this structure stores the address 4024, or in other words, the address given by **a + 2**. This address, as you would agree, is the base address of the second structure of the array. Thus the parentheses reduce to (**a + 2**) -> **i**, or **4024 -> i**, which is 3. 3 is decremented to 2 by the -- operator, and we realise that the expression that almost succeeded in putting us off was only a camouflage for **a[2].z!** This again yields the starting address of "Kanpur", and the same is therefore displayed once again.

(9)
```c
#include <stdio.h>
int main( )
{
    struct s1
    {
        char *str ;
        struct s1 *ptr ;
    };
    static struct s1 arr[ ] = {
                                { "Nikhil", arr + 1 },
                                { "Aditya", arr + 2 },
                                { "Sudheer", arr }
                              };
    struct s1 *p[3] ;
    int i ;
    for ( i = 0 ; i <= 2 ; i++ )
        p[i] = arr[i].ptr ;
    printf ( "%s\n", p[0] -> str ) ;
```

```
        printf ( "%s\n", ( *p ) -> str ) ;
        printf ( "%s\n", ( **p ) ) ;
        return 0 ;
}
```

Output

Aditya
Aditya
Aditya

Explanation

struct s1 comprises of 2 pointers; one a **char** pointer and another, a pointer to **struct s1. arr[ ]**, an array of such structures, is declared and initialised. Next, an array of pointers to structures, **p[3]** is declared. What this means is that each element of array **p[ ]** will hold the address of a structure of the type **struct s1**.

The first time in the **for** loop, **arr[0].ptr** is assigned to **p[0]**, which is the zeroth element of the array of pointers to structures. **arr[0].ptr** contains the address 4008 as per Figure 4.17. Likewise, **p[1]** is assigned the address 4016 and **p[2]**, the address 4000.

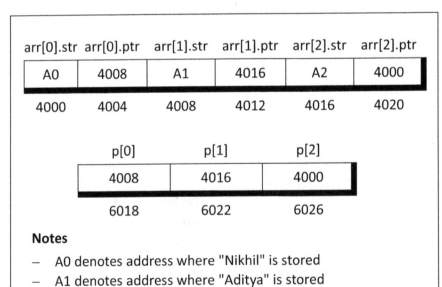

Notes
  −   A0 denotes address where "Nikhil" is stored
  −   A1 denotes address where "Aditya" is stored
  −   A2 denotes address where "Sudheer" is stored

Figure 4.17

Following this, the **printf( )**s get executed. In the first one, the string at **p[0] -> str** is printed. As **p[0]** is equal to 4008, the expression refers to the element **str** of the first structure, which stores A1, the starting address of "Aditya". Hence the name "Aditya" gets printed for the first time.

In the second **printf( )**, mentioning **p** gives the base address of the array **p[ ]**. This address according to the figure is 6018. Hence ***p** would give the value at address 6018, which is nothing but 4008. Thus **(*p) -> str** evaluates to **4008 -> str**, which yields A1, the base address of "Aditya". This outputs "Aditya" once again.

Finally, let us analyse the expression ****p**. A quick glance at the figure would confirm that ***p** gives the address 4008, and ****p** therefore gives the address at 4008. This address this time too turns out to be A1. Thus "Aditya" gets printed out through this **printf( )** too.

```
(10)  #include <stdio.h>
      void swap ( struct s1 *, struct s1 * ) ;
      struct s1
      {
          char *str ;   struct s1 *next ;
      };
      int main( )
      {
          static struct s1 arr[ ] = {
                                    { "Akhil", arr + 1 },
                                    { "Nikhil", arr + 2 },
                                    { "Anant", arr }
                                  };
          struct s1 *p[3] ;
          int i ;
          for ( i = 0 ; i <= 2 ; i++ )
              p[i] = arr[i].next ;
          printf ( "%s %s %s\n", p[0] -> str, ( *p ) -> str, ( **p ).str ) ;
          swap ( *p, arr ) ;
          printf ( "%s\n", p[0] -> str ) ;
          printf ( "%s\n", ( *p ) -> str ) ;
          printf ( "%s\n", ( *p ) -> next -> str ) ;
          swap ( p[0], p[0] -> next ) ;
          printf ( "%s\n", p[0] -> str ) ;
```

```
    printf ( "%s\n", ( *++p[0] ).str ) ;
    printf ( "%s\n", ++( *++( *p ) -> next ).str ) ;
    return 0 ;
}
void swap ( struct s1 *p1, struct s1 *p2 )
{
    char *temp ;
    temp = p1 -> str ;
    p1 -> str = p2 -> str ;
    p2 -> str = temp ;
}
```

Output

```
Nikhil Nikhil Nikhil
Akhil
Akhil
Anant
Anant
Akhil
nant
```

Explanation

You can by now take the setting up of the arrays of structures and pointers to structures in your stride. In the **for** loop the array **p[ ]** is set up with the addresses 4008, 4016 and 4000, as per Figure 4. 18.

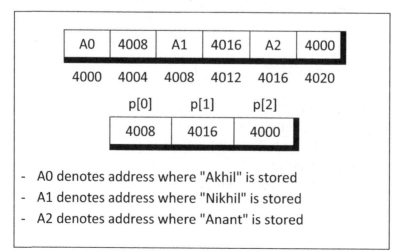

- A0 denotes address where "Akhil" is stored
- A1 denotes address where "Nikhil" is stored
- A2 denotes address where "Anant" is stored

Figure 4.18

In the first **printf( )**, **p[0] -> str** is same as **(4008 -> str)**. As 4008 denotes the base address of the first structure, **str** corresponds to the address A1, which is the base address of "Nikhil". Hence this **printf( )** prints the first string "Nikhil".

*p is another way of referring to the same element **p[0]** (as you would recall that **n[i]** is equal to ***(n + i)**). Thus, corresponding to ***p -> str**, "Nikhil" is outputted once again.

The third expression uses ****p**, which is equal to ***(p[0])**, i.e. ***(4008)**, which can also be expressed as ***(arr + 1)**. But the expression ***(arr + 1)** is same as **arr[1]**. Thus the expression ****p.str** can also be thought of as **arr[1].str**. As can be confirmed from the figure, **arr[1].str** gives A1, which is the base address of the string "Nikhil". Hence "Nikhil" gets printed through the **printf( )**.

After this, a function **swap( )** is called, which takes as its arguments the base addresses of two structures, **arr + 1** (as ***p** equals **arr + 1**) and **arr**. Hence, in **swap( )**, **p1** and **p2** have been declared as **struct** pointers. Using an auxiliary pointer **temp**, the strings at **(arr + 1) -> str** and **arr -> str** are exchanged. Thus, "Akhil" is now present where "Nikhil" was and vice versa. The current contents of the array **arr[ ]** are now changed to:

```
{
    { "Nikhil", arr + 1 },
    { "Akhil", arr + 2 },
    { "Anant", arr }
}
```

Thus, "Akhil" shows up for the next two **printf( )**s.

Let us now analyse the expression **(*p) -> next -> str**. ***p -> next** is same as **p[0] -> next**. Since **p[0]** contains the address 4008, the term can be expressed as **4008 -> next**, which yields the address 4016. Next, **4016 -> str** yields A2, the base address of "Anant". Hence the **printf( )** outputs "Anant".

After this, **swap( )** is called once again with arguments **p[0]** and **p[0] -> next** This time **p[0]** contains the address 4008, while **p[0] -> next** contains the address 4016. 4008 and 4016 represent the base addresses of the first and second structures of the array **arr[ ]**. In the function **swap( )** the strings in these two structures are interchanged. So the array now looks like:

```
{
    { "Nikhil", arr + 1 },
    { "Anant", arr + 2 },
    { "Akhil", arr }
}
```

With this changed array, let's look at the last set of **printf( )**s. The first of these is quite simple. **p[0] -> str**, i.e. **4008 -> str** yields "Anant" in keeping with the latest contents of the array.

Next is the expression **(*++p[0]).str**. In the parentheses **p[0]** is incremented by the **++** operator. Thus, **p[0]**, storing **(arr + 1)**, now contains **(arr + 2)**. Now, ***(arr + 2)** can be expressed as **arr[2]**. Hence the **printf( )** prints **arr[2].str**, which yields "Akhil".

Not allowing ourselves to be impressed by the length of the last **printf( )**'s argument, we start within the parentheses, on the left of the arrow operator. ***p**, i.e. **p[0]**, having been incremented in the preceding **printf( )**, currently contains **(arr + 2)**. Since the **->** operator enjoys a higher priority than the **++**, **(arr + 2) -> next** gets evaluated next, yielding address **arr**. Now the **++** operator goes to work and we get the address **arr + 1**.

The expression can now be rewritten as **++(*(arr + 1)).str**. As ***(arr + 1)** is same as **arr[1]**, the expression is reduced to **++arr[1].str**. **arr[1].str** gives the starting address of "Anant". The **++** operator increments this so that the address of the first 'n' of "Anant" is reached. Since this is the address supplied to **printf( )**, the string is printed 'n' onwards. This corresponds to the last output "nant".

Exercise

[A] What will be the output of the following program segments:

(1)
```c
#include <stdio.h>
int main( )
{
    struct a
    {
        char *str ;
        struct a *ptr ;
    } ;
    static struct a arr[ ] = {
                                { "Niranjan", arr + 2 },
                                { "Praveen", arr },
                                { "Ashish", arr + 1 }
                            } ;
    struct a *p[3] ;
    int i ;
    for ( i = 0 ; i <= 2 ; i++ )
        p[i] = arr[i].ptr ;
    printf ( "%s\n", p[0] -> str ) ;
    printf ( "%s\n", ( *p ) -> str ) ;
    printf ( "%s\n", ( **p ) ) ;
    return 0 ;
}
```

(2)
```c
#include <malloc.h>
#include <stdio.h>
int main( )
{
    struct a
    {
        struct a *next ;
        int data ;
    } ;
    struct a *ptr[3] ;
    int i ;
    ptr[0] = ( struct a * ) malloc ( sizeof ( struct a ) ) ;
    ptr[1] = ( struct a * ) malloc ( sizeof ( struct a ) ) ;
    ptr[2] = ( struct a * ) malloc ( sizeof ( struct a ) ) ;
    ptr[0] -> data = 10 ;
```

```
            ptr[1] -> data = 20 ;
            ptr[2] -> data = 50 ;
            ptr[0] -> next = ptr[1] ;
            ptr[1] -> next = ptr[2] ;
            ptr[2] -> next = NULL ;
            while ( ptr[0] != NULL )
            {
                   printf( "%d\n", ptr[0] -> data ) ;
                   ptr[0] = ptr[0] ->  next ;
            }
            return 0 ;
      }
(3)   #include <stdio.h>
      struct a
      {
            char city[3][20] ;
            char state[3][20] ;
      } ;
      int main( )
      {
            struct a arr = {
                                 {
                                       "Nagpur",
                                       "Mumbai",
                                       "Bangalore"
                                 },
                                 {
                                       "Maharashtra",
                                       "Maharashtra",
                                       "Karnataka"
                                 }
                          } ;
            printf ( "%s %s\n", arr.city, arr.state ) ;
            printf ( "%s %s\n", arr.city + 2, arr.state + 2 ) ;
            return 0 ;
      }
(4)   #include <stdio.h>
      int main( )
      {
            struct a
```

```
        {
            struct b
            {
                char name[10] ;
                int age ;
            } bb ;
            struct c
            {
                char address[50] ;
                int sal ;
            } cc ;
    } ;
    struct a *ptr ;
    struct a aa = {
                        { "George", 30 },
                        { "86, Vermalayout, Nagpur", 4000 }
                    } ;
        ptr = &aa ;
        printf ( "%s %s %d %d\n", ptr -> bb.name, ptr -> cc.address,
                    ptr -> bb.age, ptr -> cc.sal ) ;
        return 0 ;
    }
```

(5)
```
    #include <stdio.h>
    void print ( struct b * ) ;
    struct b
    {
        char name[10] ;
        char address[50] ;
    } ;
    int main( )
    {
        struct b bb = {
                        "Niranjan",
                        "Samarth Apartment, TTnagar, Nagpur"
                    } ;
        print ( &bb ) ;
        return 0 ;
    }
    void print ( struct b *bb )
    {
        printf ( "%s\n", bb -> name ) ;
```

```
    printf ( "%s\n", bb -> address ) ;
}
```

## CHAPTER 05

Understanding
Pointers in
C & C++

Pointers and Data Structures

Choice of right Data Structure separates a good program from a bad program. To implement most of the commonly used data structures one needs pointer, as you would see in this chapter...

In Computer science a Data Structure refers to the way of arrangement of data in memory. There are several data structures available, each with its set of advantages and limitations. Array, String, Linked List, Stack, Queue, Tree and Graph are some of the more popularly used data structures. We have already seen how pointers go hand in hand with Array and String. In this chapter we propose to explore the rest of the data structures. Let us begin with linked list.

Linked Lists

Often the list of items to be stored in an array is either too small or too big as compared to the declared size of the array. Moreover, during program execution the list cannot grow beyond the size of the declared array. Also, operations like insertion and deletion at a specified location in a list requires a lot of movement of data, thereby leading to an inefficient and time consuming algorithm.

All these disadvantages of arrays can be overcome using a data structure called Linked List. A linked list can grow and shrink in size dynamically. In particular, the linked list's maximum size need not be known in advance. Also, linked lists provide flexibility in rearranging the items in the list efficiently. This flexibility is gained at the expense of quick access to any arbitrary item in the list.

Linked list is often used to store similar data in memory. While the elements of an array occupy contiguous memory locations, those of a linked list are not constrained to be stored in adjacent locations. The individual elements are stored "somewhere" in memory, rather like a family dispersed, but still bound together. The order of the elements is maintained by explicit links between them. For instance, the marks obtained by different students can be stored in a linked list as shown in Figure 5.1.

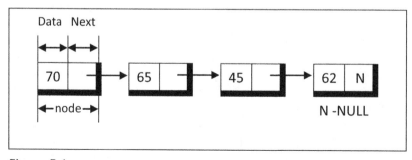

Figure 5.1

Observe that the linked list is a collection of elements called nodes, each of which stores two items of information—an element of the list and a link. A link is a pointer or an address that indicates explicitly the location of the node containing the successor of the list element. In Figure 5.1, the arrows represent the links. The **Data** part of each node consists of the marks obtained by a student and the **Next** part is a pointer to the next node. The NULL in the last node indicates that this is the last node in the list.

There are several operations that we can think of performing on linked lists. The following program shows how to build a linked list by adding new nodes at the beginning, at the end or in the middle of the linked list. It also contains a function **display( )** which displays all the nodes present in the linked list and a function **delete( )** which can delete any node in the linked list. Go through the program carefully, a step at a time.

```
/* Program 47 */
/* Program to maintain a linked list */
#include <stdlib.h>
#include <stdio.h>
struct node
{
    int data ;
    struct node *link ;
} ;
void append ( struct node **, int ) ;
void addatbeg ( struct node **, int ) ;
void addafter ( struct node *, int, int ) ;
void display ( struct node * ) ;
int count ( struct node * ) ;
void delnode ( struct node **, int ) ;
int main( )
{
    struct node *p ;
    p = NULL ;  /* empty linked list */
    printf ( "No. of elements in the Linked List = %d\n", count ( p ) ) ;
    append ( &p, 1 ) ;
    append ( &p, 2 ) ;
    append ( &p, 3 ) ;
    append ( &p, 4 ) ;
    append ( &p, 17) ;
```

```
        display ( p ) ;
        addatbeg ( &p, 999 ) ;
        addatbeg ( &p, 888 ) ;
        addatbeg ( &p, 777 ) ;
        display ( p ) ;
        addafter ( p, 7, 0 ) ;
        addafter ( p, 2, 1 ) ;
        addafter ( p, 1, 99 ) ;
        display ( p ) ;
        printf ( "\nNo. of elements in the Linked List = %d\n", count ( p ) ) ;
        delnode ( &p, 888 ) ;
        delnode ( &p, 1 ) ;
        delnode (&p, 10 ) ;
        display ( p ) ;
        printf ( "\nNo. of elements in the linked list = %d\n", count ( p ) ) ;
        return 0 ;
}

/* adds a node at the end of a linked list */
void append ( struct node **q, int num )
{
    struct node *temp, *r ;
    temp = *q ;
    if ( *q == NULL ) /* if the list is empty, create first node */
    {
        temp = ( struct node * ) malloc ( sizeof ( struct node ) ) ;
        temp -> data = num ;
        temp -> link = NULL ;
        *q = temp ;
    }
    else
    {
        temp = *q ;
        /* go to last node */
        while ( temp -> link != NULL )
            temp = temp -> link ;
        /* add node at the end */
        r = ( struct node * ) malloc ( sizeof ( struct node ) ) ;
        r -> data = num ;
        r -> link = NULL ;
        temp -> link = r ;
```

```
        }
}

/* adds a new node at the beginning of the linked list */
void addatbeg ( struct node **q, int num )
{
    struct node *temp ;
    /* add new node */
    temp = ( struct node * ) malloc ( sizeof ( struct node ) ) ;
    temp -> data = num ;
    temp -> link = *q ;
    *q = temp ;
}

/* adds a new node after the specified number of nodes */
void addafter ( struct node *q, int loc, int num )
{
    struct node *temp, *r ;
    int i ;
    temp = q ;
    /* skip to desired portion */
    for ( i = 0 ; i < loc ; i++ )
    {
        temp = temp -> link ;
        /* if end of linked list is encountered */
        if ( temp == NULL)
        {
            printf ( "There are less than %d elements in list\n", loc ) ;
            return ;
        }
    }
    /* insert new node */
    r = ( struct node * ) malloc ( sizeof ( struct node ) ) ;
    r -> data = num ;
    r -> link = temp -> link ;
    temp -> link = r ;
}

/* displays the contents of the linked list */
void display ( struct node *q )
{
```

```
        printf ( "\n" ) ;
        /* traverse the entire linked list */
        while ( q != NULL )
        {
            printf ( "%d ", q-> data ) ;
            q = q -> link ;
        }
}

/* counts the number of nodes present in the linked list */
int count ( struct node *q )
{
    int c = 0 ;
    /* traverse the entire linked list */
    while ( q != NULL )
    {
        q = q -> link ;
        c++ ;
    }
    return c ;
}

/* deletes the specified node from the linked list */
void delnode ( struct node **q, int num )
{
    struct node *old, *temp ;
    temp = *q ;
    while ( temp != NULL )
    {
        if ( temp -> data == num )
        {
            /* if node to be deleted is the first node */
            if ( temp == *q )
            {
                *q = temp -> link ;
                /* free the memory occupied by the node */
                free ( temp ) ;
                return ;
            }

            /* deletes the intermediate nodes in the linked list */
```

```
        else
        {
            old -> link = temp -> link ;
            free ( temp ) ;
            return ;
        }
    }
    /* traverse the linked list till the last node is reached */
    else
    {
        old = temp ; /* old points to the previous node */
        temp = temp -> link ; /* go to the next node */
    }
}
printf ( "Element %d not found\n", num ) ;
}
```

To begin with we have defined a structure for a node. It contains a data part and a link part. The variable **p** has been declared as pointer to a node. We have used this pointer as pointer to the first node in the linked list. No matter how many nodes get added to the linked list, **p** would continue to pointer to the first node in the list. When no node has been added to the list, **p** has been set to NULL to indicate that the list is empty.

The **append( )** function has to deal with two situations:

(a)　The node is being added to an empty list.
(b)　The node is being added at the end of an existing list.

In the first case, the condition

if (*q == NULL)

gets satisfied. Hence, space is allocated for the node using **malloc( )**. Data and the link part of this node are set up using the statements:

temp -> data = num ;
temp -> link = NULL ;

Lastly **p** is made to point to this node, since the first node has been added to the list and **p** must always point to the first node. Note that ***q** is nothing but equal to **p**.

In the other case, when the linked list is not empty, the condition

if (*q == NULL)

would fail, since ***q** (i.e. **p** is non-NULL). Now **temp** is made to point to the first node in the list through the statement

temp = *q ;

Then using **temp** we have traversed through the entire linked list using the statements:

while (temp -> link != NULL)
    temp = temp -> link ;

The position of the pointers before and after traversing the linked list is shown in Figure 5.2.

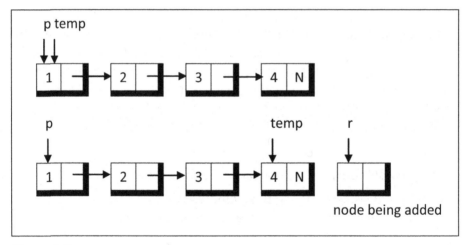

Figure 5.2

Each time through the loop the statement **temp = temp -> link** makes **temp** point to the next node in the list. When **temp** reaches the last node the condition **temp -> link != NULL** would fail. Once outside the loop we allocate space for the new node through the statement

r = (struct node *) malloc (sizeof (struct node)) ;

Once the space has been allocated for the new node its **data** part is stuffed with **num** and the link part with NULL. Note that this node is now going to be the last Node in the list.

All that now remains to be done is connecting the previous last node with the new last node. The previous last node is being pointed to by **temp** and the new last node is being pointed to by **r**. They are connected through the statement

temp -> link = r ;

this link gets established

There is often confusion as to how the statement **temp = temp -> link** makes **temp** point to the next node in the list. Let us understand this with the help of an example. Suppose in a linked list containing 4 nodes **temp** is pointing at the first node. This is shown in Figure 5.3.

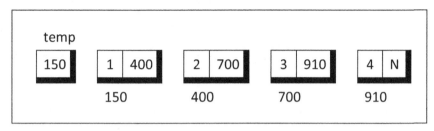

Figure 5.3

Instead of showing the links to the next node I have shown the addresses of the next node in the link part of each node.

When we execute the statement

temp = temp -> link ;

the right hand side yields 400. This address is now stored in **temp**. As a result, **temp** starts pointing to the node present at address 400. In effect the statement has shifted **temp** so that it has started pointing to the next node in the list.

Let us now understand the **addatbeg( )** function. Suppose there are already 5 nodes in the list and we wish to add a new node at the beginning of this existing linked list. This situation is shown in Figure 5.4.

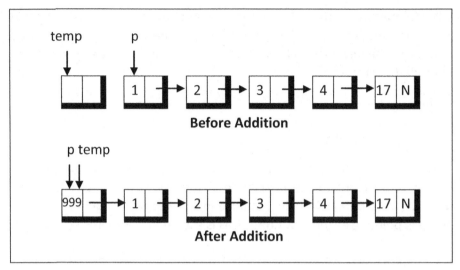

Figure 5.4

For adding a new node at the beginning, firstly space is allocated for this node and data is stored in it through the statement

temp -> data = num ;

Now we need to make the **link** part of this node point to the existing first node. This has been achieved through the statement

temp -> link = *q ;

Lastly, this new node must be made the first node in the list. This has been attained through the statement

*q = temp ;

The **addafter( )** function permits us to add a new node after a specified number of node in the linked list. To begin with, through a loop we skip the desired number of nodes after which a new node is to be added. Suppose we wish to add a new node containing data as 99 after the 3rd node in the list. The position of pointers once the control reaches outside the **for** loop is shown in the Figure 5.4. Now space is allocated for the node to be inserted and 99 is stored in the data part of it. All that remains to be done is readjustment of links such that 99 goes in between 3 and 4. This is achieved through the statements

r -> link = temp -> link ;
temp -> link = r ;

The first statement makes link part of node containing 99 to point to the node containing 4. The second statement ensures that the link part of node containing 3 points to the node containing 99. On execution of the second statement the earlier link between 3 and 4 is severed. So now 3 no longer points to 4, it points to 99.

The **display( )** and **count( )** functions are straight forward. I leave them for you to understand.

That brings us to the last function in the program i.e. **delete( )**. In this function through the **while** loop, we have traversed the linked list, checking at each node, whether it is the node to be deleted. If so, we have checked if the node being deleted is the first node in the linked list. If it is so, we have simply shifted **p** (which is same as ***q**) to the next node and then deleted the earlier node.

If the node to be deleted is an intermediate node, then the position of various pointers and links before and after the deletion is shown in Figure 5.5.

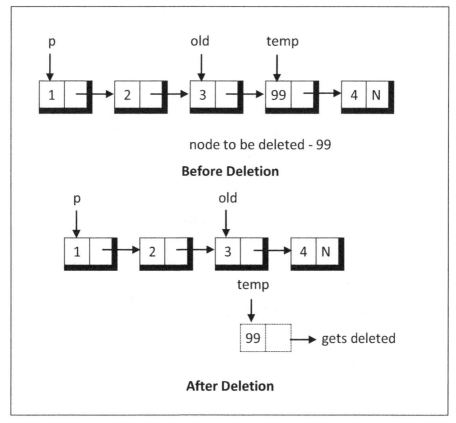

Figure 5.5

The **addafter( )** function permits us to add a new node after a specified number of node in the linked list.

To begin with, through a loop we skip the desired number of nodes after which a new node is to be added. Suppose we wish to add a new node containing data as 99 after the 3rd node in the list. The position of pointers once the control reaches outside the **for** loop is shown in the Figure 5.6(a).

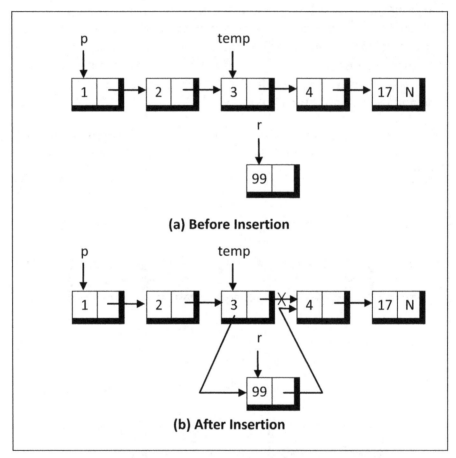

(a) Before Insertion

(b) After Insertion

Figure 5.6

A common and a wrong impression that beginners carry is that a linked list is used only for storing integers. However, a linked list can virtually be used for storing any similar data. For example, there can exist a linked list of floats, a linked list of names, or even a linked list of records, where each record contains name, age and salary of an employee.

Stacks and Queues

Stacks and queues are two very common and popular data structures. These data structures are often implemented using arrays since most programming languages provide array as a predefined data type, and such an implementation is therefore quite easy. However, when implemented as an array, these data structures suffer from the basic limitation of an array—that its size cannot be increased or decreased once it is declared. As a result, one ends up reserving either too much space or too less space for an array and in turn for a stack or a queue. This difficulty is eliminated when we implement these data structures using linked lists.

Before we do so, let us formally define these data structures. A stack is a data structure in which addition of new element or deletion of existing element always takes place at the same end. This end is often known as 'top' of stack. This situation can be compared to a stack of plates in a cafeteria where every new plate added to the stack is added at the 'top'. Similarly, every new plate taken off the stack is also from the 'top' of the stack. There are several applications where stack can be put to use. For example, recursion, keeping track of function calls, evaluation of expressions etc.

Unlike a stack, in a queue the addition of new element takes place at the end (called 'rear' of queue) whereas deletion takes place at the other end (called 'front' of queue). Figure 5.7 shows these two data structures. A stack is often called a Last-In-First-Out (LIFO) structure, whereas a queue is called a First-In-First-Out (FIFO) structure.

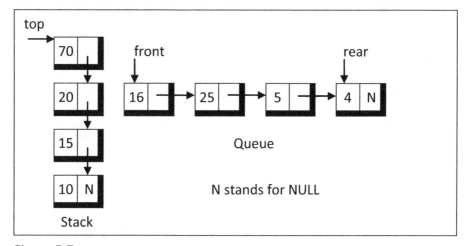

Figure 5.7

And now a program, which implements the stack and the queue using linked lists.

```c
/* Program 48 */
/* Program to implement a stack as a linked list */
#include <stdlib.h>
#include <stdio.h>
struct node
{
int data ;
struct node *link ;
} ;
void push ( struct node **, int ) ;
int pop ( struct node ** ) ;
void stack_display ( struct node * ) ;
int count ( struct node * ) ;
int main( )
{
    struct node *top ; /* top will always point to top of a stack */
    int item ;
    top = NULL; /* empty stack*/
    push ( &top, 11 ) ;
    push ( &top, 12 ) ;
    push ( &top, 13 ) ;
    push ( &top, 14 ) ;
    push ( &top, 15 ) ;
    push ( &top, 16 ) ;
    push ( &top, 17 ) ;
    stack_display ( top ) ;
    printf ( "No. of items in stack = %d\n", count ( top ) ) ;
    printf ( "Items extracted from stack : " ) ;
    item = pop ( &top ) ;
    if ( item != NULL )
        printf ( "%d ", item ) ;
    item = pop ( &top ) ;
    if ( item != NULL )
        printf ( "%d ", item ) ;
    item = pop ( &top ) ;
    if ( item != NULL )
        printf ( "%d ", item ) ;
    stack_display ( top ) ;
```

```
        printf ( "No. of items in stack = %d\n" , count ( top ) ) ;
        return 0 ;
}


/* adds a new element on the top of stack */
void push ( struct node **s, int item )
{
        struct node *q ;
        q = ( struct node * ) malloc ( sizeof ( struct node ) ) ;
        if ( q == NULL )
        {
                printf ( "\nstack is full\n" ) ;
                return ;
        }
        q -> data = item ;
        q -> link = *s ;
        *s = q ;
}


/* removes an element from top of stack */
int pop ( struct node **s )
{
        int item ;
        struct node *q ;
        /* if stack is empty */
        if ( *s == NULL )
        {
                printf ( "\nstack is empty\n" ) ;
                return NULL ;
        }
        else
        {
                q = *s ;
                item = q -> data ;
                *s = q -> link ;
                free ( q ) ;
                return ( item ) ;
        }
}


/* displays whole of the stack */
```

```
void stack_display ( struct node *q )
{
    printf ( "\n" ) ;
    /* traverse the entire linked list */
    while ( q != NULL )
    {
        printf ( "%2d ", q -> data ) ;
        q = q -> link ;
    }
    printf ( "\n" ) ;
}

/* counts no. of nodes present in the linked list representing a stack */
int count ( struct node * q )
{
    int c = 0 ;
    /* traverse the entire linked list */
    while ( q != NULL )
    {
        q = q -> link ;
        c++ ;
    }
    return c ;
}
```

If you observe carefully, you would note that, the process of pushing and popping is similar to adding a node at the beginning of a linked list and deleting a node from the beginning of the linked list.

Let us now implement the queue data structure using a linked list.

```
/* Program 49 */
/* Program to implement a queue as a linked list */
#include <windows.h>
#include <stdlib.h>
#include <stdio.h>
struct node
{
    int data ;
    struct node *link ;
} ;
void addq ( struct node **, struct node **, int ) ;
```

```
int delq ( struct node **, struct node ** ) ;
void q_display ( struct node * ) ;
int count ( struct node * ) ;
int main( )
{
    struct node *front , *rear ;
    int item ;
    front = rear = NULL ;   /* empty queue */
    addq ( &front, &rear, 11 ) ;
    addq ( &front, &rear, 12 ) ;
    addq ( &front, &rear, 13 ) ;
    addq ( &front, &rear, 14 ) ;
    addq ( &front, &rear, 15 ) ;
    addq ( &front, &rear, 16 ) ;
    addq ( &front, &rear, 17 ) ;
    q_display ( front ) ;
    printf ( "No. of items in queue = %d\n" , count ( front ) ) ;
    printf ( "Items extracted from queue :\n" ) ;
    item = delq ( &front, &rear ) ;
    if ( item != NULL )
        printf ( "%d ", item ) ;
    item = delq ( &front, &rear ) ;
    if ( item != NULL )
        printf ( "%d ", item ) ;
    item = delq ( &front, &rear ) ;
    if ( item != NULL )
        printf ( "%d ", item ) ;
    printf ( "\n" ) ;
    q_display ( front ) ;
    printf ( "No. of items in queue = %d\n", count ( front ) ) ;
    return 0 ;
}

/* adds a new element at the end of queue */
void addq ( struct node **f, struct node **r, int item )
{
    struct node *q ;
    /* create new node */
    q = ( struct node * ) malloc ( sizeof ( struct node ) ) ;
    if ( q == NULL )
    {
```

```
        printf ( "\nqueue is full\n" ) ;
        return ;
    }
    q -> data = item ;
    q -> link = NULL ;
    /* if the queue is empty */
    if ( *f == NULL )
        *f = q ;
    else
        ( *r ) -> link = q ;
    *r = q ;
}

/* removes an element from front of queue */
int delq ( struct node **f, struct node **r )
{
    struct node *q ;
    int item ;
    /* if queue is empty*/
    if ( *f == NULL )
    {
        printf ( "\nqueue is empty\n" ) ;
        return NULL ;
    }
    else
    {
        /* delete the node */
        q = *f ;
        item = q -> data ;
        *f = q -> link ;
        free ( q ) ;
        /* if on deletion the queue has become empty */
        if ( *f == NULL )
            *r = NULL ;
        return ( item ) ;
    }
}

/* displays all elements of the queue */
void q_display ( struct node *q )
{
```

```
    /* traverse the entire linked list */
    while ( q != NULL )
    {
        printf ( "%2d ", q -> data ) ;
        q = q -> link ;
    }
    printf ( "\n" ) ;
}


/* counts the number of nodes in the linked list representing a queue */
int count ( struct node * q )
{
    int c = 0 ;
    /* traverse the entire linked list */
    while ( q != NULL )
    {
        q = q -> link ;
        c++ ;
    }
    return c ;
}
```

Note that, the addition of a node to queue is similar to adding a node at the end of the linked list. After adding a new node the **rear** is made to point to this node. To begin with, **front** and **rear** both are set to NULL to indicate emptiness of the queue.

Deleting a node from the queue is same as deleting the first node from the linked list. If on deletion of the node, the queue becomes empty, then **front** as well as **rear** should be set to NULL.

A double-ended queue or a deque is a queue in which elements can be added or deleted from both the ends i.e. front and rear. I would leave it for you to implement it in a program.

Doubly Linked Lists

In the linked lists that we have used so far each node provides information about where is the next node in the list. It has no knowledge about where the previous node lies in memory. If we are at say the 15th node in the list, then to reach the 14th node we have to traverse the list right from the first node. To avoid this we can store in each node not only the address of next node but also the address of the previous node in the linked list. This arrangement is often known as a 'Doubly Linked List' and is shown in the following figure.

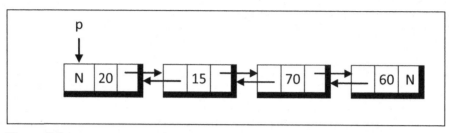

Figure 5.8

Trees

The data structures arrays, strings, linked lists, stacks, and queues were linear data structures. As against this, trees are non-linear data structures. In a tree each node may point to several other nodes (which may then point to several other nodes, etc.). Thus a tree is a very flexible and powerful data structure that can be used for a wide variety of applications.

Although the nodes in a general tree may contain any number of pointers to the other tree nodes, a large number of data structures have at the most two pointers to the other tree nodes. This type of a tree is called a **binary tree**. In this chapter we would restrict our discussion of trees to only binary trees.

Binary Trees

Let us begin our study of binary trees by discussing some basic concepts. A simple binary tree is shown in Figure 5.9.

A binary tree is a finite set of elements that is either empty or is partitioned into three disjoint subsets. The first subset contains a single clement called the **root** of the tree. The other two subsets are themselves binary trees, called the **left** and **right subtrees** of the original tree. A left or right subtree can be empty. Each element of a binary tree is called a **node** of the tree.

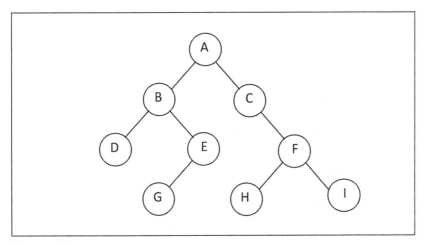

Figure 5.9

Traversal of a Binary Tree

The traversal of a binary tree means visiting each node in the tree exactly once. There are three popular methods of binary tree traversal. These are known as **inorder** traversal, **preorder** traversal and **postorder** traversal. The functions used to traverse a tree using these methods can be kept quite short if we understand the recursive nature of the binary tree. A binary tree is recursive in that each subtree is really a binary tree itself. Thus traversing a binary tree involves visiting the root node and traversing its left and right subtrees. The only difference among the methods is the order in which these three operations are performed.

To traverse a nonempty binary tree in **preorder**, we perform the following three operations:

(1) Visit the root.
(2) Traverse the left subtree in preorder.
(3) Traverse the right subtree in preorder.

To traverse a nonempty binary tree in **inorder** (or symmetric order):

(1) Traverse the left subtree in inorder.
(2) Visit the root.
(3) Traverse the right subtree in inorder.

To traverse a nonempty binary tree in **postorder**:

(1) Traverse the left subtree in postorder.
(2) Traverse the right subtree in postorder.
(3) Visit the root.

Many algorithms that use binary trees proceed in two phases. The first phase builds a binary tree, and the second traverses the tree. As an example of such an algorithm, consider the following sorting method. Given a list of numbers in an input file, we wish to print them in ascending order. As we read the numbers, they can be inserted into a binary tree such as the one of Figure 5.10. When a number is compared with the contents of a node in the tree, a left branch is taken if the number is smaller than the contents of the node and a right branch if it is greater or equal to the contents of the node. Thus if the input list is

20 17 6 8 10 7 18 13 12 5

the binary tree of Figure 5.10 is produced.

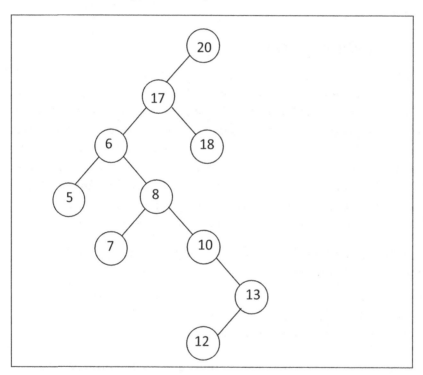

Figure 5.10

Such a binary tree has the property that all elements in the left subtree of a node **n** are less than the contents of **n**, and all elements in the right subtree of **n** are greater than or equal to the contents of **n**. A binary tree that has these properties is called a **Binary Search tree**. If a binary search tree is traversed in inorder (left, root, right) and the contents of each node are printed as the node is visited, the numbers are printed in ascending order. Convince yourself that this is the case for the binary search tree of Figure 5.10. The program to implement this algorithm is given below.

```
/* Program 50 */
/* Program to implement a binary tree */
#include <stdlib.h>
#include <stdio.h>
struct btreenode
{
    struct btreenode *leftchild ;
    int data ;
    struct btreenode *rightchild ;
} ;
void insert ( struct btreenode **, int ) ;
void inorder ( struct btreenode * ) ;
void preorder ( struct btreenode * ) ;
void postorder ( struct btreenode * ) ;
int main( )
{
    struct btreenode *bt ;
    int req, i = 1, num ;
    bt = NULL ; /* empty tree */
    printf ( "Specify the number of data items to be inserted : " ) ;
    scanf ( "%d", &req ) ;
    while ( i++ <= req )
    {
        printf ( "Enter the data : " ) ;
        scanf ( "%d", &num ) ;
        insert ( &bt, num ) ;
    }
    printf ( "\nInorder Traversal: \n" ) ;
    inorder ( bt ) ;
    printf ( "\nPreorder Traversal: \n" ) ;
    preorder ( bt ) ;
    printf ( "\nPostorder Traversal: \n" ) ;
    postorder ( bt ) ;
    return 0 ;
}

/* inserts a new node in a binary search tree */
void insert ( struct btreenode **sr, int num )
{
```

```
        if ( *sr == NULL )
        {
            *sr = ( struct btreenode * ) malloc ( sizeof ( struct btreenode ) ) ;
            ( *sr ) -> leftchild = NULL ;
            ( *sr ) -> data = num ;
            ( *sr ) -> rightchild = NULL ;
            return ;
        }
        else    /* search the node to which new node will be attached */
        {
            /* if new data is less, traverse to left */
            if ( num < ( *sr ) -> data )
                insert ( &( ( *sr ) -> leftchild ), num ) ;
            else
                /* else traverse to right */
                insert ( &( ( *sr ) -> rightchild ), num ) ;
        }
    }

/* traverse a binary search tree in a LDR (Left-Data-Right) fashion */
void inorder ( struct btreenode *sr )
{
    if ( sr != NULL )
    {
        inorder ( sr -> leftchild ) ;
        /* print the data of the node whose leftchild is NULL or the path
            has already been traversed */
        printf ( "%d ", sr -> data ) ;
        inorder ( sr -> rightchild ) ;
    }
    else
        return ;
}

/* traverse a binary search tree in a DLR (Data-Left-right) fashion */
void preorder ( struct btreenode *sr )
{
    if ( sr != NULL )
    {
        /* print the data of a node */
        printf ( "%d ", sr -> data ) ;
```

```
        /* traverse till leftchild is not NULL */
        preorder ( sr -> leftchild ) ;
        /* traverse till rightchild is not NULL */
        preorder ( sr -> rightchild ) ;
    }
    else
        return ;
}

/* traverse a binary search tree in LRD (Left-Right-Data} fashion */
void postorder ( struct btreenode *sr )
{
    if ( sr != NULL )
    {
        postorder ( sr -> leftchild ) ;
        postorder ( sr -> rightchild ) ;
        printf ( "%d ", sr -> data ) ;
    }
    else
        return ;
}
```

Graphs

The only non-linear data structure that we have seen so far is tree. A tree in fact is a special type of graph. Graphs are data structures which have wide-ranging applications in real life like, Analysis of electrical circuits, Finding shortest routes, Statistical analysis, etc. To be able to understand and use the graph data structure one must first get familiar with the definitions and terms used in association with graphs. These are discussed below.

A graph consists of two sets **v** and **e** where, **v** is a finite, non-empty set of vertices and **e** is a set of pairs of vertices. The pairs of vertices are called edges. A Graph can be of two types: Undirected graph and Directed graph.

In an undirected graph the pair of vertices representing any edge is unordered. Thus, the pairs **(v1, v2)** and **(v2, v1)** represent the same edge.

In a directed graph each edge is represented by a directed pair **<v1, v2>**. **v1** is the tail and **v2** the head of the edge. Therefore **<v2, v1>** and **<v1,**

v2> represent two different edges. A directed graph is also called Digraph. In Figure 5.11 the graph **G1** is an undirected graph whereas graph **G2** is a directed graph.

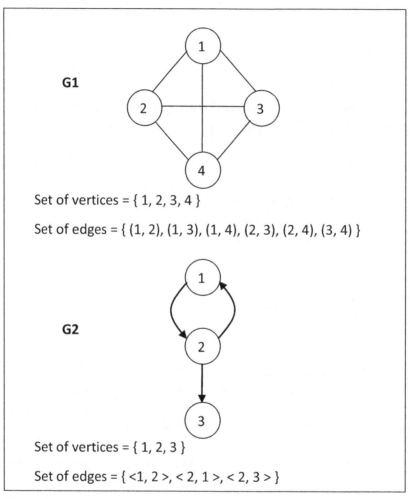

G1

Set of vertices = { 1, 2, 3, 4 }

Set of edges = { (1, 2), (1, 3), (1, 4), (2, 3), (2, 4), (3, 4) }

G2

Set of vertices = { 1, 2, 3 }

Set of edges = { <1, 2 >, < 2, 1 >, < 2, 3 > }

Figure 5.11

Note that the edges of a directed graph are drawn with an arrow from the tail to the head.

In an undirected graph if **(v1, v2)** is an edge in the set of edges, then the vertices **v1** and **v2** are said to be adjacent and that the edge **(v1, v2)** is **incident on** vertices **v1** and **v2**. The vertex 2 in **G1** is **adjacent to** vertices 1, 3, and 4. The edges **incident on** vertex 3 in **G1** are **(1, 3)**, **(2, 3)** and **(4, 3)**.

If **<v1, v2>** is a directed edge, then vertex **v1** is said to be **adjacent to v2** while **v2** is **adjacent from v1**. The edge **<v1, v2>** is **incident to v1** and **v2**. In **G2** the edges **incident to** vertex 2 are **<1, 2>, < 2, 1 >** and **< 2, 3 >**.

The most commonly used representations for graphs are Adjacency lists. In this representation there is one linked list for each vertex in the graph. The nodes in list **i** represent the vertices that are adjacent from vertex **i**. Each list has a head node. The head nodes are sequential providing easy random access to the adjacency list for any particular vertex. The adjacency lists for graphs **G1** and **G2** are shown below.

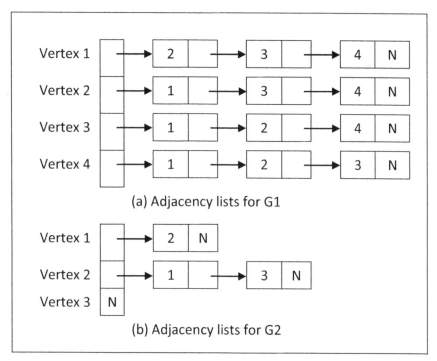

(a) Adjacency lists for G1

(b) Adjacency lists for G2

Figure 5.12

Given the root node of a binary tree, one of the most common operation performed is visiting every node of the tree in some order. Similarly, given a vertex in a directed or undirected graph we may wish to visit all vertices in the graph that are reachable from this vertex. This can be done in two ways—using the Depth First Search and the Breadth First Search algorithm.

Depth First Search

Depth first search of an undirected graph proceeds as follows. The start vertex **v** is visited. Next an unvisited vertex **w** adjacent to **v** is selected and a depth first search from **w** is initiated. When a vertex **u** is reached such that all its adjacent vertices have been visited, we back up to the last vertex visited which has an unvisited vertex **w** adjacent to it and initiate a depth first search from **w**. The search terminates when no unvisited vertex can be reached from any of the visited ones. This procedure is best-described recursively and has been implemented in the program given below.

```c
/* Program 51 */
#include <stdlib.h>
#include <stdio.h>
#define TRUE 1
#define FALSE 0
#define MAX 8
int visited[ MAX ] ;
int q[ 8 ] ;
struct node
{
    int data ;
    struct node *next ;
} ;
struct node *newnode ;
void dfs ( int, struct node **, int ) ;
struct node * getnode_write ( int ) ;
int main( )
{
    struct node *arr[ MAX ] ;
    struct node * getnode_write ( int val ) ;
    struct node *v1, *v2, *v3, *v4 ;
    v1 = getnode_write ( 2 ) ;
    arr[ 0 ] = v1 ;
    v1 -> next = v2 = getnode_write ( 3 ) ;
    v2-> next = NULL ;
    v1 = getnode_write ( 1 ) ;
    arr[ 1 ] = v1 ;
    v1 -> next = v2 = getnode_write ( 4 ) ;
    v2 -> next = v3 = getnode_write ( 5 ) ;
    v3 -> next = NULL ;
    v1 = getnode_write ( 1 ) ;
    arr[ 2 ] = v1 ;
    v1 -> next = v2 = getnode_write ( 6 ) ;
    v2 -> next = v3 = getnode_write ( 7 ) ;
```

```
        v3 -> next = NULL ;
        v1 = getnode_write ( 2 ) ;
        arr[ 3 ] = v1 ;
        v1 -> next = v2 = getnode_write ( 8 ) ;
        v2 -> next = NULL ;
        v1 = getnode_write ( 2 ) ;
        arr[ 4 ] = v1 ;
        v1 -> next = v2 = getnode_write ( 8 ) ;
        v2 -> next = NULL ;
        v1 = getnode_write ( 3 ) ;
        arr[ 5 ] = v1 ;
        v1 -> next = v2 = getnode_write ( 8 ) ;
        v2 -> next = NULL ;
        v1 = getnode_write ( 3 ) ;
        arr[ 6 ] = v1 ;
        v1 -> next = v2 = getnode_write ( 8 ) ;
        v2 -> next = NULL ;
        v1 = getnode_write ( 4 ) ;
        arr[ 7 ] = v1 ;
        v1 -> next = v2 = getnode_write ( 5 ) ;
        v2 -> next = v3 = getnode_write ( 6 ) ;
        v3 -> next = v4 = getnode_write ( 7 ) ;
        v4 -> next = NULL ;
        dfs ( 1, arr, 8 ) ;
        return 0 ;
}
void dfs ( int v, struct node **p, int n )
{
        struct node *q ;
        visited [ v - 1 ] = TRUE ;
        printf ( " %d", v ) ;
        q = * ( p + v - 1 ) ;
        while ( q != NULL )
        {
            if ( visited [ q -> data - 1 ] == FALSE )
                dfs ( q -> data, p, n ) ;
            else
                q = q -> next ;
        }
}
struct node * getnode_write ( int val )
```

```
{
    newnode = ( struct node * ) malloc ( sizeof ( struct node ) ) ;
    newnode -> data = val ;
    return newnode ;
}
```

The graph **G** in Figure 5.13 (a) is represented by its adjacency lists shown in Figure 5.13 (b). If a depth first search is initiated from vertex **v1**, then the vertices of **G** are visited in the order: $v_1, v_2, v_4, v_8, v_5, v_6, v_3, v_7$.

Breadth First Search

Starting at vertex **v** and marking it as visited, breadth first search differs from depth first search in that all unvisited vertices adjacent to **v**, are visited next. Then unvisited vertices adjacent to these vertices are visited and so on. A breadth first search beginning at vertex v_1 of Figure 5.13 (a) would first visit v_1 and then v_2 and v_3. Next vertices v_4, v_5, v_6 and v_7 will be visited and finally v_8.

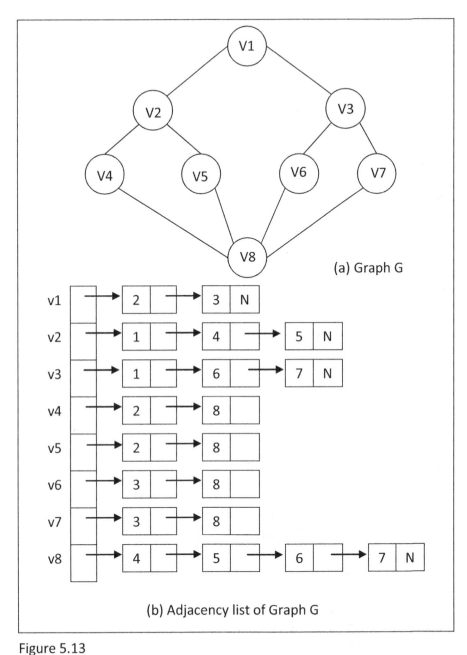

(a) Graph G

(b) Adjacency list of Graph G

Figure 5.13

The following program implements this algorithm.

```
/* Program 52 */
#include <stdlib.h>
#include <stdio.h>
#define TRUE 1
#define FALSE 0
```

```
#define MAX 8
struct node
{
    int data ;
    struct node *next ;
} ;
struct node *newnode ;
void bfs ( int, struct node **, int ) ;
struct node * getnode_write ( int ) ;
void addqueue ( int ) ;
int deletequeue( ) ;
int isempty( ) ;
int visited [ MAX ] ;
int q[ 8 ] ;
int front, rear ;
int main( )
{
    struct node *arr[ MAX] ;
    struct node *getnode_write ( int val ) ;
    struct node *v1, *v2, *v3, *v4 ;
    v1 = getnode_write ( 2 ) ;
    arr[ 0 ] = v1 ;
    v1 -> next = v2 = getnode_write ( 3 ) ;
    v2 -> next = NULL ;
    v1 = getnode_write ( 1 ) ;
    arr[ 1 ]  = v1 ;
    v1 -> next = v2 = getnode_write ( 4 ) ;
    v2 -> next = v3 = getnode_write ( 5 ) ;
    v3 -> next = NULL ;
    v1 = getnode_write ( 1 ) ;
    arr[ 2 ] = v1 ;
    v1 -> next = v2 = getnode_write ( 6 ) ;
    v2 -> next = v3 = getnode_write ( 7 ) ;
    v3 -> next = NULL ;
    v1 = getnode_write ( 2 ) ;
    arr[ 3 ] = v1 ;
    v1 -> next = v2 = getnode_write ( 8 ) ;
    v2 -> next = NULL ;
    v1 = getnode_write ( 2 ) ;
    arr[ 4 ] = v1 ;
    v1 -> next = v2 = getnode_write ( 8 ) ;
```

```
        v2 -> next = NULL ;
        v1 = getnode_write ( 3 ) ;
        arr[ 5 ] = v1 ;
        v1 -> next = v2 = getnode_write ( 8 ) ;
        v2 -> next = NULL ;
        v1 = getnode_write ( 3 ) ;
        arr[ 6 ] = v1 ;
        v1 -> next = v2 = getnode_write ( 8 ) ;
        v2 -> next = NULL ;
        v1 = getnode_write ( 4 ) ;
        arr[ 7 ] = v1 ;
        v1 -> next = v2 = getnode_write ( 5 ) ;
        v2 -> next = v3 = getnode_write ( 6 ) ;
        v3 -> next = v4 = getnode_write ( 7 ) ;
        v4 -> next = NULL ;
        front = rear = -1 ;
        bfs ( 1, arr, 8 ) ;
        return 0 ;
}
void bfs ( int v, struct node **p, int n )
{
        struct node *u ;
        visited [ v - 1 ] = TRUE ;
        printf ( " %d", v ) ;
        addqueue ( v ) ;
        while ( isempty( ) == FALSE )
        {
                v = deletequeue( ) ;
                u = * ( p + v - 1 ) ;
                while ( u != NULL )
                {
                        if ( visited [ u -> data - 1 ] == FALSE )
                        {
                                addqueue ( u -> data ) ;
                                visited [ u -> data - 1 ] = TRUE ;
                                printf ( " %d", u -> data ) ;
                        }
                        u = u -> next ;
                }
        }
}
```

```
struct node * getnode_write ( int val )
{
    newnode = ( struct node * ) malloc ( sizeof ( struct node ) ) ;
    newnode -> data = val ;
    return newnode ;
}
void addqueue ( int vertex )
{
    if ( rear == MAX - 1)
    {
        printf ( "Queue Overflow\n" ) ;
        exit ( 0 ) ;
    }
    rear++ ;
    q[ rear ] = vertex ;
    if ( front == -1 )
        front = 0 ;
}
int deletequeue( )
{
    int data ;
    if ( front == -1 )
    {
        printf ( "Queue Underflow\n" ) ;
        exit ( 0 ) ;
    }
    data = q[ front ] ;
    if ( front == rear )
        front = rear = -1 ;
    else
        front++ ;
    return data ;
}
int isempty( )
{
    if ( front == -1 )
        return TRUE ;
    return FALSE ;
}
```

Solved Problems

[A] What will be the output of the following programs:

(1) #include <stdlib.h>
     #include <stdio.h>
     int main( )
     {
         struct node
         {
             int data ;
             struct node *link ;
         } ;
         struct node *p, *q ;
         p = (struct node *) malloc (sizeof (struct node)) ;
         q = (struct node *) malloc (sizeof (struct node)) ;
         printf ("%d %d\n", sizeof (p), sizeof (q)) ;
         return 0 ;
     }

Output

4 4

Explanation

p and **q** have been declared as pointers to structures of the type **struct node**. In the next statement we come across **malloc( )**, which is a standard library function. It reserves as many locations in memory as its argument specifies. Unlike arrays, which put aside a fixed number of bytes specified at the time of declaration, **malloc( )** can be given a variable as an argument, thus allowing flexibility in the size of memory to be allocated.

The **struct node** engages four bytes for **data** and four for **link**, hence the size of **struct node** is 8. Therefore when the calls to **malloc( )** are made, the argument that is passed is 8. Hence each time, **malloc( )** reserves 8 bytes in memory. These bytes would always be in contiguous memory locations. Having successfully reserved the bytes, **malloc( )** returns the base address of these 8 bytes. The base address returned during the first call to **malloc( )** is collected in **p** and the one returned during the second call, in **q**. As **p** and **q** are both 4-byte addresses, saying **sizeof (p)** and **sizeof (q)** results in 4 and 4 being outputted.

(2)
```
#include <stdio.h>
#include <stdlib.h>
int main( )
{
    struct node
    {
        int data ;
        struct node *link ;
    } ;
    struct node *p, *q ;
    p = ( struct node * ) malloc ( sizeof ( struct node ) ) ;
    q = ( struct node * ) malloc ( sizeof ( struct node ) ) ;
    p -> data = 30 ;
    p -> link = q ;
    q -> data = 40 ;
    q -> link = NULL ;
    printf ( "%d\n", p -> data ) ;
    p = p -> link ;
    printf ( "%d\n", p -> data ) ;
    return 0 ;
}
```

Output

30
40

Explanation

p and **q** are returned the starting addresses of two slots of memory allocated by the two **malloc( )**s for structures of the type **struct node**. When we say **p -> data**, we are referring to the first four bytes starting from the address in **p**, where 30 is assigned. In **p -> link** is stored the address present in **q**, which is the base address of the area of memory allocated by the second **malloc( )**. In the structure starting from address contained in **q**, 40 and NULL are stored. NULL is defined as 0 in the file 'stdlib.h'. On printing **p -> data**, we find the 30 stored there. Now we change the contents of **p**

to **p** -> **link**, so that **p** is now equal to **q**. Thus **p** -> **data** now evaluates to 40, and on printing the same this time we get 40.

The arrangement of the data types in this problem conforms to the popular 'linked list' data structure. This arrangement is shown in Figure 5.14, where the arrow represents the pointer to the next node.

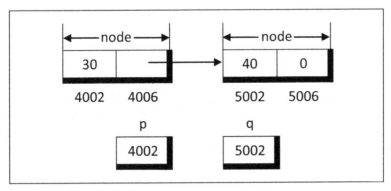

Figure 5.14

(3) ```
#include <stdlib.h>
#include <stdio.h>
int main( )
{
    struct node
    {
        struct node *previous ;
        int data ;
        struct node *next ;
    } ;
    struct node *p, *q ;
    p = (struct node *) malloc (sizeof (struct node)) ;
    q = (struct node *) malloc (sizeof (struct node)) ;
    p -> data = 75 ;
    q -> data = 90 ;
    p -> previous = NULL ;
    p -> next = q ;
    q -> previous = p ;
    q -> next = NULL ;
    while (p != NULL)
    {
        printf ("%d\n", p -> data) ;
        p = p -> next ;
```
```

```
    }
    return 0 ;
}
```

Output

75
90

Explanation

The structure comprises of an integer **data** and two **struct** pointers, **previous** and **next**. The in **malloc( )**s allocate 2 blocks of memory starting at addresses 4002 and 5002 as per Figure 5.15. The whole arrangement can be thought of as a chain of 2 structures. As the variable names suggest, **previous** of **p**, assigned NULL, indicates there is no structure prior to the one at **p**. **next** of **p** stores the address of the structure at **q**. Similarly, **previous** of **q** points to the structure preceding it in the chain, which is present at **p**, and **next** of **q** is assigned NULL, signifying that there are no more structures after the one at **q**. This arrangement is nothing but a 'doubly linked list'.

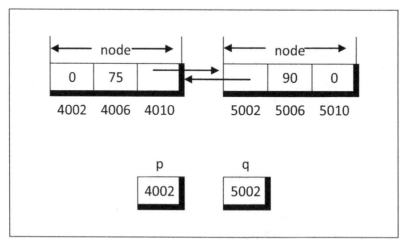

Figure 5.15

The body of the **while** loop is executed subject to the condition that **p** is not equal to NULL, i.e. 0. Since **p** contains 4002, this condition is satisfied for the first time, hence **p -> data**, which is 75, gets outputted. Next **p** is assigned **p -> next**, which is equal to 5002. This is as good as shifting **p** so that it now points to the next node. Since

p now contains 5002, the condition in the loop would once again be satisfied, and this time around the **printf( )** prints out 90. In the next statement, **p -> next** is assigned to **p**. But this time **p -> next** contains 0 (NULL), so **p** is assigned the value 0. The condition in **while** now fails, and the program is terminated.

(4)   #include <stdlib.h>
      #include <stdio.h>
      int main( )
      {
            struct node
            {
                  int data ;
                  struct node *next ;
            } ;
            struct node *p, *q ;
            p = (struct node *) malloc (sizeof (struct node)) ;
            q = (struct node *) malloc (sizeof (struct node)) ;
            p -> data =10 ;
            q -> data = 20 ;
            p -> next = q ;
            q -> next = p ;
            while (p != NULL)
            {
                  printf ("%d\n", p -> data) ;
                  p = p -> next ;
            }
            return 0 ;
      }

Output

10
20
10
20
10
20
...
...
...

Explanation

p and q are declared as pointers to structures of the type **struct node**. With the use of **malloc( )**, two areas in memory, each of the same size as that of **struct node** are reserved, p and q collect the starting addresses of these areas. According to Figure 5.16, these addresses are 4002 and 5002. Now 10 and 20 are assigned to the **data** parts within the two structures. Next, **p -> next** is assigned the contents of **q**, i.e. the address 5002, and **q -> next** is assigned the contents of **p**, which is the address 4002.

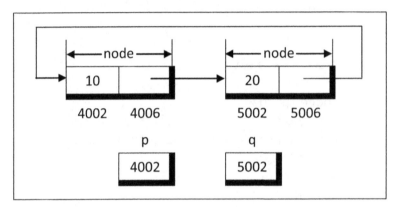

Figure 5.16

The **while** checks the contents of **p** for its execution. The first time since the condition is satisfied, **p -> data**, which is 10, gets printed. Now **p** is assigned **p -> next**, which is 5002. Thus **p** now points to the second structure. Hence the condition in **while** gets satisfied, and so this time **p -> data** yields 20. After this **p** is assigned the value of **p -> next**. Since **p** right now contains 5002, **p -> next** this time turns out to be 4002 (refer figure). Thus **p** is assigned the address 4002, and **p** now points to the first structure. The integer **data** within the first structure stores 10, which again gets printed when the **printf( )** is executed. Once again the address 5002 is assigned to **p** through the statement **p = p -> next**. Thus contents of **p** toggle between 4002 and 5002. And since **p** never becomes NULL, defined earlier as 0, the loop is an indefinite one.

[B] Attempt the following:

(1) Write a program to erase all the nodes of a linked list.

Program

```
/* Program to erase all nodes present in a linked list */
#include <stdlib.h>
#include <stdio.h>
struct node
{
    int data ;
    struct node *link ;
} ;
void append ( struct node **, int ) ;
void display ( struct node * ) ;
int count ( struct node * ) ;
struct node *erase ( struct node * ) ;
int main( )
{
    struct node *first ;
    first = NULL ;
    append ( &first, 0 ) ;
    append ( &first, 1 ) ;
    append ( &first, 2 ) ;
    append ( &first, 3 ) ;
    append ( &first, 4 ) ;
    append ( &first, 5 ) ;
    display ( first ) ;
    printf ( "\nNo. of elements in Linked List before erasing = %d\n",
                count ( first ) ) ;
    first = erase ( first ) ;
    printf ( "\nNo. of elements in Linked List after erasing = %d\n",
                count ( first ) ) ;
    return 0 ;
}

/* adds a node at the end of a linked list */
void append ( struct node **q, int num )
{
    struct node *temp ;
    temp = *q ;
    if ( *q == NULL )     /* if the list is empty, create first node */
    {
        *q = ( struct node * ) malloc ( sizeof ( struct node ) ) ;
        temp = *q ;
    }
```

```
        else
        {
            /* go to last node */
            while ( temp -> link != NULL )
                temp = temp -> link ;

            /* add node at the end */
            temp -> link = ( struct node * ) malloc ( sizeof ( struct node ) )
            ;
            temp = temp -> link ;
        }
        /* assign data to the last node */
        temp -> data = num ;
        temp -> link = NULL ;
    }

    /* displays the contents of the linked list */
    void display ( struct node *q )
    {
        printf ( "\n" ) ;
        /*traverse the entire linked list */
        while ( q != NULL )
        {
            printf ( "%d ", q -> data ) ;
            q = q -> link ;
        }
    }

    /* counts the number of nodes present in the linked list */
    int count ( struct node *q )
    {
        int c = 0 ;
        /* traverse the entire linked list */
        while ( q != NULL )
        {
            q = q -> link ;
            c++ ;
        }
        return c ;
    }
```

```
/* erases all the nodes from a linked list */
struct node *erase ( struct node *q )
{
    struct node *temp ;
    /* traverse till the end erasing each node */
    while ( q != NULL )
    {
        temp = q ;
        q = q -> link ;
        free ( temp ) ;   /* free the memory occupied by the node */
    }
    return NULL ;
}
```

(2) Write a program to find number of nodes in a linked list using recursion.

Program

```
/* Program to find the number of nodes in the linked list
        using recursion */
#include <stdlib.h>
#include <stdio.h>
struct node
{
    int data ;
    struct node *link ;
} ;
void append ( struct node **, int ) ;
int length ( struct node * ) ;
int main( )
{
    struct node *p ;
    p = NULL ;  /* empty linked list*/
    append ( &p, 1 ) ;
    append ( &p, 2 ) ;
    append ( &p, 3 ) ;
    append ( &p, 4 ) ;
    append ( &p, 5 ) ;
    printf ( "Length of linked list = %d\n", length ( p ) ) ;
    return 0 ;
}
```

```c
/* adds a node at the end of a linked list */
void append ( struct node **q, int num )
{
    struct node *temp ;
    temp = *q ;
    if ( *q == NULL ) /* if the list is empty, create first node */
    {
        *q = ( struct node * ) malloc ( sizeof ( struct node ) ) ;
        temp = *q ;
    }
    else
    {
        /* go to last node */
        while ( temp -> link != NULL )
            temp = temp -> link ;
        /* add node at the end */
        temp -> link = ( struct node * ) malloc ( sizeof ( struct node ));
        temp = temp -> link ;
    }
    /* assign data to the last node */
    temp -> data = num ;
    temp -> link = NULL ;
}

/* counts the number of nodes in a linked list */
int length ( struct node *q )
{
    static int l ;
    /* if list is empty or if NULL is encountered */
    if ( q == NULL )
        return ( 0 ) ;
    else
    {
        /* go to next node */
        l = 1 + length ( q -> link ) ;
        return ( l ) ;
    }
}
```

(3) Write a program to compare two linked lists using recursion

Program

```c
/* Program to compare two linked lists using recursion */
#include <stdlib.h>
#include <stdio.h>
struct node
{
    int data ;
    struct node *link ;
} ;
void append ( struct node **, int ) ;
int compare ( struct node *, struct node * ) ;
int main( )
{
    struct node *first, *second ;
    first = second = NULL ; /* empty linked lists */
    append ( &first, 1 ) ;
    append ( &first, 2 ) ;
    append ( &first, 3 ) ;
    append ( &second, 1 ) ;
    append ( &second, 2 ) ;
    append ( &second, 3 ) ;
    if ( compare ( first, second ) )
        printf ( "Both linked lists are EQUAL" ) ;
    else
        printf ( "Linked lists are DIFFERENT" ) ;
    return 0 ;
}

/* adds a node at the end of a linked list */
void append ( struct node **q, int num )
{
    struct node *temp ;
    temp = *q ;
    if ( *q == NULL )    /* if the list is empty, create first node */
    {
        *q = ( struct node * ) malloc ( sizeof ( struct node ) ) ;
        temp = *q ;
    }
    else
```

```
    {
        /* go to last node */
        while ( temp -> link != NULL )
            temp = temp -> link ;
        /* add node at the end */
        temp -> link = ( struct node * ) malloc( sizeof ( struct node )) ;
        temp = temp -> link ;
    }
    /* assign data to the last node */
    temp -> data = num ;
    temp -> link = NULL ;
}

/* compares 2 linked lists, returns 1 if equal and 0 if unequal */
int compare ( struct node *q, struct node *r )
{
    static int flag ;
    if ( ( q == NULL ) && ( r == NULL ) )
        flag = 1 ;
    else
    {
        if (q == NULL || r == NULL )
            flag = 0 ;
        if ( q-> data != r -> data )
            flag = 0 ;
        else
            compare ( q -> link, r -> link ) ;
    }
    return ( flag ) ;
}
```

(4) Write a program to copy one linked list into another using recursion.

Program

```
/* Program to copy one linked list into another using recursion */
#include <stdlib.h>
#include <stdio.h>
/* structure containing a data part and link part */
struct node
{
```

```
            int data ;
            struct node *link ;
        } ;
        void append ( struct node **, int ) ;
        void copy ( struct node *, struct node ** ) ;
        void display ( struct node * ) ;
        int main( )
        {
            struct node *first, *second ;
            first = second = NULL ; /* empty linked lists */
            append ( &first, 1 ) ;
            append ( &first, 2 ) ;
            append ( &first, 3 ) ;
            append ( &first, 4 ) ;
            append ( &first, 5 ) ;
            append ( &first, 6 ) ;
            append ( &first, 7 ) ;
            display ( first ) ;
            copy ( first, &second ) ;
            display ( second ) ;
            return 0 ;
        }

        /* adds a node at the end of the linked list */
        void append ( struct node **q, int num )
        {
            struct node *temp ;
            temp = *q ;
            if ( *q == NULL )    /* if the list is empty, create first node */
            {
                *q = ( struct node * ) malloc ( sizeof ( struct node ) ) ;
                temp = *q ;
            }
            else
            {
                /* go to last node */
                while ( temp -> link != NULL)
                    temp = temp -> link ;
                /* add node at the end */
                temp -> link = ( struct node * ) malloc( sizeof ( struct node ) );
                temp = temp -> link ;
```

```
        }

        /* assign data to the last node */
        temp -> data = num ;
        temp -> link = NULL ;
    }

    /* copies a linked list into another */
    void copy ( struct node *q, struct node **s )
    {
        if ( q != NULL )
        {
            *s = ( struct node * ) malloc ( sizeof ( struct node ) ) ;
            ( *s ) -> data = q -> data ;
            ( *s ) -> link = NULL ;
            copy ( q -> link, &( ( *s ) -> link ) ) ;
        }
    }

    /* displays the contents of the linked list */
    void display ( struct node *q )
    {
        printf ( "\n" ) ;
        /* traverse the entire linked list */
        while ( q != NULL )
        {
            printf ( "%d ", q -> data ) ;
            q = q -> link ;
        }
    }
```

(5)   Using recursion write a program to add a new node at the end of the linked list.

Program

```
/* Program to add a new node at the end of linked list using
    recursion*/
#include <stdlib.h>
#include <stdio.h>
struct node
{
```

```
    int data ;
    struct node *link ;
} ;
void addatend ( struct node **, int ) ;
void display ( struct node * ) ;
int main( )
{
    struct node *p ;
    p = NULL ;
    addatend ( &p, 1 ) ;
    addatend ( &p, 2 ) ;
    addatend ( &p, 3 ) ;
    addatend ( &p, 4 ) ;
    addatend ( &p, 5 ) ;
    addatend ( &p, 6 ) ;
    addatend ( &p, 10 ) ;
    display ( p ) ;
    return 0 ;
}

/* adds a new node at the end of the linked list */
void addatend ( struct node **s, int num )
{
    if ( *s == NULL )
    {
        *s = ( struct node * ) malloc ( sizeof ( struct node ) ) ;
        ( *s ) -> data = num ;
        ( *s ) -> link = NULL ;
    }
    else
        addatend ( &( ( *s ) -> link ), num ) ;
}

/* displays the contents of the linked list */
void display ( struct node *q )
{
    printf ( "\n" ) ;
    /* traverse the entire linked list */
    while ( q != NULL )
    {
        printf ( "%d ", q -> data ) ;
```

```
            q = q -> link ;
        }
    }

(6) Write a program to traverse a binary tree using inorder traversal
    method without using recursion.
```

Program

```
/* Program to traverse a binary search tree using inorder
        traversal without recursion */
#include <stdlib.h>
#include <stdio.h>
#define MAX 10
struct btreenode
{
    struct btreenode *leftchild ;
    int data ;
    struct btreenode *rightchild ;
} ;
void insert ( struct btreenode **, int ) ;
void inorder ( struct btreenode * ) ;
int main( )
{
    struct btreenode *bt ;
    int req, i = 1, num ;
    bt = NULL ; /* empty tree */
    printf ( "Specify the number of data to be inserted : " ) ;
    scanf ( "%d", &req ) ;
    while ( i++ <= req )
    {
        printf ( "Enter the data :\n" ) ;
        scanf ( "%d", &num ) ;
        insert ( &bt, num ) ;
    }
    inorder ( bt ) ;
    return 0 ;
}

/* inserts a new node in a binary search tree */
void insert ( struct btreenode **sr, int num )
{
```

```
        if ( *sr == NULL )
        {
            *sr = (struct btreenode *)malloc( sizeof ( struct btreenode )) ;
            ( *sr ) -> leftchild =  NULL ;
            ( *sr ) -> data = num ;
            ( *sr ) -> rightchild = NULL ;
            return ;
        }
        else   /* search the node to which new node will be attached */
        {
            /* if new data is less, traverse to left */
            if ( num < ( *sr ) -> data )
                insert ( &( ( *sr ) -> leftchild ), num ) ;
            else
                /* else traverse to right */
                insert ( &( ( *sr ) -> rightchild ), num ) ;
        }
        return ;
    }

    /* traverses a binary search tree in a LDR fashion */
    void inorder ( struct btreenode *currentnode )
    {
        int top = 0 ;
        struct btreenode *nodestack[ MAX ] ;
        while ( 1 )
        {
            while ( currentnode != NULL )
            {
                top++ ;

                if ( top > MAX )
                {
                    printf ( "stack is full.....\n" ) ;
                    exit ( 0 ) ;
                }
                else
                {
                    /* remembers the previous nodes whose right side is
                        yet to be traversed */
                    nodestack[top] = currentnode ;
```

```
                    currentnode = currentnode -> leftchild ;
                }
            }
            /* pop previous nodes one by one */
            if ( top != 0 )
            {
                currentnode = nodestack[top] ;
                top-- ;

                /* print the data field */
                printf ( "%d ", currentnode -> data ) ;
                currentnode = currentnode -> rightchild ;
            }
            else
                break ;
        }
    }
```

(7) Write a program to swap the contents of a binary tree.

Program

```
/* Program to swap a binary tree */
#include <stdlib.h>
#include <stdio.h>
void insert ( struct btreenode **, int ) ;
void inorder ( struct btreenode * ) ;
void swap ( struct btreenode ** ) ;
struct btreenode
{
    struct btreenode *leftchild ;
    int data ;
    struct btreenode *rightchild ;
} ;
int main( )
{
    struct btreenode *bt ;
    int req, i = 1, num ;
    bt = NULL ; /* empty tree*/
    printf ( "Specify the number of data items to be inserted: " ) ;
    scanf ( "%d", &req ) ;
    while ( i++ <= req )
```

```
    {
        printf ( "Enter the data:\n" ) ;
        scanf ( "%d", &num ) ;
        insert ( &bt, num ) ;
    }
    printf ( "Inorder Traversal before swapping:\n" ) ;
    inorder ( bt ) ;
    swap ( &bt ) ;
    printf ( "\nInorder Traversal after swapping:\n" ) ;
    inorder ( bt ) ;
    return 0 ;
}

/* inserts a new node in a binary search tree */
void insert ( struct btreenode **sr, int num )
{
    if ( *sr == NULL )
    {
        *sr = (struct btreenode *)malloc( sizeof ( struct btreenode ) );
        ( *sr ) -> leftchild = NULL ;
        ( *sr ) -> data = num ;
        ( *sr ) -> rightchild = NULL ;
        return ;
    }
    else
    /* search the node to which new node will be attached */
    {
        /* if new data is less, traverse to left */
        if ( num < ( *sr ) -> data )
            insert ( &( ( *sr ) -> leftchild ), num ) ;
        else
            insert ( &( ( *sr ) -> rightchild ), num ) ;
    }
}

/* traverse a binary search tree in a LDR (Left-Data-Right} fashion*/
void inorder ( struct btreenode *sr )
{
    if ( sr != NULL )
    {
        inorder ( sr -> leftchild ) ;
```

```
            /* print the data of the node whose leftchild is NULL or the
            path has already been traversed */
            printf ( "%d ", sr -> data ) ;
            inorder ( sr -> rightchild ) ;
        }
        else
            return ;
    }

    void swap ( struct btreenode **sr )
    {
        struct btreenode *tmp ;
        if ( *sr != NULL )
        {
            /* swap both childs */
            tmp = ( *sr ) -> leftchild ;
            ( *sr ) -> leftchild = ( *sr ) -> rightchild ;
            ( *sr ) -> rightchild = tmp ;
            swap ( &( ( *sr ) -> leftchild ) ) ;
            swap ( &( ( *sr ) -> rightchild ) ) ;
        }
        else
            return ;
    }
```

Exercise

[A] Attempt the following:

(1) Write a program for adding and deleting nodes from an ascending order linked list.

(2) Suppose we have two linked lists pointed to by two independent pointers. Write a program to merge the two lists into a third list. Ensure that those elements which are common to both the lists occur only once in the third list.

(3) Write a program that reverses the links in the existing linked list such that the last node becomes the first node and the first becomes the last.

(4) A double-ended queue or a deque is a queue in which elements can be added or deleted from both the ends i.e. front and rear. Write a program to implement a deque as a linked list.

(5) Polynomials like $5x^4+2x^3+7x^2+10x-8$ can be maintained using a linked list. To achieve this each node should consist of three elements, namely coefficient, exponent and a link to the next term. Write a program that maintains two linked lists for two polynomials and then adds the two polynomials. Result of addition should be stored in a third linked list.

(6) Write a program that maintains two linked lists for two polynomials and then multiplies the two polynomials. Result of multiplication should be stored in a third linked list.

(7) Write a program to maintain a doubly linked list.

(8) Write a program to implement stack as a circular linked list. In a circular linked list the last node's link points to the first node.

(9) Write a program to implement a doubly linked list as a circular linked list.

(10) Write a program to traverse a binary tree using preorder traversal method without using recursion.

(11) Write a program to traverse a binary tree using postorder traversal method without using recursion.

(12) Write a program to copy a binary search tree using recursion.

(13) Write a program to compare two binary search trees using recursion.

(14) Write a function to insert a node **t** as a left child of **s** in a threaded binary tree.

Understanding
Pointers in
C & C++

Pointers
Miscellany

*In principle one can write C programs without
using any of the miscellaneous features of
pointers. But once you know their utility you are
likely to get hooked on to them. So read on...*

For those of you who have reached this far, it's time to exploit the immense potential of pointers. We wouldn't be able to do so unless we know things like file pointers, far, near & huge pointers, pointers to functions, pointers and variable number of arguments etc. In this chapter we intend to look at these and a few more miscellaneous topics. Let's begin with file pointers.

File Pointers

Consider the following program. It opens a file, reads it character by character till the time its end is not encountered. On reaching the end of file, the file is closed and the count of characters present in it is printed.

```
/* Program 53 */
/* Count chars */
# include <stdio.h>
int main( )
{
    FILE *fp ;
    char ch ;
    int nol, noc = 0 ;
    fp = fopen ( "PR1.C", "r" ) ;
    while ( 1 )
    {
        ch = fgetc ( fp ) ;
        if ( ch == EOF )
            break ;
        noc++ ;
        if ( ch == EOF )
            break ;
        noc++;
    }
    fclose ( fp ) ;
    printf ( "Number of characters = %d\n", noc ) ;
    return 0 ;
}
```

Here is a sample run...

Number of characters = 125

What is **fp** in our program? Most of the time it is known as a file pointer. However, it is actually a pointer to a structure. This structure has been

typedefed into **FILE** in the header file **stdio.h**. This structure is shown below:

```
struct _iobuf
{
    char * _ptr ;
    int  _cnt ;
    char * _base ;
    int  _flag ;
    int  _file ;
    int  _charbuf ;
    int  _bufsiz ;
    char * _tmpfname ;
} ;
typedef struct _iobuf FILE ;
```

When we open a file for reading two things happen:

(a)   The contents of the file are loaded into buffer.

(b)   A **FILE** structure is created in memory, its elements are setup and address of this structure is returned.

This address we have collected in **fp**. Thus, **fp** is not pointing to the file's buffer. Within the structure to which **fp** is pointing there is a character pointer called **_ptr**. It is this pointer which is pointing to the buffer. This arrangement is shown in Figure 6.1.

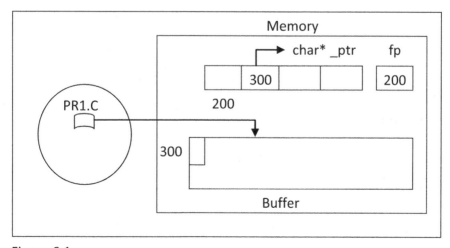

Figure 6.1

When we read a character from the file using **getc( )** we need to pass the file pointer **fp** to it. Why? Because **getc( )** must know from which file should it do the reading. Also, on reading a character using **getc( )** we never have to increment the pointer pointing to the buffer. This is because **getc( )** does this for us. Assuming that the file pointer **fp** that we have passed to **getc( )** is collected by **getc( )** in say **p**, then to increment the buffer pointer **getc( )** internally must be doing an operation of the from **p -> _ptr = p -> _ptr + 1**.

When we close the file using **fclose( )** the buffer associated with the file is freed along with the structure being pointed to by **fp**.

The above discussion is also relevant for a file opened for writing.

Pointers to Functions

Every type of variable, with the exception of register, has an address. We have seen how we can reference variables of type **char, int, float** etc. through their addresses—that is by using pointers. Pointers can also point to C functions. And why not? C functions have addresses. If we know the function's address we can point to it, which provides another way to invoke it. Let us see how this can be done.

```
/* Program 54 */
/* Demo to get address of a function */
#include <stdio.h>
int main( )
{
    int display( ) ;
    printf ( "Address of function display is %u\n", display ) ;
    display( ) ;  /* usual way of invoking  a function */
    return 0 ;
}
int display( )
{
    printf ( "Long live viruses!!\n" ) ;
    return 0 ;
}
```

The output of the program would be:

Address of function display is 1125
Long live viruses!!

Note that to obtain the address of a function all that we have to do is to mention the name of the function, as has been done in the **printf( )** statement above. This is similar to mentioning the name of the array to get its base address.

Now let us see how using the address of a function we can manage to invoke it. This is shown in the program given below:

```
/* Program 55 */
/* Invoking function using pointer to a function */
#include <stdio.h>
int main( )
{
    int display( ) ;
    int ( *func_ptr )( ) ;
    func_ptr = display ;     /* assign address of function */
    printf ( "Address of function display is %u\n", func_ptr ) ;
    ( *func_ptr )( ) ;     /* invokes the function display( ) */
    return 0 ;
}
int display( )
{
    printf ( "Long live viruses!!\n" ) ;
    return 0 ;
}
```

The output of the program would be:

Address of function display is 1125
Long live viruses!!

In **main( )** we have declared the function **display( )** as a function returning an **int**. But what are we to make of the declaration,

int (*func_ptr)( ) ;

that comes in the next line? We are obviously declaring something which, like **display( )**, will return an **int**. But what is it? And why is ***func_ptr** enclosed in parentheses?

If we glance down a few lines in our program, we see the statement,

func_ptr = display ;

So we know that **func_ptr** is being assigned the address of **display( )**. Therefore, **func_ptr** must be a pointer to the function **display( )**.

Thus, all that the declaration

int (*func_ptr)( ) ;

means is, that **func_ptr** is a pointer to a function, which returns an **int**. And to invoke the function we are just required to write the statement,

(*fun_ptr)( ) ;

Instead of this, we can also make the call to the function by simply saying,

fun_ptr( ) ;

Pointers to functions are certainly awkward and off-putting. And why use them at all when we can invoke a function in a much simpler manner? What is the possible gain of using this esoteric feature of C? There are several possible uses:

(a)   in writing device driver programs
(b)   in Windows programming to connect events to functions

These topics form interesting and powerful applications and would call for separate books on each if full justice is to be given to them. Much as I would have liked to, for want of space I would have to exclude these topics.

typedef with Function Pointers

We know that **typedef** is used to give convenient names to complicated datatypes. It is immensely useful when using pointers to functions. Given below are a few examples of its usage.

(1)   typedef int (*funcptr)( ) ;
       funcptr fptr ;

      fptr is a pointer to a function returning an **int**.

(2)   typedef int (*fret_int)(char *, char *) ;
       fret_int fri1, fri2 ;

fri1 and **fri2** are pointers to function that accepts two **char** pointers and returns an **int.**

(3) typedef void (*complex)( ) ;
complex c ;

c is a pointer to a function that doesn't accept any parameter and doesn't return anything.

(4) typedef char (* (* frpapfrc( )) [ ]) ( ) ;
frpapfrc f ;

f is a function returning a pointer to an array of pointers to functions returning a **char.**

(5) typedef int (* (*arr2d_ptr)( )) [3][4] ;
arr2d_ptr p ;

p is a pointer to a function returning a pointer to a 2-D **int** array.

(6) typedef int (* (* (* ptr2d_fptr)( )) [10])( ) ;
ptr2d_fptr p ;

p is a pointer to a function returning a pointer to an array   of 10 pointers to function returning an **int.**

(7) typedef char (* (* arr_fptr[3])( )) [10] ;
arr_fptr x ;

x is an array of 3 pointers to function returning a pointer to an array of 10 **chars**.

(8) typedef float* (* (* (* ptr_fptr)( )) [10])( ) ;
ptr_fptr q ;

q is a pointer to function returning a pointer to an array of 10 pointers to functions returning a **float** pointer.

argc and *argv*—Arguments to *main( )*

Can we not pass arguments to **main( )** the way we pass them to other functions? We can. For this we specify the arguments at command prompt when we execute the program. For example, suppose 'PR1.EXE' is the name of the executable file, and we wish to pass the arguments

'Cat', 'Dog' and 'Parrot' to **main( )** in this lie. We can do so through the following command at the command prompt:

C> PR1.EXE Cat Dog Parrot

Now if we are passing arguments to **main( )**, it must collect them in variables. Usually only two variables are used to collect these arguments. These are called **argc** and **argv**. Of these, **argc** contains the count (number) of arguments being passed to **main( )**, whereas **argv** contains addresses of strings passed to **main( )**. In the above example **argc** would contain 4, whereas **argv[0]**, **argv[1]**, **argv[2]**, and **argv[3]** would contain base addresses of PR1.EXE, Cat, Dog and Parrot respectively. If we so desire we can print these arguments from within **main( )** as shown in the following program.

```
/* Program 56 */
#include <stdio.h>
int main ( int argc, char *argv[ ] )
{
    int i ;
    for ( i = 0 ; i < argc ; i++ )
        printf ( "%s\n", argv[i] ) ;
    return 0 ;
}
```

Note the declaration of **argv[ ]**. It has been declared as an array of pointers to strings. Also observe the format specification used in **printf( )**. We are using **%s** because we wish to print out the various strings that are being passed to **main( )**.

It is not necessary that we should always use the variable names **argc** and **argv**. In place of them any other variable names can as well be used.

Pointers and Variable Number of Arguments

We use **printf( )** so often without realising how it works correctly irrespective of how many arguments we pass to it. How do we go about writing such routines, which can take variable number of arguments? And what have pointers got to do with it? There are three macros available in the file "stdarg.h" called **va_start, va_arg** and **va_list**, which allow us to handle this situation. These macros provide a method for accessing the arguments of the function when a function takes a fixed number of arguments followed by a variable number of arguments. The fixed number of arguments are accessed in the normal way, whereas the optional arguments are accessed using the macros **va_start** and **va_arg**. Out of these macros **va_start** is used to initialise a pointer to the beginning of the list of optional arguments. On the other hand the macro **va_arg** is used to advance the pointer to the next argument. Let us put these concepts into action using a program. Suppose we wish to write a function **findmax( )** which would find out the maximum value from a set of values, irrespective of the number of values passed to it.

```
/* Program 57 */
#include <stdio.h>
#Include <stdarg.h>
int findmax ( int, ... ) ;
int main( )
{
    int max ;
    max = findmax ( 5, 23, 15, 1, 92, 50 ) ;
    printf ( "Max = %d\n", max ) ;
    max = findmax ( 3, 100, 300, 29 ) ;
    printf ( "Max = %d\n", max ) ;
    return 0 ;
}
int findmax ( int tot_num, ... )
{
    int max, count, num ;
    va_list ptr ;
    va_start ( ptr, tot_num ) ;
    ax = va_arg ( ptr, int ) ;
    for ( count = 1 ; count < tot_num ; count++ )
    {
        num = va_arg ( ptr, int ) ;
        if ( num > max )
            max = num ;
    }
    return ( max ) ;
}
```

Here we are making two calls to **findmax( )** first time to find maximum out of 5 values and second time to find maximum out of 3 values. Note that for each call the first argument is the count of arguments that are being passed after the first argument. The value of the first argument passed to **findmax( )** is collected in the variable **tot_num**. **findmax( )**

begins with a declaration of pointer ptr of the type **va_list**. Observe the next statement carefully:

va_start (ptr, tot_num) ;

This statement sets up **ptr** such that it points to the first variable argument in the list. If we are considering the first call to **findmax()**, **ptr** would now point to 23. The next statement **max = va_arg (ptr, int)** would assign the integer being pointed to by **ptr** to **max**. Thus 23 would be assigned to **max**, and **ptr** would now start pointing to the next argument i.e., 15. The rest of the program is fairly straightforward. We just keep picking up successive numbers in the list and keep comparing them with the latest value in **max**, till all the arguments in the list have been scanned. The final value in **max** is then returned to **main( )**.

How about another program to fix your ideas? This one calls a function **display( )** which is capable of printing any number of arguments of any type.

```
/* Program 58 */
#include <stdio.h>
#include <stdarg.h>
void display ( int, int, ... ) ;
int main( )
{
    printf ( "\n" ) ;
    display ( 1, 2, 5, 6 ) ;
    printf ( "\n" ) ;
    display ( 2, 4, 'A', 'a', 'b', 'c' ) ;
    printf ( "\n" ) ;
    display ( 3, 3, 2.5, 299.3, -1.0 ) ;
    return 0 ;
}
void display ( int type, int num, ... )
{
    int  i, j ;
    char c ;
    float f ;
    va_list ptr ;
    va_start ( ptr, num ) ;
    switch ( type )
    {
```

```
        case 1 :
            for ( j = 1 ; j <= num ; j++ )
            {
                i = va_arg ( ptr, int ) ;
                printf ( "%d ", i ) ;
            }
            break ;
        case 2 :
            for ( j = 1 ; j <= num ; j++ )
            {
                c = va_arg ( ptr, char ) ;
                printf ( "%c ", c ) ;
            }
            break ;
        case 3 :
            for ( j = 1 ; j <= num ; j++)
            {
                f = ( float ) va_arg ( ptr, double ) ;
                printf ( "%f ", f ) ;
            }
    }
}
```

Here we are passing two fixed arguments to the function **display()**. The first one indicates the data type of the arguments to be printed and the second indicates the number of such arguments to be printed. Once again through the statement **va_start (ptr, num)** we have set up **ptr** such that it points to the first argument in the variable list of arguments. Then depending upon whether the value of **type** is 1, 2 or 3 we have printed out the arguments as **int**s, **char**s or **float**s.

near, far and *huge* Pointers

In MS-DOS a segmented memory model was used. As a result, to refer to any memory location it was necessary to mention the segment (64 KB chunk of memory) address and then the specific byte within this segment. This led to creation of three pointers—near, far and huge. With the advent of Windows OS the segment:offset memory model has become obsolete, as Windows uses a flat memory model. As a result, any memory location is referred to using a 4-byte address. Near, far and huge pointers work only with Turbo C / Turbo C++ environment. Visual Studio and gcc would report errors if these pointers are used.

Exercise

[A] Attempt the following:

(1) Write a function, which arranges the numbers passed to it in ascending/descending order making use of a variable argument list. The fixed arguments to the function should be:

- an integer indicating whether to sort numbers in ascending or descending order.
- an integer to indicate number of arguments to follow (the arguments being the numbers to be sorted).

(2) How would you declare an array of three function pointers where each function receives two **int**s and returns a **float**?

(3) Write a function that receives variable number of arguments, where the arguments are the coordinates of a point. Based on the number of arguments received, the function should display type of shape like a point, line, triangle, etc., that can be drawn.

[B] What will be the output of the following programs:

(1)
```
#include <stdio.h>
int main( )
{
    void ( *message )( ) ;
    void print( ) ;
    print( ) ;
    message = print ;
    ( *message )( ) ;
    return 0 ;
}
void print( )
{
    printf ( "Never trouble trouble till trouble troubles you\n" ) ;
}
```

(2)
```
/* Compile this program and run the executable file from command
    prompt as: PR5 aabbcc */
#include <stdio.h>
int main ( int argc, char *argv[ ] )
{
    printf ( "%c\n", ++( *( ++( *++argv ) ) ) ) ;
```

```
            return 0 ;
        }
(3)  #include <stdio.h>
     int main( )
     {
            int i, fun1( ), fun2( ), fun3( ) ;
            int ( *f[3] )( ) ;
            f[0] = fun1 ;
            f[1] = fun2 ;
            f[2] = fun3 ;

            for ( i = 0 ; i <= 2 ; i++ )
                ( *f[i] )( ) ;
            return 0 ;
        }
     int fun1( )
     {
            printf ( "Hail\n" ) ;
            return 0 ;
        }
     int fun2( )
     {
            printf ( "the\n" ) ;
            return 0 ;
        }
     int fun3( )
     {
            printf ( "viruses!\n" ) ;
            return 0 ;
        }
(4)  # include <stdio.h>
     void  show ( int, float ) ;
     int main( )
     {
          void  ( *s )( int, float ) ;
          s = show ;
          ( *s )( 10, 3.14 ) ;
          return 0 ;
        }
     void show ( int  i, float  f )
```

```
{
    printf ( "%d %f\n", i, f ) ;
}
```

Application of
Pointers

*Learning various features of pointers just because
they exist is a bad idea. You must be able to
actually put them to use in practice. That is
precisely what this chapter aims to do...*

In the previous six chapters we saw how pointers work in different garbs. Let us now put all that theory into practice. I will present here a few applications that use pointers. Let us begin with the first one.

Dictionary

Any computerized dictionary should not only be able to hold all the words but must also be able to search the requested word efficiently. In principle the words can be stored in an array. However, an array suffers from several limitations like:

(a)   The size of the array has to be defined while writing the program.

(b)   The size of the array cannot be increased or decreased during execution.

(c)   Insertion of a new element in the middle of an array is costly since it necessitates movement of existing elements of the array.

(d)   Deletion of an element also necessitates movement of array elements.

(e)   Since array elements are stored in adjacent memory locations and dictionary contains huge amount of words there is always a possibility that so many adjacent locations may not be available in memory.

We can easily overcome these limitations through usage of linked lists. I would demonstrate this through a program. This program would read a list of countries from a file and maintain them in the order of a dictionary. Later we would receive a country name from the keyboard and report whether it exists in the dictionary or not. If it is not present in the list it gets added to the dictionary at suitable position. Here is a program that achieves this. . .

```
/* Program 59 */
/* Program to implement a Dictionary */
#include <stdio.h>
#include <string.h>
#include <ctype.h>
#include <stdlib.h>
void addtolist ( int, char * ) ;
int search_list ( int, char * ) ;
```

```
struct clist
{
    char name[20] ;
    struct clist *link ;
} ;
struct clist *a[26] ;
int main( )
{
    int sflag, l ;
    char country[20], ch ;
    FILE *fp ;
    fp = fopen ( "CNAMES.TXT", "r+" ) ;
    if ( fp == NULL )
    {
        printf ( "Unable to Open\n" ) ;
        exit ( 0 ) ;
    }
    while ( fgets ( country, 20, fp ) )
    {
        l = strlen ( country ) ;
        country [ l - 1 ] = '\0' ;
        addtolist ( toupper ( country[0] ) - 65, country ) ;
    }
    while ( 1 )
    {
        printf ( "Enter the Country to Search:\n" ) ;
        fflush ( stdin ) ;
        gets ( country ) ;
        sflag = search_list ( toupper ( country[0] ) - 65, country ) ;
        if ( sflag )
            printf ( "%s is present in the List\n", country ) ;
        else
        {
            printf ( "Misspelled\n" ) ;
            printf ( "Do you want to Add it in the List (Y/N):\n" ) ;
            ch = getchar( ) ;
            if ( tolower ( ch ) == 'y' )
            {
                fseek ( fp, 0L, SEEK_END ) ;
                fputs ( country, fp ) ;
                fputs( "\n", fp ) ;
```

```
                addtolist ( toupper ( country[0] ) - 65, country ) ;
            }
        }
        printf ( "Any More Countries to Search (Y/N):\n" ) ;
        fflush ( stdin ) ;
        ch = getchar( ) ;
        if ( tolower ( ch ) != 'y' )
            break ;
    }
    fclose ( fp ) ;
    return 0 ;
}

void addtolist ( int index, char *str )
{
    struct clist *q, *r, *temp ;
    temp = q = a[index] ;
    r = ( struct clist * ) malloc ( sizeof ( struct clist ) ) ;
    strcpy ( r -> name, str ) ;
    /* if list is empty */
    if ( q == NULL || strcmp ( q -> name, str ) > 0 )
    {
        q = r ;
        q -> link = temp ;
        a[index] = q ;
    }
    else
    {
        /* traverse the list */
        while ( temp != NULL )
        {
            if ( strcmp ( temp -> name, str ) <= 0 && ( strcmp ( temp ->
                link -> name, str ) > 0 ) || ( temp -> link == NULL ) )
            {
                r -> link = temp -> link ;
                temp -> link = r ;
                return ;
            }

            temp = temp -> link ;
        }
```

```
            r -> link = NULL ;
            temp -> link = r ;
    }
}

int search_list ( int index, char *str )
{
    struct clist *p ;
    p = a[index] ;
    if ( p == NULL )
        return 0 ;
    else
    {
        while ( p != NULL )
        {
            if ( strcmp ( p -> name, str ) == 0 )
                return 1 ;
            else
                p = p -> link ;
        }
        return 0 ;
    }
}
```

To facilitate easy insertion of a new country name in the dictionary we have used linked list to maintain the names of countries. If one linked list is used to store all country names addition of a new country name to it would necessitate searching an appropriate point of insertion starting from the first name. This would involve an exhaustive search. This means if we are to insert a name like 'Zimbabwe', we will have to start the search from the first node. Ideally, we should be able to compare only those names that start with Z. Similarly, once the linked list is built, searching for a specific country in the list would again force us to start our search from the first node. Both these limitations have been overcome in our program. We have maintained 26 linked lists one for each alphabet. Each node in the linked list contains name of a country and pointer to the next node. The starting addresses of each linked list are stored in an array of pointers.

While adding a new country to the dictionary we have called the function **addtolist( )**. This function first picks up the starting address of the appropriate linked list from the array of pointers. Once this has been done it is just a matter of inserting a new node in this linked list. A similar procedure in adopted while searching for a name in the dictionary, the only difference being this time the **search_list( )** function reports the presence or absence of the name in the linked list.

Managing Database

A database file typically contains several records. Each record contains several items of information. Each item of information is known as a field. For creating and maintaining a database the fields are gathered into a structure and then the structure is written/read to/from disk using functions like **fwrite( )** and **fread()**. Often functions like **addrec( )**, **modirec( )**, **delrec( )** and **listrec( )** are written to perform operations like addition of new records, modification of existing records, deletion of existing records and listing of records respectively. However, all these operations and functions remain specific to the structure at hand. Most DBMS and RDBMS softwares permit us to create database files and perform operations on it in a more generic manner. That is we can create different database files to hold different types of structures and still perform the addition, modification, deletion and listing operations in a more generic way. We too can develop such a system easily. Given below is a program that achieves this.

```
/* Program 60 */
#include <stdio.h>
#include <stdlib.h>
#include <string.h>
#include <windows.h>
#include <ctype.h>
struct
{
    char name[11] ;
    int type ;
    int bytes ;
    int dec ;
} f[10] ;
struct header
{
    unsigned long recnum ;
    int fhsize ;
    int byte_rec ;
} ;
```

```
struct fhdr
{
    char name[11] ;
    char type ;
    char length ;
    char dec ;
} ;
struct header h ;
struct fhdr fd ;
struct integer
{
    int num ;
    int ind ;
    struct integer *link ;
} ;
struct floatnum
{
    float num ;
    int ind ;
    struct floatnum *link ;
} ;
struct string
{
    char name[20] ;
    int ind ;
    struct string *link ;
} ;
union fieldlist
{
    struct integer x ;
    struct floatnum n ;
    struct string s ;
} u ;
void create_dbf( ) ;
void create_index( ) ;
void gotoxy ( short x, short y ) ;
void list_irec( ) ;
void sort_writeindex ( union fieldlist **, FILE *, char  ) ;

int main( )
{
```

```
    char choice ;
    while ( 1 )
    {
        system ( "cls" ) ;
        gotoxy ( 30, 6 ) ;
        printf ( "1. Create Database File and Add Records" ) ;
        gotoxy ( 30, 8 ) ;
        printf ( "2. Index Database File" ) ;
        gotoxy ( 30, 10 ) ;
        printf ( "3. List Indexed Records" ) ;
        gotoxy ( 30, 12 ) ;
        printf ( "0. Exit" ) ;
        gotoxy ( 30, 14 ) ;
        printf ( "Enter Choice:\n" ) ;
        fflush ( stdin ) ;
        choice = getchar( ) ;
        switch ( choice )
        {
            case '1':
                create_dbf( ) ;
                break ;
            case '2':
                create_index( ) ;
                break ;
            case '3':
                list_irec( ) ;
                break ;
            case '0':
                exit ( 0 ) ;
        }
    }
    return 0 ;
}

void create_dbf( )
{
    FILE *fp ;
    int i = 0, j = 8, k = 0, num, numoffields = 0, len, totbyte_rec = 0, fh ;
    float decif ;
    char str[20], filename[13], ch ;
    system ( "cls" ) ;
```

```
printf ( "Enter the DataBase File to Create :\n " ) ;
fflush ( stdin ) ;
gets ( filename ) ;
filename[9] = '\0' ;
len = strlen ( filename ) ;
if ( len < 8 )
    filename[ len ] = '\0' ;
strcat ( filename, ".dbf" ) ;
fp = fopen ( filename, "wb" ) ;
if ( fp == NULL )
{
    puts ( "Unable to create database file\n" ) ;
    exit ( 1 ) ;
}
h.recnum = 0 ;
h.fhsize = 0 ;
h.byte_rec = 0 ;
fwrite ( &h, sizeof ( h ), 1, fp ) ;
gotoxy ( 32, 6 ) ;
printf ( "DataBase Structure" ) ;
gotoxy ( 20, 7 ) ;
printf ( "Name" ) ;
gotoxy ( 40, 7 ) ;
printf ( "Type" ) ;
gotoxy ( 54, 7 ) ;
printf ( "Bytes" ) ;
gotoxy ( 64, 7 ) ;
printf ( "Precision" ) ;
do
{
    gotoxy ( 20, j ) ;
    gets ( f[i].name ) ;
    if ( f[i].name[0] == '\0' )
        break ;
    gotoxy ( 40, j ) ;
    f[i].type = getchar( ) ;

    if ( f[i].type == 'i' )
    {
        gotoxy ( 54, j ) ;
        printf ( "%d", f[i].bytes = 2 ) ;
```

```
        }
        else if ( f[i].type == 'f' )
        {
            gotoxy ( 54, j ) ;
            printf ( "%d", f[i].bytes = 4 ) ;
            gotoxy ( 64, j ) ;
            scanf ( "%d", &f[i].dec ) ;
        }
        else if ( f[i].type == 's' )
        {
            gotoxy ( 54, j ) ;
            scanf ( "%d", &f[i].bytes ) ;
            if ( f[i].bytes > 20 )
                f[i].bytes = 20 ;
        }
        else
        {
            printf ( "Error" ) ;
            exit ( 2 ) ;
        }
        totbyte_rec += f[i].bytes ;
        strcpy ( fd.name, f[i].name ) ;
        fd.type = f[i].type ;
        if ( fd.type == 'f' )
            fd.dec = f[i].dec ;
        fd.length = f[i].bytes ;
        fwrite ( &fd, sizeof ( fd ), 1, fp ) ;
        i++ ;
        j++ ;
        fflush ( stdin ) ;
    } while ( i < 10 ) ;
    numoffields = i ;
    fseek ( fp, 4L, SEEK_SET ) ;
    fh = 14 * i ;
    fwrite ( &totbyte_rec, sizeof ( totbyte_rec ), 1 , fp ) ;
    fwrite ( &fh, sizeof ( fh ), 1, fp ) ;
    fseek ( fp, 0L, SEEK_END ) ;
    system ( "cls" ) ;
    for ( i = 0 ; i < numoffields ; i++ )
    {
        gotoxy ( 6 + 20 * i, 3 ) ;
```

```
            printf ( "%s", f[i].name ) ;
    }
    j = 0 ;
    k = 4 ;
    do
    {
        for ( i = 0 ; i < numoffields ; i++ )
        {
            gotoxy ( 6 + 20 * i, k ) ;
            if ( f[i].type == 'i' )
            {
                scanf ( "%d", &num ) ;
                fwrite ( &num, sizeof ( num ), 1, fp ) ;
            }
            else if ( f[i].type == 'f' )
            {
                scanf ( "%f", &decif ) ;
                fwrite ( &decif, sizeof ( decif ), 1, fp ) ;
            }
            else if ( f[i].type == 's' )
            {
                scanf ( "%s", str ) ;
                if ( f[i].bytes < 20 )
                    fwrite ( str, f[i].bytes, 1, fp ) ;
                else
                {
                    * ( str + 19 ) = '\0' ;
                    fwrite ( str, sizeof ( str ), 1, fp ) ;
                }
            }
        }
        k++ ;
        j++ ;
        gotoxy ( 1, 1 ) ;
        printf ( "Another Record (Y/N):\n" ) ;
        printf ( " \b" ) ;
        fflush ( stdin ) ;
        ch = getchar( ) ;

    } while ( tolower ( ch ) == 'y' ) ;
    h.recnum = j ;
```

```
    h.fhsize = numoffields * 14 ;
    h.byte_rec = totbyte_rec ;
    rewind ( fp ) ;
    fwrite ( &h, sizeof ( h ), 1, fp ) ;
    fclose ( fp ) ;
}

void create_index( )
{
    FILE *fp,*ft ;
    int i = 0, len, num ;
    unsigned int nfields, bytes, depth = 0 ;
    float decif ;
    char str[20], filename[13], field[11], type ;
    union fieldlist *p, *temp, *start ;
    system ( "cls" ) ;
    printf ( "Enter the DataBase File to Read :\n " ) ;
    fflush ( stdin ) ;
    gets ( filename ) ;
    fp = fopen ( filename, "rb" ) ;
    if ( fp == NULL )
    {
        puts ( "Unable to Open database file" ) ;
        return ;
    }
    fread ( &h, sizeof ( h ), 1, fp ) ;
    /* determine the field and its type */
    for ( i = 0 ; i < h.fhsize / 14 ; i++ )
    {
        fread ( &fd, sizeof ( fd ),1, fp ) ;
        strcpy ( f[i].name, fd.name ) ;
        f[i].type = fd.type ;
        f[i].bytes = fd.length ;
        if ( fd.type == 'f' )
            f[i].dec = fd.dec ;
    }
    printf ( "Enter Field Name for Indexing:\n" ) ;
    fflush ( stdin ) ;
    scanf ( "%s", field ) ;
    fp = fopen ( filename, "rb" ) ;
    if ( fp == NULL )
```

```
    {
        puts ( "Unable to open" ) ;
        return ;
    }
    strcpy ( filename, field ) ;
    strcat ( filename, ".idx" ) ;

    ft = fopen ( filename, "wb" ) ;
    if ( ft == NULL )
    {
        puts ( "Unable to open" ) ;
        return ;
    }
    fwrite ( &field, sizeof ( field ), 1, ft ) ;
    nfields = h.fhsize / 14 ;
    for ( i = 0 ; i < nfields ; i++ )
    {
        if ( strcmp ( f[i].name , field ) == 0 )
        {
            type = f[i].type ;
            len = f[i].bytes ;
            break ;
        }
        depth += f[i].bytes ;
    }
    fseek ( fp, 8L + h.fhsize, SEEK_SET ) ;
    switch ( type )
    {
        case 'i':
            fseek ( fp, depth, SEEK_CUR ) ;
            fread ( &num, sizeof ( num ), 1, fp ) ;
            fseek ( fp, h.byte_rec - depth - sizeof ( num ), SEEK_CUR ) ;
            p = ( union fieldlist * ) malloc ( sizeof ( struct integer ) ) ;
            p -> x.ind = 1 ;
            p -> x.num = num ;
            p -> x.link = NULL ;
            temp = start = p ;
            fseek ( fp, depth, SEEK_CUR ) ;
            bytes = h.byte_rec - sizeof ( num ) ;
            for ( i = 1 ; i < h.recnum ; i++ )
            {
```

```
        fread ( &num, sizeof ( num ), 1, fp ) ;
        temp = ( union fieldlist * )malloc(sizeof ( struct integer ));
        temp -> x.ind = i + 1 ;
        temp -> x.num = num ;
        temp -> x.link = NULL ;
        while ( p -> x.link != NULL )
            p = ( union fieldlist * ) p -> x.link ;
        p -> x.link = ( struct integer * ) temp ;
        p = start ;
        fseek ( fp, bytes, SEEK_CUR ) ;
    }
    sort_writeindex ( &start, ft, type ) ;
    break ;
case 'f':
    fseek ( fp, depth, SEEK_CUR ) ;
    fread ( &decif, sizeof ( decif ), 1, fp ) ;
    fseek ( fp, h.byte_rec - depth - sizeof ( decif ), SEEK_CUR ) ;
    p = ( union fieldlist * ) malloc ( sizeof ( struct floatnum ) ) ;
    p -> n.ind = 1 ;
    p -> n.num = decif ;
    p -> n.link = NULL ;
    temp = start = p ;
    fseek ( fp, depth, SEEK_CUR ) ;
    bytes = h.byte_rec - sizeof ( decif ) ;
    for ( i = 1 ; i < h.recnum ; i++ )
    {
        fread ( &decif, sizeof ( decif ), 1, fp ) ;
        temp = ( union fieldlist* )malloc(sizeof( struct floatnum));
        temp -> n.ind = i + 1 ;
        temp -> n.num = decif ;
        temp -> n.link = NULL ;
        while ( p -> n.link != NULL )
            p = ( union fieldlist * ) p -> n.link ;
        p -> n.link = ( struct floatnum * ) temp ;
        fseek ( fp, bytes, SEEK_CUR) ;
        fseek ( fp, 0L, SEEK_CUR ) ;
    }
    sort_writeindex ( &start, ft, type ) ;
    break ;
case 's':
    fseek ( fp, depth, SEEK_CUR ) ;
```

```
          fread ( str, len, 1, fp ) ;
          fseek ( fp, h.byte_rec - depth - len, SEEK_CUR ) ;
          p = ( union fieldlist * ) malloc ( sizeof ( struct string ) ) ;
          p -> s.ind = 1 ;
          strcpy ( p -> s.name, str ) ;
          p -> s.link = NULL ;
          temp = start = p ;
          fseek ( fp, depth, SEEK_CUR ) ;
          bytes = h.byte_rec - len ;
          for ( i = 1 ; i < h.recnum ; i++ )
          {
              fread ( str, len, 1, fp ) ;
              temp = ( union fieldlist * ) malloc ( sizeof( struct string ) );
              temp -> s.ind = i + 1 ;
              strcpy ( temp -> s.name, str ) ;
              temp -> s.link = NULL ;
              while ( p -> s.link != NULL )
                    p = ( union fieldlist * ) p -> s.link ;
              p -> s.link = ( struct string * ) temp ;
              fseek ( fp, bytes, SEEK_CUR ) ;
          }
          sort_writeindex ( &start, ft, type ) ;
          break ;
      }
    fclose ( fp ) ;
    fclose ( ft ) ;
}

void sort_writeindex ( union fieldlist **start, FILE *ft, char type )
{
    union fieldlist *p, *q, *r, *s, *temp ;
    s = NULL ;
    p = *start ;
    /* r precedes p and s for sentinel node for inner loop */
    while ( 1 )
    {
        if ( type == 'i' && s == ( union fieldlist * ) ( *start ) -> x.link )
            break ;
        if ( type == 'f' && s == ( union fieldlist * ) ( *start ) -> n.link )
            break ;
        if ( type == 's' && s == ( union fieldlist * ) ( *start ) -> s.link )
```

```
      break ;
r = p = *start ;
if ( type == 's' )
     q = ( union fieldlist * ) p -> s.link ;
else if ( type == 'f' )
     q = ( union fieldlist * ) p -> n.link ;
else
     q = ( union fieldlist * ) p -> x.link ;
while ( ( union fieldlist * ) p -> x.link != s ||
          ( union fieldlist * ) p -> n.link != s ||
            ( union fieldlist * ) p -> s.link != s )
{
    if ( type == 'i' && p -> x.num > q -> x.num )
    {
        if ( p == *start )
        {
            temp = ( union fieldlist * ) q -> x.link ;
            q -> x.link = &( p -> x ) ;
            p -> x.link = ( struct integer * ) temp ;
            *start = q ;
            r = q ;
        }
        else
        {
            temp = ( union fieldlist * ) q -> x.link ;
            q -> x.link = &( p -> x ) ;
            p -> x.link = ( struct integer * ) temp ;
            r -> x.link = &( q -> x ) ;
            r = q ;
        }
    }
    else if ( type == 'f' && p -> n.num > q -> n.num )
    {
        if ( p == *start )
        {
            temp = ( union fieldlist * ) q -> n.link ;
            q -> n.link = &( p -> n ) ;
            p -> n.link = ( struct floatnum * ) temp ;
            *start = q ;
            r = q ;
        }
```

```
            else
            {
                temp = ( union fieldlist * ) q -> n.link ;
                q -> n.link = &( p -> n ) ;
                p -> n.link = ( struct floatnum * ) temp ;
                r -> n.link = &( q -> n ) ;
                r = q ;
            }
        }
        else if ( type == 's' && strcmp (p -> s.name, q -> s.name ) > 0 )
        {
            if ( p == *start )
            {
                temp = ( union fieldlist * ) q -> s.link ;
                q -> s.link = &( p -> s ) ;
                p -> s.link = ( struct string * ) temp ;
                *start = q ;
                r = q ;
            }
            else
            {
                temp = ( union fieldlist * ) q -> s.link ;
                q -> s.link = &( p -> s ) ;
                p -> s.link = ( struct string * ) temp ;
                r -> s.link = &( q -> s ) ;
                r = q ;
            }
        }
        else
        {
            r = p ;
            if ( type == 'i' )
                p = ( union fieldlist * ) p -> x.link ;
            if ( type == 'f' )
                p = ( union fieldlist * ) p -> n.link ;
            if ( type == 's' )
                p = ( union fieldlist * ) p -> s.link ;
        }
        if ( type == 'i' )
            q = ( union fieldlist * ) p -> x.link ;
        if ( type == 'f' )
```

```
                    q = ( union fieldlist * ) p -> n.link ;
              if ( type == 's' )
                    q = ( union fieldlist * ) p -> s.link ;
              if ( q == NULL || q == s )
              {
                    s = p ;
                    break ;
              }
         }
    }
    p = *start ;
    if ( type == 's' )
    {
         while ( p != NULL )
         {
              fwrite ( &p -> s.ind, sizeof ( p -> s.ind ), 1, ft ) ;

              p = ( union fieldlist * ) p -> s.link ;
         }
    }
    else if ( type == 'f' )
    {
         while ( p != NULL )
         {
              fwrite ( &p -> n.ind, sizeof ( p -> n.ind ), 1 , ft ) ;
              p = ( union fieldlist * ) p -> n.link ;
         }
    }
    else
    {
         while ( p != NULL )
         {
              fwrite ( &p -> x.ind, sizeof ( p -> x.ind ), 1, ft ) ;

              p = ( union fieldlist * ) p -> x.link ;
         }
    }
}

void list_irec( )
{
```

```
FILE *fp, *ft ;
int i = 0, j = 8, k = 0 ;
int num, ind ;
float decif ;
char str[20], filename[13] ;
system ( "cls" ) ;
printf ( "Enter the DataBase File to Read :\n" ) ;
fflush ( stdin ) ;
gets ( filename ) ;
fp = fopen ( filename, "rb" ) ;
if ( fp == NULL )
{
    puts ( "Unable to Open" ) ;
    exit ( 0 ) ;
}
printf ( "Enter the Index File to Use:\n " ) ;
fflush ( stdin ) ;
gets ( filename ) ;
ft = fopen ( filename, "rb" ) ;
if ( ft == NULL )
{
    puts ( "Unable to open index file" ) ;
    exit ( 3 ) ;
}
fseek ( ft,11L, SEEK_SET ) ;
fseek ( fp, 0L, SEEK_CUR ) ;
fread ( &h, sizeof ( h ), 1, fp ) ;
for ( i = 0 ; i < h.fhsize / 14 ; i++ )
{
    fread ( &fd, sizeof ( fd ), 1, fp ) ;
    strcpy ( f[i].name, fd.name ) ;
    f[i].type = fd.type ;
    f[i].bytes = fd.length ;
    if ( fd.type == 'f' )
        f[i].dec = fd.dec ;
}

system ( "cls" ) ;
for ( i = 0 ; i < h.fhsize / 14 ; i++ )
{
    gotoxy ( 6 + 10 * i, 3 ) ;
```

```
            printf ( "%s", f[i].name ) ;
      }
      j = 0 ;
      k = 4 ;
      fseek ( fp, 8L + h.fhsize, SEEK_SET ) ;
      while ( fread ( &ind, sizeof ( ind ), 1 , ft ) == 1 )
      {
            fseek ( fp, ( ind - 1 ) * h.byte_rec, SEEK_CUR ) ;
            for ( i = 0 ; i < h.fhsize / 14 ; i++ )
            {
                  gotoxy ( 6 + 10 * i, k ) ;
                  if ( f[i].type == 'i' )
                  {
                        if ( fread ( &num,  sizeof ( num ), 1, fp ) )
                              printf ("%d", num ) ;
                  }
                  else if ( f[i].type == 'f' )
                  {
                        if ( fread ( &decif, sizeof ( decif ), 1, fp ) )
                              printf ( "%f", f[i].dec, decif ) ;
                  }
                  else if ( f[i].type == 's' )
                  {
                        if ( fread ( &str, f[i].bytes, 1, fp ) == 1 )
                              printf ( "%s", str ) ;
                  }
            }
            fseek ( fp, 8L + h.fhsize, SEEK_SET ) ;
            k++ ;
            j++ ;
      }
      getchar( ) ;
      fclose ( fp ) ;
      fclose ( ft ) ;
}

void gotoxy ( short int col, short int row )
{
   HANDLE hStdout = GetStdHandle ( STD_OUTPUT_HANDLE ) ;
   COORD position = { col, row } ;
```

```
    SetConsoleCursorPosition ( hStdout, position ) ;
}
```

On executing the program a menu containing the following items pops up:

1. Create Database File and Add Records
2. Index Database File
3. List Indexed Records
0. Exit

On selecting the first item we are asked to build the structure of the records to be stored in the file. While building this structure we can create fields of types string, integer, or float. For the sake of programming convenience we have restricted the number of fields that can be added to the structure to 10. Each time you add a field you are prompted to enter its name, type, size and precision. If field type is integer or float the size of the field is assumed to be 2 and 4 bytes respectively. Precision indicates number of places after the decimal point and hence is relevant only for a field of the type float. To indicate the type of the field you must type 's' for string, 'i' for integer and 'f' for float. To indicate that you are through with entry of fields you should simply hit enter in the field **Name**. Once the structure has been created you are asked to enter records.

After this we can create an index file for the database by selecting the second menu option. While indexing the records we have the choice of creating an index based on any one field. Once the index file has been created we can list the records indexed according to the index file.

To help maintain a generic structure we have stored in the database file the information about the fields and a header containing the total number of records and the record size. The index file contains the name of the field on which the database has been indexed. This is followed by the positions of records in the database file had they been sorted according to the index field.

As the user enters the records they are written to the database file on a record-by-record basis. While creating the index file the records are read and a linked list is created. This linked list doesn't contain the entire record read from the database file. Instead, every node contains only the field value on which database is being indexed and position of the record in the database. While creating the index file the linked list is sorted and then the indexes are stored in an index file along with the field name on which the database has been indexed.

While listing the records firstly the database file and the index files are opened. Then one by one the positions of the records are picked up from the index file and the appropriate records are read from the database file. Every record read from the database file is then displayed on the screen.

Infix to Postfix

When higher level programming languages came into existence one of the major hurdles faced by the computer scientists was to generate machine language instructions that would properly evaluate any arithmetic expression. To convert a complex assignment statement such as:

X = A / B + C * D - F * G / Q

into a correct instruction sequence was a formidable task. That it is no longer considered so formidable is a tribute to the elegant and simple solutions that the computer scientists came out with. As of today, this conversion is considered to be one of the minor aspects of compiler writing.

To fix the order of evaluation of an expression each language assigns to each operator a priority. Even after assigning priorities how can a compiler accept an expression and produce correct code? For this the expression is reworked into a form called 'postfix' notation. If **e** is an expression with operators and operands, the conventional way of writing **e** is called infix, because the operators come in between the operands. (Unary operators precede their operand.) The postfix form of an expression calls for each operator to appear after its operands. For example, the postfix form of the infix expression A * B / C is A B * C / .

If we study the postfix form we see that the multiplication comes immediately after its two operands A and B. Now imagine that A * B is computed and stored in T. Then we have the division operator (/), coming immediately after its two operands T and C.

Notice three features of the postfix expression:

-   The operands maintain the same order as in the equivalent infix expression.

- Parentheses are not needed to designate the expression unambiguously.
- While evaluating the postfix expression the priority of the operators is no longer relevant.

Given below is a program that converts an infix expression into its postfix form.

```
/* Program 61 */
#include <stdio.h>
#include <string.h>
#include <ctype.h>
#define MAX 50
struct infix
{
    char target[MAX] ;
    char stack[MAX] ;
    char *s, *t ;
    int top ;
} ;
void initinfix ( struct infix * ) ;
void setexpr ( struct infix *, char * ) ;
void push ( struct infix *, char ) ;
char pop ( struct infix * ) ;
void convert ( struct infix * ) ;
int priority ( char ) ;
void show ( struct infix ) ;
void main( )
{
    struct infix p ;
    char expr[MAX] ;
    initinfix ( &p ) ;
    printf ( "\nEnter an expression in infix form: " ) ;
    gets ( expr ) ;
    setexpr ( &p, expr ) ;
    convert ( &p ) ;

    printf ( "The postfix expression is: " ) ;
    show ( p ) ;
}

/* initializes structure elements */
```

```
void initinfix ( struct infix *p )
{
    p -> top = -1 ;
    strcpy ( p -> target, "" ) ;
    strcpy ( p -> stack, "" ) ;
    p -> t = p -> target ;
    p -> s = "" ;
}

/* sets s to point to given expr. */
void setexpr ( struct infix *p, char *str )
{
    p -> s = str ;
}

/* adds an operator to the stack */
void push ( struct infix *p, char c )
{
    if ( p -> top == MAX )
        printf ( "\nStack is full.\n" ) ;
    else
    {
        p -> top++ ;
        p -> stack[p -> top] = c ;
    }
}

/* pops an operator from the stack */
char pop ( struct infix *p )
{
    if ( p -> top == -1 )
    {
        printf ( "\nStack is empty.\n" ) ;
        return -1 ;
    }
    else
    {
        char item = p -> stack[p -> top] ;
        p -> top-- ;
        return item ;
    }
```

```
}

/* converts the given expr. from infix to postfix form */
void convert ( struct infix *p )
{
    char opr ;
    while ( *( p -> s ) )
    {
        if ( *( p -> s ) == ' ' || *( p -> s ) == '\t' )
        {
            p -> s++ ;
            continue ;
        }
        if ( isdigit ( *( p -> s ) ) || isalpha ( *( p -> s ) ) )
        {
            while ( isdigit ( *( p -> s ) ) || isalpha ( *( p -> s ) ) )
            {
                *( p -> t ) = *( p -> s ) ;
                p -> s++ ;
                p -> t++ ;
            }
        }
        if ( *( p -> s ) == '(' )
        {
            push ( p, *( p -> s ) ) ;
            p -> s++ ;
        }
        if ( *( p -> s ) == '*' || *( p -> s ) == '+' || *( p -> s ) == '/' ||
            *( p -> s ) == '%' || *( p -> s ) == '-' || *( p -> s ) == '$' )
        {
            if ( p -> top != -1 )
            {
                opr = pop ( p ) ;
                while ( priority ( opr ) >= priority ( *( p -> s ) ) )
                {
                    *( p -> t ) = opr ;
                    p -> t++ ;
                    opr = pop ( p ) ;
                }
                push ( p, opr ) ;
                push ( p, *( p -> s ) ) ;
```

```
        }
        else
            push ( p, *( p -> s ) );
        p -> s++ ;
    }
    if ( *( p -> s ) == ')' )
    {
        opr = pop ( p );
        while ( ( opr ) != '(' )
        {
            *( p -> t ) = opr ;
            p -> t++ ;
            opr = pop ( p );
        }
        p -> s++ ;
    }
}
while ( p -> top != -1 )
{
    char opr = pop ( p );
    *( p -> t ) = opr ;
    p -> t++ ;
}
*( p -> t ) = '\0' ;
}

/* returns the priority of an operator */
int priority ( char c )
{
    if ( c == '$' )
        return 3 ;
    if ( c == '*' || c == '/' || c == '%' )
        return 2 ;
    else
    {
        if ( c == '+' || c == '-' )
            return 1 ;
        else
            return 0 ;
    }
}
```

```
/* displays the postfix form of given expr. */
void show ( struct infix p )
{
    printf ( " %s", p.target ) ;
}
```

Evaluation of Postfix Expression

In the last section we saw a program that could translate an infix expression to the postfix form. The virtue of postfix notation is that it enables easy evaluation of expressions. To begin with, the need for parentheses is eliminated. Secondly, the priority of the operators is no longer relevant. The expression can be evaluated by making a left to right scan, stacking operands, and evaluating operators using as operands the correct numbers from the stack and finally placing the result onto the stack. This evaluation process is much simpler than attempting a direct evaluation of infix notation. The following program implements the postfix expression evaluation algorithm.

```
/* Program 62 */
#include <stdio.h>
#include <stdlib.h>
#define MAX 25
void push ( int *, int *, int ) ;
int pop ( int *, int * ) ;
int main( )
{
    char str[MAX], *s ;
    int n1, n2, n3, nn ;
    int stack[MAX], top = -1 ;
    printf ( "Enter the postfix expression to be evaluated:\n" ) ;
    gets ( str ) ;

    s = str ;
    while ( *s )
    {
        /* skip whitespace, if any */
        if ( *s == ' ' || *s == '\t' )
        {
            s++ ;
            continue ;
```

```
        }
        /* if digit is encountered */
        if ( *s >= 48 && *s <= 57 )
        {
            nn = *s - '0' ;
            push ( stack, &top, nn ) ;
        }
        else
        {
            /* if operator is encountered */
            n1 = pop ( stack,  &top ) ;
            n2 = pop ( stack, &top ) ;
            switch ( *s )
            {
                case '+' :
                    n3 = n2 + n1 ;
                    break ;
                case '-' :
                    n3 = n2 - n1 ;
                    break ;
                case '/' :
                    n3 = n2 / n1 ;
                    break ;
                case '*' :
                    n3 = n2 * n1;
                    break ;
                case '%' :
                    n3 = n2 % n1 ;
                    break ;
                default :
                    printf ( "Unknown operator\n" ) ;
                    exit ( 1 ) ;
            }
            push ( stack, &top, n3 ) ;
        }
        s++ ;
    }
    printf ( "Result is : %d\n", pop ( stack, &top ) ) ;
    return 0 ;
}
```

```
void push ( int *stk, int *sp, int item )
{
    if ( *sp == MAX )
        printf ( "Stack is full\n" ) ;
    else
    {
        *sp = *sp + 1 ;
        stk[ *sp ] = item ;
    }
}

int pop ( int *stk, int *sp )
{
    int item ;
    if ( *sp == -1 )
    {
        printf ( "Stack is empty\n" ) ;
        return ( -1 ) ;
    }
    else
    {
        item = stk[ *sp ] ;
        *sp = *sp - 1 ;
        return ( item ) ;
    }
}
```

Hashing

Suppose you want to write an application that generates 1000 random numbers in the range 1 to 32,767. All the random numbers are required to be unique. For example, once the number 511 is generated, it can't be generated again. You propose to use a random number generating function **rand( )** that doesn't generate unique numbers and devise a scheme to reject the previously generated random numbers. Hence you need to remember the random numbers that you generate. It is wasteful to use a 32,767-element boolean array for this purpose. And if you use linked list, the amount of time to figure out if the number is already generated increases as the linked list grows. In such a situation a technique **hashing** can be used. Here we will partition the hash table into 32 buckets. Each bucket will hold numbers in a specific range. For example, random numbers in the range 0 to 1000 would be stored in bucket 0, numbers in the range 1001 to 2000 would be stored in bucket 1, etc. We will store these numbers in a linked list attached to each bucket. This arrangement is shown in the following Figure 7.1.

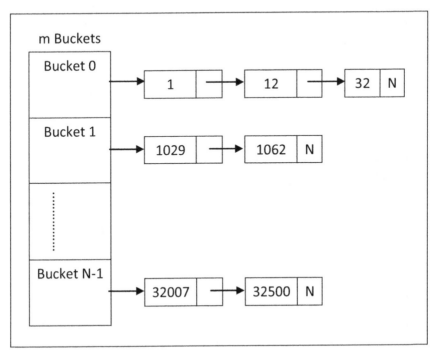

Figure 7.1

While searching a number first we would reach an appropriate bucket and then search the number in the linked list associated with it. Given below is a program that implements this hashing technique.

```
/* Program 63 */
/* program to generate unique random numbers using hashing */
#include <stdio.h>
#include <stdlib.h>
#include <ctype.h>
#include <time.h>
struct node
{
    int data ;
    struct node *link ;
} ;
struct node *bucks[33] ;
void addtolist ( int, int ) ;
void printlist ( void ) ;
```

```
int search_list ( int, int ) ;
int main( )
{
    int num, sflag ;
    char ch ;
    srand ( ( unsigned ) time ( NULL ) ) ;
    while ( 1 )
    {
        printlist( ) ;
        printf ( "\nDo you want to generate a random num ? (Y/N): " ) ;
        fflush ( stdin ) ;
        ch = tolower ( getchar( ) ) ;
        if ( ch != 'y' )
            break ;
        num = rand( ) ;
        printf ( "Random no. is %d", num ) ;
        sflag = search_list ( num / 1000, num ) ;
        if ( sflag )
            printf ( "\n%d is present in the List", num ) ;
        else
        {
            printf ( "\n%d not present in the list", num ) ;
            printf ( "\nAdd it in the List (Y/N): " ) ;
            fflush ( stdin ) ;
            ch = getchar( ) ;
            if ( tolower ( ch ) == 'y' )
                addtolist ( num / 1000, num ) ;
        }
    }
    return 0 ;
}

void addtolist ( int index, int data )
{
    struct node *q, *r, *temp ;
    temp = q = bucks [ index ] ;
    r = ( struct node * ) malloc ( sizeof ( struct node ) ) ;
    r -> data = data ;
    /* if list is empty */
    if ( q == NULL || q -> data > data)
    {
```

```
        q = r ;
        q -> link = temp ;
        bucks[ index ] = q ;
    }
    else
    {
        /* traverse the list */
        while ( temp != NULL)
        {
            if ( ( temp -> data < data ) && ( temp -> link -> data > data )
                            || ( temp -> link == NULL) )
            {
                r -> link = temp -> link ;
                temp -> link = r ;
                return ;
            }
            temp = temp -> link ;
        }
        r -> link = NULL ;
        temp -> link = r ;
    }
}

int search_list ( int index, int data )
{
    struct node *p ;
    p = bucks[ index ] ;

    if ( p == NULL )
        return 0 ;
    else
    {
        while ( p != NULL )
        {
            if ( p -> data == data )
                return 1 ;
            else
                p = p -> link ;
        }
        return 0 ;
    }
```

```
}

void printlist ( void )
{
    struct node *p ;
    int i ;
    printf ( "list:\n" ) ;
    for ( i = 0 ; i < 33 ; i++ )
    {
        p = bucks[i] ;

        while ( p != NULL )
        {
            printf ( "%d  ",p -> data ) ;
            p = p -> link ;
        }
    }
}
```

We have generated random numbers using the standard library function **random( ).** The statement **struct node* bucks[33]** defines an array of pointers. Each pointer in this array points to the linked list associated with that bucket. Thus **bucks[0]** will point to the linked list holding numbers in range of 0 to 1000, **bucks[1]** will point to the linked list holding numbers in range of 1001 to 2000, and so on. The array is declared global so that initially the all elements point to NULL.

While storing the random number we first go to the appropriate hash bucket and then search the number in the linked list associated with the bucket.

Solved Problems

[A] Attempt the following:

(1) Suppose Fundu Parking Garage contains 10 parking lanes, each with a capacity to hold 10 cars at a time. As each car arrives/departs, the values A/D (representing arrival /departure) is entered along with the car registration number. If a car is departing the data should get updated. If a new car is arriving then on the screen a message should be displayed indicating suitable parking slot for the car. Cars arrive at the south end of the garage and leave from the north end. If a customer arrives to pick up a car that is not the nothernmost, all cars to the north of the car are moved out, the car is driven out, and the other cars are restored in the same order that they were in originally. Whenever a car leaves, all cars to the south are moved forward so that at all times all the empty spaces are in the south part of the garage. Write a program that implements this parking system.

Program

```
/* Car garage simulation using de-queue */
#include <stdio.h>
#include <stdlib.h>
#define TOP 1
#define BOT 2
struct node
{
    char plate[15] ;
    struct node *link ;
} *front[5], *rear[5] ;
char plate[15], temp[15] ;
int i ;
void add_dq ( struct node**, struct node**, int, char* ) ;
char* del_dq ( struct node**, struct node**, int ) ;
void push ( struct node**, char* ) ;
char* pop ( struct node** ) ;
int search ( struct node *, char * ) ;
int count ( struct node * ) ;
void q_display ( struct node * ) ;

int main( )
```

```
{
    char ad ;
    int s, lane = -1, min ;
    while ( 1 )
    {
        for ( i = 0 ; i < 5 ; i++ )
        {
            printf ( "lane %d: ", i ) ;
            q_display ( front[i] ) ;
        }
        printf ( "Arrival/Departure/Quit? ( A/D/Q ): " ) ;
        fflush ( stdin ) ;
        ad = getchar( ) ;
        if ( ad == 'Q' || ad == 'q' )
            exit ( 1 ) ;
        printf ( "Enter license plate number: " ) ;
        fflush ( stdin ) ;
        gets ( plate ) ;
        ad = toupper ( ad ) ;
        if ( ad == 'A' || ad == 'a' ) /* arrival of car */
        {
            lane = -1 ; /* assume no lane is available */
            min = 10 ;
            for ( i = 0 ; i < 5 ; i++ )
            {
                s = count ( front[i] ) ;
                if ( s < min )
                {
                    min = s ;
                    lane = i ;
                }
            }
            if ( lane == -1 )
                printf ( "No room available\n" ) ;
            else
            {
                add_dq( &front[ lane ], &rear[ lane ], BOT, plate);
                printf ( "park car at lane %d slot %d\n", lane, s ) ;
            }
        }
        else if ( ad == 'D' || ad == 'd' ) /* departure of car */
```

```
        {
            for ( i = 0 ; i < 5 ; ++i )
            {
                s = search ( front[i], plate ) ;
                if ( s != -1 )
                {
                    lane = i ;
                    break ;
                }
            }
            if ( i == 5 )
                printf ( "No such car!!\n" ) ;
            else
            {
                printf( "Car found at lane %d slot %d\n", lane, s ) ;
                del_dq ( &front[ lane ], &rear[ lane ], s ) ;
            }
        }
        else if ( ad == 'Q' )
            exit ( 1 ) ;
    }
    return 0 ;
}

/* adds a new element at the end of queue */
void add_dq ( struct node **f, struct node **r, int tb, char *p )
{
    struct node *q ;
    /* create new node */
    q = malloc ( sizeof ( struct node ) ) ;
    strcpy ( q -> plate, p ) ;
    q -> link = NULL ;
    /* if the queue is empty*/
    if ( *f == NULL )
        *f = q ;
    else
    {
        if ( tb == BOT )
            ( *r ) -> link = q ;
        else
        {
```

```
                q ->link = *f ;
                *f = q ;
                return ;
            }
        }
        *r = q ;
    }

char* del_dq ( struct node **f, struct node **r, int n )
{
    struct node *q, *top = NULL ;
    /* if queue is empty */
    if ( *f == NULL )
    {
        printf ( "queue is empty\n" ) ;
        return NULL ;
    }
    else
    {
        if ( n == 0 )
        {
            strcpy ( temp, ( *f ) -> plate ) ;
            q = *f ;
            *f = ( *f ) -> link ;
            free ( q ) ;
            return temp ;
        }
        /* locate node */
        for ( i = 0 ; i < n ; i++ )
        {
            /* drive out cars */
            push ( &top, ( *f ) -> plate ) ;
            /* delete the node */
            q = *f ;
            *f = q -> link ;
            free ( q ) ;
        }
        /* delete the nth node */
        q = *f ;
        *f = q -> link ;
        free ( q ) ;
```

```
                for ( i = 0 ; i < n ; i++ )
                {
                        strcpy ( temp, pop ( &top ) ) ;
                        /* add the node*/
                        add_dq ( f, r, TOP, temp ) ;
                }
        }
}

int count ( struct node *q )
{
        int c = 0 ;
        /* traverse the entire linked list */
        while ( q != NULL )
        {
                q = q -> link ;
                c++ ;
        }
        return c ;
}

int search ( struct node *q, char *p )
{
        int s = -1,c = 0 ;
        while ( q != NULL )
        {
                if ( strcmp ( p, q -> plate ) == 0 )
                {
                        s = c ;
                        break ;
                }
                else
                {
                        q = q -> link ;
                        c++ ;
                }
        }
        return ( s ) ;
}

/* adds a new element to the top of stack */
```

```
void push ( struct node **s, char* item )
{
    struct node *q ;
    q = ( struct node* ) malloc ( sizeof ( struct node ) ) ;
    strcpy ( q  -> plate, item ) ;
    q -> link = *s ;
    *s = q ;
}

/* removes an element from top of stack */
char* pop ( struct node **s )
{
    struct node *q ;
    /* if stack is empty */
    if ( *s == NULL )
        return NULL ;
    else
    {
        q = *s ;
        strcpy ( temp, q -> plate ) ;
        *s = q -> link ;
        free ( q ) ;
        return ( temp ) ;
    }
}

void q_display ( struct node *q )
{
    while ( q != NULL )
    {
        printf ( "%s ", q -> plate ) ;
        q = q -> link ;
    }
    printf( "\n" ) ;
}
```

Understanding
Pointers in
C & C ++

Pointers in
C++

Experience is a great teacher. So true in life, so also in programming. C++ supports all existing features of pointers and adds a few more of its own. These features are explored in this chapter...

So far we have seen pointers and their usage in C programs. C++ too has pointers. As it happens in the process of evolution pointers too have more features to it in C++. This chapter explores all these new enhancements to pointers in C++ and some of the minor differences in their working in C and C++. This chapter assumes that you have a basic understanding of classes and objects.

void Pointers

The keyword **void** can be used to define a pointer to a generic term. Unlike C, in C++ special care has to be taken to handle the assignment of **void** pointers to other pointer types. This is shown in the following code fragment.

```
void *p ;
char *s ;
p = s ;
s = p ;
```

Here, the second assignment would flag an error indicating a type mismatch. While you can assign a pointer of any type to a **void** pointer, the reverse is not true unless you specifically typecast it as shown below:

```
s = ( char * ) p ;
```

The *this* Pointer

The member functions of every object have access to a pointer named **this**, which points to the object itself. When we call a member function, it comes into existence with the value of **this** set to the address of the object for which it was called. The **this** pointer can be treated like any other pointer to an object.

Using a **this** pointer any member function can find out the address of the object of which it is a member. It can also be used to access the data in the object it points to. The following program shows the working of the **this** pointer.

```
/* Program 64 */
#include <iostream>
using namespace std ;
class example
{
```

```
        private :
            int i ;
        public :
            void setdata ( int ii )
            {
                i = ii ;  // one way to set data
                cout << endl << "my object's address is " << this ;
                this->i = ii ;  // another way to set data
            }
            void showdata( )
            {
                cout << i ;  // one way to display data
                cout << endl << "my object's address is " << this << endl ;
                cout << this->i << endl ;  // another way to display data
            }
};
int main( )
{
    example e1 ;
    e1.setdata ( 10 ) ;
    e1.showdata( ) ;
    return 0 ;
}
```

Here is the output of the program...

```
my object's address is 0012FF6010
my object's address is 0012FF60
10
```

From the output we can confirm that each time the address of the same object **e1** got printed. Since the **this** pointer contains the address of the object, using it we can reach the data member of the **example** class through statements like:

```
this->i = ii ;  // another way to set data
cout << this->i ;  // another way to display data
```

Let us now get back to our overloaded **operator +( )** function of the last section. In it we had a statement,

```
t.real = real + c.real ;
```

This statement internally is treated as:

t.real = this->real + c.real ;

When the **operator +( )** function is called through the statement

c3 = c1.operator + (c2) ;

the **this** pointer would contain the **c1** object's address. As a result, **this->real** would refer to **c1**'s **real**.

A more practical use of **this** is in returning values from member functions and overloaded operators. Let us now understand this utility of **this** pointer. Consider the following program.

```
/* Program 65 */
#include <iostream>
using namespace std ;
class circle
{
    private :
        int radius ;
        float x, y ;
    public :
        circle( )
        {
        }
        circle ( int rr, float xx, float yy )
        {
            radius = rr ;
            x = xx ;
            y = yy ;
        }
        circle operator = ( circle& c )
        {
            cout << endl << "Assignment operator invoked" ;
            radius = c.radius ;
            x = c.x ;
            y = c.y ;
            return circle ( radius, x, y ) ;
        }
        void showdata( )
        {
```

```
                cout << endl << "\nRadius = " << radius ;
                cout << endl << "X-Coordinate = " << x ;
                cout << endl << "Y-Coordinate = " << y << endl ;
        }
} ;
int main( )
{
    circle c1 ( 10, 2.5, 2.5 ) ;
    circle c2, c3 ;
    c3 = c2 = c1 ;
    c1.showdata( ) ;
    c2.showdata( ) ;
    c3.showdata( ) ;
    return 0 ;
}
```

Most of the program is straightforward. What is important here is the function **operator = ( )**, which overloads the = operator. The overloaded operator function gets called when the statement **c3 = c2 = c1 ;** gets executed. The overloaded = operator does the copying of the member data from one object to another. It also prints the 'Assignment operator invoked' message so that we can keep track of when it executes.

We have passed the argument to overloaded operator function by reference. Though not absolutely necessary, this is often desirable. Had the argument been passed by value it would have generated a copy of itself in the function. In our program it would not have mattered much, but in case of large objects this would lead to considerable wastage of memory.

The **operator = ( )** function in our program returns a value by creating a temporary **circle** object and initialising it using the three-argument constructor. Note that the value returned is a copy of the object of which the overloaded = operator is a member. Returning a value makes it possible to chain = operators in **c4 = c2 = c1**.

However, returning by value creates an extra copy of the object, which means wastage of memory space. We know that when an object is returned by reference, no new object is created.

Then can we not return the value from the overloaded operator function by reference using a declaration like circle& operator = (circle & c)

Unfortunately, we can't use reference returns on variables that are local to a function since the local variables are destroyed when the function returns. This problem can be overcome using a **this** pointer as shown below:

```
circle& operator = ( circle& c )
{
    cout << endl << "Assignment operator invoked" ;
    radius = c.radius ;
    x = c.x ;
    y = c.y ;
    return *this ;
}
```

Since **this** is a pointer to the object of which the above function is a member, ***this** naturally is that object itself. The statement

return *this ;

returns this object by reference.

new and *delete* Operators

While doing dynamic memory allocation in C the memory is allocated from **heap**. Thus heap is a pool of memory from which standard library C functions like **malloc( )** and **calloc( )** allocate memory. The memory allocated from system heap using **malloc( )**, **calloc( )** and **realloc( )** is vacated (deallocated) using the function **free( )**.

C++ offers a better way to accomplish the same job through the use of the **new** and **delete** operators. The **new** operator allocates memory from free store (in the C++ lexicon, heap is called **free store**)., whereas, the **delete** operator returns the allocated memory back to the free store. Thus the **new** and **delete** operators perform the job of **malloc( )** and **free( )**. These operators associate the allocation of memory with the way we use it.

The **new** operator, when used with the pointer to a data type, a structure, or an array, allocates memory for the item and assigns the address of that memory to the pointer. The **delete** operator does the reverse. It returns to the free store the memory owned by the object.

The following code snippet shows the **new** and **delete** operators at work.

```
int *p1 ;
struct employee
{
    char name[20] ;
    int age ;
    float sal ;
} *p2 ;
p1 = new int ;          // allocates 4 bytes
p2 = new employee ;  // allocates 28 bytes
int *p3 ;
p3 = new int[30] ; // allocates memory for storing 30 integers
// some code that uses p1, p2 and p3
delete p1 ;
delete p2 ;
delete [ ] p3 ;
```

Note the last usage of the **delete** operator:

```
delete [ ] p3 ;
```

It indicates that we are not deleting a **thing** but an array of **things** (**thing**s being integers in this case) pointed to by the pointer **p3**. Would a simple

```
delete p3 ;
```

not work in this case? The compiler may not flag an error, but whether it would work successfully or not would vary from compiler to compiler. In some compilers the heap may get corrupted, in some others only the first object in the array would get deleted. In short, you would be better off if you use **delete [ ]** whenever you allocate memory using **new [ ]**. Otherwise be prepared for a disaster.

Instead of using the **new** operator to allocate memory had we used **malloc( )** the allocation statements would have looked like this:

```
p1 = ( int * ) malloc ( sizeof ( int ) ) ;
p2 = ( stuct employee * ) malloc ( sizeof ( struct employee ) ) ;
p3 = ( int * ) malloc ( sizeof ( int ) * 30 ) ;
```

Note that since **malloc( )** returns a **void** pointer it is necessary to typecast it into an appropriate type depending on the type of pointer we have on the left hand side of the assignment operator. This gets completely avoided when we are using the **new** operator.

Look at the last allocation done using **new**. Here the **new** operator accepts a data type with an array dimension. The dimension that we gave was a constant 30, representing the number of integers. You can, however, supply a variable dimension, and the **new** operator allocates the correct amount of memory as shown below:

```
int n ;
cin >> n ;
int *p = new int[n] ;
// some code that uses p
delete [ ] p ;
```

When you run this code you type in the size of the array. The **new** operator uses the value that you enter to establish the size of memory to be allocated. The program builds the array by using the **new** operator and deletes the array by using the **delete** operator.

Can we **free( )** the memory allocated with **new** or **delete** the pointers allocated with **malloc( )**? No. They are incompatible with one another. Memory allocated using **new** should be freed only using **delete**. Similarly, memory allocated using **malloc( )** should be freed only using **free( )**.

malloc( )/free( ) Versus *new/delete*

The program in the last section may have given you an impression that the only advantages of using **new/delete** over **malloc( )/free( )** are their easier syntax and ability to work with variety of data types without being required to do some clumsy typecasting. However, there is more to **new** and **delete** than meets the eye. Consider the following program to understand this.

```
/* Program 66 */
#include <iostream>
#include <string>
using namespace std ;
class employee
{
```

```
        private :
            char name[20] ;
            int age ;
            float sal ;

        public :
            employee( )
            {
                cout << endl << "reached zero-argument constructor" ;
                strcpy ( name, "" ) ;
                age = 0 ;
                sal = 0.0 ;
            }
            employee ( char *n, int a, float s )
            {
                cout << endl << "reached three-argument constructor" ;
                strcpy ( name, n ) ;
                age = a ;
                sal = s ;
            }
            void setdata ( char *n, int a, float s )
            {
                strcpy ( name, n ) ;
                age = a ;
                sal = s ;
            }
            void showdata( )
            {
                cout << endl << name << "\t" << age << "\t" << sal ;
            }
            ~employee( )
            {
                cout << endl << "reached destructor" << endl ;
            }
};
int main( )
{
    employee *p ;
    p = new employee ;
    p -> setdata ( "sanjay", 23, 4500.50 ) ;
    employee *q ;
```

```
        q = new employee ( "ajay", 24, 3400.50 ) ;
        p -> showdata( ) ;
        q -> showdata( ) ;

        delete p ;
        delete q ;
        return 0 ;
}
```

The output of the program looks like this...

```
reached one-argument constructor
reached three-argument constructor
sanjay  23  4500.5
ajay        24  3400.5
reached destructor
reached destructor
```

From the output it is obvious that when we allocated memory for objects pointed to by **p** and **q** not only the memory allocation took place but the zero-argument and the three-argument constructors also got called. Similarly, on using **delete** not only did the memory got deallocated, but the destructor of the class also got called. Thus **new** and **delete** create and destroy objects. In contrast **malloc( )** and **free( )** merely allocate and deallocate memory.

Smart Pointers

A **container** is a way to organize data in memory. Hence stacks, linked lists, arrays are all containers. An **iterator** is an object that moves through a container accessing various elements of the container. The process of moving from element to element is called **iteration**. Hence the object that permits you to do this is called an **iterator**.

We can iterate through an ordinary C++ array by using a pointer as shown below.

```
/* Program 67 */
#include <iostream>
using namespace std ;
int main( )
{
        const int MAX = 5 ;
```

```
    int arr[ MAX] = { 10, 20, 30, 40, 50 } ;
    int *p ;
    p = arr ;
    for ( int i = 0 ; i < MAX ; i++ )
    {
        cout << *p << endl ;
        p++ ;
    }
    return 0 ;
}
```

However, with more sophisticated containers plain C++ pointers won't work. If the items stored in a container are not placed in adjacent memory locations, incrementing the pointer becomes complicated. For example, moving to the next node in the linked list doesn't merely involve incrementing a pointer. We have to follow the link to the next node. The solution to this is to create a class of **smart** pointers.

An object of a smart pointer class wraps its member functions around an ordinary pointer. The + and the * operator are overloaded in this class. So it knows how to tackle situations when the container elements are not in adjacent memory locations. Iterators are thus nothing but objects of the smart pointer class. The typical skeleton of the smart pointer class is shown below.

```
class smartpointer
{
    private :
        int *p ; // ordinary pointer
    public :
        int operator ++ ( int n )
        {
        }
        int operator * ( )
        {
        }
} ;
```

The following program illustrates the use so smart pointers in accessing various nodes of a linked list.

```
/* Program 68 */
#include <iostream>
```

```cpp
using namespace std ;
class container
{
    private :
        struct node
        {
            int data ;
            node *link ;
        } *head, *current ;
        int count ;
    public :
        container( )
        {
            head = current = NULL ;
            count = 0 ;
        }
        void add ( int n )
        {
            node *temp = new node ;
            temp -> data = n ;
            temp -> link = NULL ;
            if ( head == NULL )
                head = current = temp ;
            else
            {
                node *q ;
                q = head ;
                while ( q -> link != NULL )
                    q = q -> link ;
                q -> link = temp ;
            }
            count++ ;
        }
        int getcount( )
        {
            return count ;
        }
        friend class smartpointer ;
};

class smartpointer
```

```
{
    private :
        container *cptr ;
    public :
        smartpointer ( container *t )
        {
            cptr = t ;
        }
        int operator *( )
        {
            if ( cptr->current == NULL )
                return NULL ;
            else
            {
                int i = cptr->current->data ;
                return i ;
            }
        }
        void operator ++ ( int n )
        {
            if ( cptr->current != NULL )
                cptr->current = cptr->current->link ;
        }
};
int main( )
{
    container c ;
    c.add ( 10 ) ;
    c.add ( 20 ) ;
    c.add ( 0 ) ;
    c.add ( -40 ) ;
    c.add ( 50 ) ;
    smartpointer sptr ( &c ) ;
    for ( int i = 0 ; i < c.getcount( ) ; i++ )
    {
        cout << *sptr << endl ;
        sptr++ ;
    }
    return 0 ;
}
```

Here the **container** class implements the linked list. It has three data members: **head, current** and **count**. Of these, **head** and **current** are pointers to nodes, whereas **count** is an integer. The **head** pointer always points to the first node in the linked list. If the linked list is empty, **head** contains NULL. As the name suggests, **current** always points to the current node in the list. The 'current node' means the one which would be returned if we say ***current**. **count** keeps track of the number of nodes in the linked list. Every time a new node is added, the value of **count** is incremented by **1**.

The **smartpointer** class has been declared as a **friend** of the **container** class. This in effect means that all the member functions of the **smartpointer** class would have an access to the **private** data members of the **container** class.

In the **smartpointer** class we have two overloaded operator functions. The **operator * ( )** function returns the integer in the current node. The **operator ++ ( )** function advances the **current** pointer to point to the next node in the linked list.

In **main( )** we have added nodes to the linked list. Then we have built an object of **smartpointer** class through the statement

smartpointer sptr (&c) ;

The constructor sets up the **container c**'s address being passed to it in a **container** pointer. Using this pointer the member functions can access the **private** data members of the **container**.

The crux of the program is the **for** loop.

```
for ( int i = 0 ; i < c.getcount( ) ; i++ )
{
    cout << endl << *sptr ;
    sptr++ ;
}
```

Here **getcount( )** returns the number of nodes currently in the linked list. **cout << *sptr** invokes the overloaded **operator * ( )** function. This returns the integer contained in the node at which **current** is currently pointing. Through **sptr++** the **operator ++ ( )** function gets called. It moves **current** to make it point to the next node in the linked list.

Pointers to Members

We know that to access a structure member we use a '.' or a '->' operator. Also, to dereference a pointer we use the * operator. Following example shows this at work.

```
int i ;
int *ptr ;
struct emp
{
    char name ;
    int age ;
} ;
emp e, *empptr ;
ptr = &i ;
cout << *ptr ; // dereferencing
cout << e.name ; // access
cout << empptr -> name ; // access
```

If we want we can set up pointers to particular members of a structure. Since the elements of a structure are laid out in contiguous memory locations, the address of any structure element is really an offset from the starting address of the structure. Now to access the structure element through this pointer we need '.' or '->' to reach the element and '*' to dereference the pointer. To carry out the access and the dereferencing simultaneously, C++ provides two new operators: '.*' and '->*'. These are known as **pointer to member** operators. The following program shows their usage.

```
/* Program 69 */
#include <iostream>
using namespace std ;
struct sample
{
    int a ;
    float b ;
} ;
int main( )
{
    int sample::*p1 = &sample::a ;
    float sample::*p2 = &sample::b ;
    sample so = { 10, 3.14f } ;
```

```
        cout << endl << so.*p1 << endl << so.*p2 ;
        sample *sp ;
        sp = &so ;
        cout << endl << sp->*p1 << endl << sp->*p2 ;
        // we can even assign new values
        so.*p1 = 20 ;
        sp->*p2 = 6.28f ;
        cout << endl << so.*p1 << endl << so.*p2 ;
        cout << endl << sp->*p1 << endl << sp->*p2 ;

        sample soarr[ ] = {
                            { 30, 9.22f },
                            { 40, 7.33f },
                            { 60, 8.88f }
                    } ;
        for ( int i =0 ; i <= 2 ; i++ )
            cout << soarr[i].*p1 << endl << soarr[i].*p2 << endl ;
        return 0 ;
}
```

Note the definition of the pointers **p1** and **p2**:

```
int sample::*p1 = &sample::a ;
float sample::*p2 = &sample::b
```

Consider the part before the assignment operator. The stars indicate that **p1** and **p2** are pointers. **sample::** indicates they are pointers to an **int** and a **float** within **sample**. We have also initialised these pointers while declaring them, with addresses of **a** and **b** respectively.

Really speaking there is no "address of" **sample::a** because we are referring to a class and not to an object of that class. **&sample::a** merely produces an offset into the class. The actual address would be produced when we combine that offset with the starting address of a particular object.

Hence **&sample::a** is nothing more than the syntax of pointer to member. If we use **p1** and **p2** with one object we would get one set of values, if we use it with another we would get another set of values. This is what is shown towards the end of the program, where we have built an array of objects and accessed all objects' elements using **p1** and **p2**. Moral is that the pointers to members are not tied with any specific object.

On the left hand side of '.*' there would always be a structure variable (object) or a reference and on the left hand side of '->*' there would always be a pointer to a structure (object).

Go through the following program carefully. I think it would help you fix your ideas about pointers to members.

```cpp
/* Program 70 */
#include <iostream>
using namespace std ;
struct sample
{
    int a ;
    float b ;
    int *c ;
    float *d ;
    int **e ;
    float **f ;
};
int main( )
{
    int sample::*p1 = &sample::a ;
    float sample::*p2 = &sample::b ;
    int * sample::*p3 = &sample::c ;
    float * sample::*p4 = &sample::d ;
    int ** sample::*p5 = &sample::e ;
    float ** sample::*p6 = &sample::f ;
    sample so = { 10, 3.14f, &so.a, &so.b, &so.c, &so.d } ;
    sample *sp ;
    sp = &so ;
    cout << endl << so.*p1 << endl << so.*p2 ;
    cout << endl << * ( so.*p3 ) << endl << *(so.*p4) ;
    cout << endl << ** ( so.*p5 ) << endl << ** ( so.*p6 ) ;
    cout << endl << sp->*p1 << endl << sp->*p2 ;
    cout << endl << * ( sp->*p3 ) << endl << * ( sp->*p4 ) ;
    cout << endl << ** ( sp->*p5 ) << endl << ** ( sp->*p6 ) ;
    // store new values
    * ( so.*p3 ) = 20 ;
    ** ( sp->*p6 ) = 6.28f ;
    // output changed values through p1 and p2
    cout << endl << so.*p1 << endl << so.*p2 << endl ;
```

```
        return 0 ;
}
```

You may have understood the concept of pointers to members, but two questions still remain unanswered:

(a) Why should we use them?

(b) If we use them with classes then won't we be required to make our data **public**?

Let me answer the second one first. We would certainly be required to make the data **public**. And this would violate the rules of encapsulation. Hence pointer to members are more often used with member functions (which are usually **public**) rather than the data members of a class.

Now the answer to the first one. By using pointers to members we can have the flexibility of choosing a member function to be called, at run time. This permits us to select or change the behaviour at run time. Sounds abstract? Well, you would soon understand it. For that firstly we will have to understand a pointer to a function. The following program shows how it works.

```
/* Program 71 */
#include <iostream>
using namespace std ;
int main( )
{
    void fun ( int, float ) ;
    void ( *p ) ( int, float ) ;
    p = fun ;
    ( *p ) ( 10, 3.14f ) ;
    return 0 ;
}
void fun ( int a, float b )
{
    cout << endl << a << endl << b << endl ;
}
```

Here **p** is a pointer to a function that receives an **int** and a **float** and returns a **void**. Note that the parentheses around ***p** are necessary. In their absence **p** would become a function that receives an **int** and a **float** and return a **void ***.

We have initialised **p** to address of the function **fun( )**. Mentioning the function name without a pair of parentheses gives its address in memory. If we want, we can still use the **&** operator to take the address:

p = &fun ;

The syntax for calling **fun( )** using **p** is as follows:
(*p)(10, 3.14) ;

If we want we can have even an array of pointers to functions and then call each function in turn using this array. The following code snippet shows this.

```
void ( *p[3] ) ( int, float ) = { fun1, fun2, fun3 } ;
for ( int i = 0 ; i <= 2 ; i++ )
    ( *p[ i ] ) ( 14 + i, 5.54 + i ) ;
```

One basic condition for this code to work is that the prototypes of functions **fun1( )**, **fun2( )** and **fun3( )** must be same, otherwise we cannot gather their addresses in the array **p[ ]**.

Let's now go a step further. Let's make **fun1( )**, **fun2( )** and **fun3( ) public** members of class **sample** and then try to call them in a manner similar to the one shown above.

```
/* Program 72 */
#include <iostream>
using namespace std ;
class sample
{
    public :
        void fun1( )
        {
            cout << endl << " In Fun1" ;
        }
        void fun2( )
        {
            cout << endl << " In Fun2" ;
        }
        void fun3( )
        {
            cout << endl << " In Fun3" ;
        }
```

```
} ;
int main( )
{
    sample so ;
    void ( *p[3] )( ) = { fun1, fun2, fun3 } ;
    for ( int i = 0 ; i <= 2 ;i++ )
        ( so.*p[ i ] )( ) ;
    }
    return 0 ;
}
```

This program would not clear even the compilation hurdle. An error would be reported in the declaration of **p[ ]**. This is to be expected since we cannot refer to the member functions directly. The following two declarations would also be wrong.

```
void ( *p[3] )( ) = { fun1, fun2, fun3 } ;
void ( *p[3] )( ) = { so.fun1, so.fun2, so.fun3 } ;
```

The only way we can make the declaration work is:

```
void ( sample::*p[3] )( ) = { &sample::fun1, &sample::fun2,
&sample::fun3 } ;
```

Now if we are to call the member functions using **p[ ]** the only way to do so is by using the **pointer to member** syntax. The following program shows how this can be done.

```
/* Program 73 */
#include <iostream>
using namespace std ;
class sample
{
    public :
        void fun1( )
        {
            cout << endl << this << " In fun1" ;
        }
        void fun2( )
        {
            cout << endl << this << " In fun2" ;
        }
        void fun3( )
```

```
        {
             cout << endl << this << "  In fun3" ;
        }
};
int main( )
{
    sample so[4] ;
    void (sample::*p[3] )( ) = { &sample::fun1, &sample::fun2,
                              &sample::fun3 } ;
    for ( int j = 0 ; j <= 3 ;j++ )
    {
        for ( int i = 0 ; i <= 2 ; i++ )
            ( so[ j ].*p[ i ] )( ) ;
    }
    return 0 ;
}
```

Using the '.*' syntax now we can call different member functions using
different objects. While doing so we have also printed the address of
each object with reference to whom the member function is being
called. The output looks like this...

```
0x1feffff2  In fun1
0x1feffff2  In fun2
0x1feffff2  In fun3
0x1feffff3  In fun1
0x1feffff3  In fun2
0x1feffff3  In fun3
0x1feffff4  In fun1
0x1feffff4  In fun2
0x1feffff4  In fun3
0x1feffff5  In fun1
0x1feffff5  In fun2
0x1feffff5  In fun3
```

Pointer Misquotes

No natural resource should go waste. Books are built out of trees. So why waste even a page of it. With that motive, given below are a few misquotes on pointers to tickle you.

"Pointers can be made to work if you fiddle with them long enough. If you fiddle with anything long enough, you will ultimately end up messing it."

"An expert C Programmer is one who avoids all errors except those related with pointers."

"The likelihood of a program crashing is in direct proportion to the number of pointers used in it."

"No matter how much time you have spent with pointers you would always find some application of it that would leave you guessing."

"If Nothing Works, Try Pointers!"

"Know Pointers, Will travel!"

Appendix A

Compilation and Execution

In principle you don't need an IDE to create, compile, assemble and debug C programs. It is like saying, well, you don't need an airplane to crisscross India, you can do it in a bullock-cart. Crap! Modern times need modern solutions. IDE is the solution for modern times. This chapter shows how to use it...

To gain confidence while working with pointers you would be required to type programs in this book using an Editor and then compile them using a Compiler. Compiler vendors provide an Integrated Development Environment (IDE) which consists of an Editor as well as the Compiler. These IDEs are discussed in this appendix.

IDEs

There are several such IDEs available, each targeted towards different processor and operating system combinations. Given below is a brief description of the popular IDEs along with the links from where they can be downloaded.

Turbo C/C++ under Windows

If you wish to use Turbo C/C++ it is available at

https://www.developerinsider.in/download-turbo-c-for-windows-7-8-8-1-and-windows-10-32-64-bit-full-screen/

It is very easy to install and it works for Windows 7, 8, 8.1 and Windows 10 (32-64 bit) with full/window screen mode.

NetBeans under Windows

NetBeans is not a compiler. It is merely an IDE. It's Windows version can be downloaded from

http://www.netbeans.org

For developing C programs using NetBeans under Windows, you would also have to install Cygwin software. Cygwin comes with GCC compiler. It is available at

https://www.cygwin.com/

There are nice tutorials available at the following links should you face any difficulty in setting up Cygwin and NetBeans:

https://netbeans.org/community/releases/80/cpp-setup-instructions.html

https://www.wikihow.com/Run-C/C%2B%2B-Program-in-Netbeans-on-Windows

NetBeans under Linux

If you propose to use NetBeans under Linux you won't need Cygwin as with most Linux installations (like say, Ubuntu) GCC compiler comes preinstalled. So you need to just download and install NetBeans for Linux environment.

Visual Studio under Windows

If you wish to use VisualStudio Express it is available at

https://www.visualstudio.com/vs/express/

You are free to use any of the IDEs mentioned above for compiling programs in this book. If you wish to know my personal choice, I would prefer NetBeans + Cygwin or Visual Studio Express Edition. All the IDEs are easy to use and are available free of cost.

Compilation and Execution Steps

The compilation and execution process with each of the IDEs mentioned in the previous section are a bit different. So for your benefit I am giving below these steps for each IDE.

Compilation and Execution using Turbo C++

Carry out the following steps to compile and execute programs using Turbo C++:

(a) Start NetBeans from Start | All Programs | Turbo C++.

(b) Click 'Start Turbo C++' from the dialog that appears.

(c) Select File | New from menu.

(d) Type the program.

(e) Save the program using F2 under a proper name (say Program1.c).

(f) Use Ctrl + F9 to compile and execute the program.

(g) Use Alt + F5 to view the output.

Compilation and Execution using NetBeans

Carry out the following steps to compile and execute programs using NetBeans:

(a) Start NetBeans from Start | All Programs | NetBeans.

(b) Select File | New Project... from the File menu. Select Project Category as C/C++ and Project Type as C/C++ Application from the dialog that pops up. Click Next button.

(c) Type a suitable project name (say Program1) in Project Name TextBox. Click Finish.

(d) Type the program.

(e) Save the program using **Ctrl + S.**

(f) Use **F6** to compile and execute the program.

Compilation and Execution using Visual Studio Express

Carry out the following steps to compile and execute programs using Visual Studio Express:

(a) Start Visual Studio Express from Start | All Programs | Microsoft Visual C++ Express.

(b) Select File | New Project... from the File menu. Select Project Type as Visual C++ | Win32 Console Application from the dialog that pops up. Type a suitable project name (say Program1) in Name TextBox. Click OK and Finish.

(c) Type the program.

(d) Save the program using **Ctrl+S.**

(e) Use **Ctrl+F5** to compile and execute the program.

When you use Visual Studio to create a Win32 Console Application for the above program the wizard would insert the following code by default:

```
#include "stdafx.h"
int _tmain ( int argc, _TCHAR* argv[ ] )
{
    return 0 ;
}
```

You can delete this code and type your program in its place. If you now compile the program using Ctrl+F5 you would get the following error:

Fatal error C1010:
unexpected end of file while looking for precompiled header.
Did you forget to add '#include "stdafx.h"' to your source?

If you add #include "stdafx.h" at the top of your program then it would compile and run successfully. However, including this file makes the program Visual Studio-centric and would not get compiled with other compilers. This is not good, as the program no longer remains portable. To eliminate this error, you need to make a setting in Visual Studio. To make this setting carry out the following steps:

(a) Go to 'Solution Explorer'.

(b) Right click on the project name and select 'Properties' from the menu that pops up. On doing so, a dialog box called 'Property Pages' would appear.

(c) From the left pane of this dialog first select 'Configuration Properties' followed by 'C/C++'.

(d) Select 'Precompiled Headers'.

(e) From the right pane of the dialog click on 'Create/Use Precompiled Header'. On doing so in the value for this option a triangle would appear.

(f) Click on this triangle and a drop-down list box would appear.

(g) From the list box select 'Not using Precompiled Header'.

(h) Click on OK button to make the setting effective.

In addition to this, you need to make one more setting. By default Visual Studio believes that your program is a C++ program and not a C program. So by making a setting you need to tell it that your program is a C program and not a C++ program. Carry out the following steps to make this setting:

(a) Go to 'Solution Explorer' window.

(b) Right click on the project name and select 'Properties' from the menu that pops up. On doing so, a 'Property Pages' dialog box would appear.

(c) From the left pane of this dialog box first select 'Configuration Properties' followed by 'C/C++'.

(d) In C/C++ options select 'Advanced'.

(e) Change the 'Compile As' option to 'Compile as C code (/TC)'.

Once this setting is made you can now compile the program using Ctrl+F5. This time no error would be flagged, and the program would compile and execute successfully.

Compilation and Execution at Linux Command-line

C programs can be compiled and executed even at command-line, i.e. without using any IDE. Many programmers prefer this mode. In such cases we need to use an editor to type the program and a compiler to compile it. For example, if you wish to compile and execute programs at Linux command prompt, then you may use an editor like vi or Vim and a compiler like GCC. In such as case you need to follow the following steps to compile and execute your program.

(a) Type the program and save it under a suitable name, 'hello.c'.

(b) At the command prompt switch to the directory containing 'hello.c' using the **cd** command.

(c) Compile the program using **GCC** compiler as shown below.

```
$ gcc  hello.c
```

(d) On successful compilation, **GCC** produces a file named 'a.out'. This file contains the machine language code of the program which can now be executed.

(e) Execute the program using the following command:

```
$ ./a.out
```

Index

If you search for an entry in this index and cannot find it, you will earn yourself a place in Indexer's heaven!

Made in the USA
Middletown, DE
16 May 2020